Political arithmetic. Containing observations on the present state of Great Britain; and the principles of her policy in the encouragement of agriculture. ... By Arthur Young, ...

Arthur Young

Political arithmetic. Containing observations on the present state of Great Britain; and the principles of her policy in the encouragement of agriculture. ... By Arthur Young, ...
Young, Arthur
ESTCID: T078929
Reproduction from British Library
With a final advertisement leaf.
London : printed for W. Nicoll, 1774.
xii,[4],366,[2]p. ; 8°

Gale ECCO Print Editions

Relive history with *Eighteenth Century Collections Online*, now available in print for the independent historian and collector. This series includes the most significant English-language and foreign-language works printed in Great Britain during the eighteenth century, and is organized in seven different subject areas including literature and language; medicine, science, and technology; and religion and philosophy. The collection also includes thousands of important works from the Americas.

The eighteenth century has been called "The Age of Enlightenment." It was a period of rapid advance in print culture and publishing, in world exploration, and in the rapid growth of science and technology – all of which had a profound impact on the political and cultural landscape. At the end of the century the American Revolution, French Revolution and Industrial Revolution, perhaps three of the most significant events in modern history, set in motion developments that eventually dominated world political, economic, and social life.

In a groundbreaking effort, Gale initiated a revolution of its own: digitization of epic proportions to preserve these invaluable works in the largest online archive of its kind. Contributions from major world libraries constitute over 175,000 original printed works. Scanned images of the actual pages, rather than transcriptions, recreate the works ***as they first appeared.***

Now for the first time, these high-quality digital scans of original works are available via print-on-demand, making them readily accessible to libraries, students, independent scholars, and readers of all ages.

For our initial release we have created seven robust collections to form one the world's most comprehensive catalogs of 18th century works.

Initial Gale ECCO Print Editions collections include:

> ***History and Geography***
> Rich in titles on English life and social history, this collection spans the world as it was known to eighteenth-century historians and explorers. Titles include a wealth of travel accounts and diaries, histories of nations from throughout the world, and maps and charts of a world that was still being discovered. Students of the War of American Independence will find fascinating accounts from the British side of conflict.

Social Science

Delve into what it was like to live during the eighteenth century by reading the first-hand accounts of everyday people, including city dwellers and farmers, businessmen and bankers, artisans and merchants, artists and their patrons, politicians and their constituents. Original texts make the American, French, and Industrial revolutions vividly contemporary.

Medicine, Science and Technology

Medical theory and practice of the 1700s developed rapidly, as is evidenced by the extensive collection, which includes descriptions of diseases, their conditions, and treatments. Books on science and technology, agriculture, military technology, natural philosophy, even cookbooks, are all contained here.

Literature and Language

Western literary study flows out of eighteenth-century works by Alexander Pope, Daniel Defoe, Henry Fielding, Frances Burney, Denis Diderot, Johann Gottfried Herder, Johann Wolfgang von Goethe, and others. Experience the birth of the modern novel, or compare the development of language using dictionaries and grammar discourses.

Religion and Philosophy

The Age of Enlightenment profoundly enriched religious and philosophical understanding and continues to influence present-day thinking. Works collected here include masterpieces by David Hume, Immanuel Kant, and Jean-Jacques Rousseau, as well as religious sermons and moral debates on the issues of the day, such as the slave trade. The Age of Reason saw conflict between Protestantism and Catholicism transformed into one between faith and logic -- a debate that continues in the twenty-first century.

Law and Reference

This collection reveals the history of English common law and Empire law in a vastly changing world of British expansion. Dominating the legal field is the *Commentaries of the Law of England* by Sir William Blackstone, which first appeared in 1765. Reference works such as almanacs and catalogues continue to educate us by revealing the day-to-day workings of society.

Fine Arts

The eighteenth-century fascination with Greek and Roman antiquity followed the systematic excavation of the ruins at Pompeii and Herculaneum in southern Italy; and after 1750 a neoclassical style dominated all artistic fields. The titles here trace developments in mostly English-language works on painting, sculpture, architecture, music, theater, and other disciplines. Instructional works on musical instruments, catalogs of art objects, comic operas, and more are also included.

POLITICAL ARITHMETIC.

CONTAINING

OBSERVATIONS

ON THE PRESENT STATE OF

GREAT BRITAIN;

AND THE

PRINCIPLES OF HER POLICY

IN THE

ENCOURAGEMENT OF AGRICULTURE.

Addressed to the

ŒCONOMICAL SOCIETIES established in EUROPE.

TO WHICH IS ADDED,

A MEMOIR on the CORN TRADE:

Drawn up and laid before the COMMISSIONERS of the TREASURY.

By GOVERNOR POWNALL.

By ARTHUR YOUNG, Esq. F.R.S.
AUTHOR of the TOURS through ENGLAND—
Honorary Member of the Societies of DUBLIN, YORK, and MANCHESTER, and of the Œconomical Society of BERNE in SWITZERLAND.

LONDON.

Printed for W. NICOLL, at No 51, in St. Paul's Church-Yard. MDCCLXXIV.

TO THE SOCIETIES

ESTABLISHED IN

DIFFERENT PARTS OF EUROPE

FOR THE

ENCOURAGEMENT OF AGRICULTURE,

THIS TREATISE

ON THE PRINCIPLES OF

BRITISH POLICY

RELATIVE TO

THAT IMPORTANT DESIGN,

IS INSCRIBED,

BY THEIR

MOST OBEDIENT,

AND DEVOTED SERVANT,

ARTHUR YOUNG.

North Mims, near Hatfield, Hertfordshire, April 15, 1774.

PREFACE.

THE great encouragement which agriculture at preſent meets with in *Europe* has been either the cauſe or effect (probably both) of many publications upon that part of political œconomy which concerns the culture of the earth. In ſeveral of theſe writings I have remarked, in ſome important inſtances, ſuch a turn of thought, and ſuch recommendations to ſovereigns as appeared to me to be founded upon principles extremely falſe: At the ſame time, I met with many paſſages in the works of foreign writers, wherein they

 quoted

quoted the example of *England*, but under great miſrepreſentations. Theſe circumſtances induced me to attempt a plain explanation of the ſyſtem of *Great Britain* in the encouragement of agriculture, in order for an opportunity to point out as well as I was able the principles of that policy which has wrought thoſe effects in this country, and which give foreign authors an idea of our proſperity; *Britiſh* ones, a conviction of our declenſion and ruin.

If ſuch a plan is executed with ability, it can hardly fail of being beneficial; for a train of conduct falſe in the very foundations of its policy, being recommended by writers of conſiderable reputation, may be ſuppoſed to be liſtened

to

to by ſtateſmen and legiſlators: —to point out ſuch errors is incumbent on a lover of agriculture, who thinks he ſees them—the world muſt be his judge if miſtaken. At the ſame time to find others recommending ideas becauſe they are realized in *England*—which in truth have no ſuch foundation, inſtigates one farther to ſhew in what principles conſiſts this branch of *Britiſh* policy. All this will be allowed to be an important ſubject; I wiſh it had been in more able hands; but others not having undertaken the taſk, is the reaſon that the reader finds me engaged in it.

In executing this deſign, it was neceſſary to give ſome account of our preſent ſtate, in reſpect of agriculture, arts, manufactures, commerce, luxury, population, wealth, and the prices of commodities. I have dwelt upon these no farther than was necessary to shew that the principles explained had been attended with such and such effects. I had already done something of this sort in the observations annexed to the registers of my Tours through *England*, and therefore avoided repetitions; this part of the work would have been very short, had not the assertions and opinions of some writers among ourselves (gentlemen for whose abilities I have an high respect) been so very contrary to the positions I was laying down, that it would have been affectation gravely to explain principles as if undeniable, without removing the objections of men of repute, who denied their existence.

The obſervations I made in my journies through the kingdom, fixed my opinions concerning population —the incloſure and diviſion of landed property—the prices of the earth's products, &c. I found the language of plain facts ſo clear, that I could not but liſten and be convinced, and I laid the facts before the world on which I founded my opinions: In oppoſition to theſe facts, thoſe writers have offered reaſon upon reaſon, argument upon argument, and have given elaborate diſquiſitions on ſubjects which demanded facts alone. This has occaſioned my ſhewing in the preſent treatiſe how the facts I before gave are conſiſtent with, and even naturally ariſing from firſt principles. This I eſteemed a neceſſary

part

part of my undertaking—for if I could not ſucceed here, it would be in vain to offer circumſtances in our national conduct to the imitation of foreigners, which were not clearly deſerving their attention.

The ſubjects here treated are the moſt important that can demand the attention of our legiſlature—and it is of the higheſt conſequence that gentlemen ſhould have right ideas of them; ſince giving into vulgar errors, and miſtaken notions on population, prices of proviſions, luxury, ſize of farms, incloſures, &c. muſt have ill effects. If the parliaments of this kingdom once adopt the errors I here endeavour to refute, it will be a ſignal of national decay; ſince thoſe principles

ciples of our policy which have made us the envy of the world, will then, inſtead of being revered, become active againſt us.

I am very ſenſible that throughout theſe calculations I have taken the unpopular ſide of the queſtion. A work (unleſs conducted with uncommon abilities) rarely ſucceeds, whoſe principal aim is to perſuade a nation to be eaſy and ſatisfied under preſent circumſtances; and to convince them that they have almoſt every reaſon to be pleaſed: ſuch a taſk has nothing in it that flatters the multitude — you run counter to public prejudice, and all the reward you can hope for, is the approbation of a few ſenſible individuals.

* * * *

Governor *Pownall* was ſo obliging as to permit me to take copies of ſome important papers relative to the corn trade. His memoir on the uncertainty of the ſtatutes, and the means of aſcertaining the prices of corn for the purpoſes of exportation, proves, in the cleareſt manner, his uncommon attention to that ſubject, and his ability in diſcuſſing it. He likewiſe favoured me with the table of the expence of ſhipping corn to and from *Holland* at page 28; that of the prices at which flour from *New-York* and *Penſylvania* can be landed in *England*, page 280, 281, and 282. Alſo that of the prices of flour in thoſe colonies, page 340.

CONTENTS.

CHAPTER I.

CHAP. II.

CONTENTS.

CONTENTS.

POLITICAL

POLITICAL ARITHMETICK.

INTRODUCTION.

IF ever the encouragement of agriculture was a principal object of attention in the several governments of *Europe*, it is at present, when we every day see establishments, institutions, or laws framed with this great and laudable view. It is a spirit which does much honour to the present age, and will certainly be attended with excellent effects. Having in many foreign publications seen various accounts of these exertions in most of the neighbouring countries; read several dissertations on what the French call the *Oeconomical Science*; and reflected on the propositions which have been best received in those countries, I am induced to offer a few observations to the public—speaking to other nations as well as to my countrymen. There are instances in which appear much more merit in the general design of encouraging agriculture, than in the particular means taken to effect it; arising, I should suppose, from a want of information: This must give concern to one who wishes so well to the cause. Desirous of being as good a citizen of the world as my station in life will allow; and seeing that the foreign writers frequently quote the case of *England*—and are eager to copy her, let me endeavour to explain, as far as I am able, the principles which have advanced the husbandry of this country to its present height—Let me observe wherein foreigners should imitate us—and wherein their imitation can be of no service to them. We cannot well understand this without improving the knowledge of our own interests. I shall do it with the greater readiness, as I believe the ingenious writers, who have published so much upon these subjects in *France*, *Italy*, and *Germany*, have, in several cases, formed mistaken ideas of the policy and practice of *England*; both have been the objects of my particular attention, and though I may fail in minutely tracing many effects to their true causes, yet a slight examination relative to foreigners adopting what they call our system, may, I think, have its use to ourselves.

In the progreſs of explaining what I take to be our national advantages, and our national obſtacles, I ſhall naturally be led to examine ſome popular opinions ſtarted lately among ourſelves by other writers, as ſome of them are ſuch as appear to me utterly deſtructive of the ends I propoſe in this enquiry.

CHAP. I.

ENCOURAGEMENT OF AGRICULTURE IN GREAT-BRITAIN.

THE circumſtances to which our farmers owe moſt, are,

1. Liberty.
2. Taxation.
3. Leaſes.
4. Tythe not generally gathered.
5. A freedom from perſonal ſervice.
6. Corn Laws.
7. General wealth of the kingdom.
8. Incloſures
9. Conſumption of meat.

SECT. I.

LIBERTY.

THE advance which the agriculture of this country has made, is owing primarily to the excellency of our conſtitution—to that general liberty which is diffuſed among all ranks of the people, and which enſures the legal poſſeſſions of every man

man from the hand of violence and power: This is the original and animating ſoul that enlivens the huſbandry of *Britain*. But it is not owing to this alone that we have attained to an high degree of excellence; other cauſes alſo have operated, and very powerful ones, for freedom alone will not do, as we ſee by *Scotland*, where the conſtitution is the ſame, but agriculture abundantly different. This we ſee alſo in *Ireland*.—Our farmers, and all the people employed by them, enjoy that general freedom and ſecurity which is the birth-right, I will not ſay of *Britons*, but of all mankind. The operations of a correct and ſpirited agriculture require conſiderable expence; the returns of which are ſome years before they come in; ſuch a buſineſs, above moſt others, requires every favour that legiſlation can ſhew A great degree of ſecurity of poſſeſſion is neceſſary in ſuch a caſe, not only from the effects of arbitrary power, but alſo from all oppreſſions that the nobility, gentry, and wealthy landlords can throw upon their tenants. An *Engliſh* farmer, with a leaſe, is as independent of his landlord, as the landlord is of the farmer; and if he has no leaſe, we may be ſure he is favoured in the rent proportionably to ſuch circumſtance. This general liberty, which our farmers enjoy in common with the reſt of their fellow-ſubjects, it muſt be evident, to all attentive obſervers, cannot fail of being of the higheſt conſequence to the promotion of good huſbandry. It is impoſſible to enter into a full explanation of all the advantages they receive under this general head; which, in fact, is of all others the greateſt encouragement, not only to agriculture, but equally ſo to arts, manufactures, commerce, and, in a word, every ſpecies of induſtry in the ſtate *.

SECT. II.

TAXATION.

THE public revenue of *Britain* is raiſed by ſuch a mode of taxation, that little of the weight falls on huſbandry. The great

* Le travail eſt le pere de l'opulence La terre inepuiſable dans ſes dons, recompenſe toujours la ſueur de l'homme laborieux qui la ſollicite, en le comblant de richeſſes a proportion de ſes ſoins & de ſes peines Mais l'appas ſeul des jouiſſances encourage le travail L'aſſurance qu'on à d'echanger à ſon gré le ſuperflu, eſt ce qui cree le ſuperflu. C'eſt cette cauſe active qui fertiliſe les champs, fait fouiller les mines, enfante les inventions, les découvertes et tout ce qui rend une nation floriſante et redoutable. *Théorie du Luxe*, 1771, tom 1. p 170.

great divifion of our taxes is into: 1. Land; 2. Parifh, 3. Windows; 4. Excifes; 5. Cuftoms. As to the fmaller objects of ftamps, licences, poft-office, &c. none of them bear the leaft upon one fet of men more than another, nor are they burthenfome to any.

The land-tax is raifed abfolutely and totally upon the landlord, though paid by the tenant. In all cafes it is the fame thing to the farmer, whether he pays his rent immediately to his landlord, or to the King in taxes; the latter are firft carried to account, and the ballance to his landlord is always proportioned to what he has already paid for land-tax. Whether it is one fhilling or four in the pound, it is juft the fame to the farmer—the landlord is the only one concerned.

If he farms his own eftate, he pays it himfelf, which makes no other difference than the mere trouble of the payment.

An immenfe advantage is the amount of the tax being fixed: If I buy or inherit an eftate confifting of wafte, or poorly cultivated tracts, which let only for an hundred pounds a year, and pay a tax of five pounds to the ftate; and if after, by fpirited exertions, I advance the annual value of my eftate to a thoufand pounds a year, the tax remains juft as it was before—no increafe.

crease. This is an advantage, and an encouragement to improvements which no system can exceed *.

Several *English* writers have pleaded for a new and more equal land-tax; which might be perhaps a good measure if there was an absolute certainty of its then remaining unchangeable for at least a century; but as we cannot have such certainty, I must esteem it a most dangerous idea; for if the tax was by a general new assessment made an equal and fair one, then there would not be the same reason as at present for opposing alterations. A tax of so much in the pound, varying according to rent, would be at once a tythe, and the most pernicious system that could be invented, because an improver would be TAXED IN PROPORTION TO HIS IMPROVEMENTS. Let therefore the tax remain upon its present footing: it is now perfectly innocent, if altered, we know not where the alterations would stop.

Another

* In one respect this is not so fully the case, the sums which parishes are assessed always remain the same, but the officers may vary the assessment on individuals, but then they must know at what rent a farm is let before they can raise any person's tax, and the person so raised may appeal, if every other person in the parish is not equally taxed, which makes such alterations in the assessment rare.

Another circumſtance which renders our land-tax ſo little burthenſome to the agriculture of the kingdom, is its being laid abſolutely upon *rent:* The aſſeſſors cannot tax the landlord for any ſuppoſed or viſible value: if a farm is ever ſo rich, or ſupports ever ſo many cattle, it is nothing to the aſſeſſor, he can tax the rent only: and if the landlord farms it himſelf, he can only be taxed according to the rent the laſt time the farm was let, though an hundred years ago, and would at preſent let for quadruple the ſum; if the old rent cannot be diſcovered, the old aſſeſſment is continued, without enquiring on what foundation it was formed.

From this ſlight review of the land-tax of *England*, it appears to be no burthen on agriculture:—no ſyſtem of taxing land could have been invented that would injure it ſo little.

It is not ſo with the pariſh taxes; they are laid immediatcly on the farmer, and prove a burthen to him in proportion to their weight: They conſiſt of the poor's rate, or the ſums raiſed for the ſupport of the chargeable poor: The church rate, for keeping in repair the pariſh church: The highway rate, raiſed by the ſurveyors for the repair of the roads. The latter is not general, as the ſtatute duty of ſix days work with their teams, is commonly more

than

than ſufficient; and in no caſe, by act of parliament, more than a rate of ſix-pence in the pound of rent can be laid in aid of the duty: this is the only reſemblance we have in *England* of the *Corvees* of *France*, and the monſtrous perſonal ſervice which is ſo deſtructive to the agriculture of *Germany* and *Poland*. The amount in *England* cannot be called burthenſome; ſince the ſix days work are performed only at a leiſure time of the year, and may be generally compounded for at a fourth part of the real value.

With the poor's rate there is uſually a few other ſmall taxes thrown together, ſuch as the conſtable's expences, which however are trivial, and the county rate, being a county expence for certain bridges and other general expences which concern the county at large; when divided among all the pariſhes it is a very ſmall amount. The poor's tax, with theſe additions, including the church rate, are uſually all thrown together, and raiſed by a ſingle rate, in which every occupier of lands or houſes are charged in proportion to his rent. The average of them in my Northern Tour, came only to 1 *s.* 1 *d.* in the pound; and in the Eaſtern Tour to 2 *s.* 8 *d.*; average of both 1 *s.* 10 ½ *d.* But in manufacturing,

turing, and many other particular places, they riſe much higher.

The reader will obſerve that this tax is entirely regulated by the rent of the land, which is a circumſtance that renders the burthen comparatively light: If a man hires an hundred acres of land for thirty pounds a year, during a leaſe of forty years, and by improvement raiſes the land to the annual value of an hundred pounds, ſtill he can be rated only at thirty pounds a year, as the value or goodneſs of the land, and the largeneſs of the farmer's ſtock have nothing to do in the account; he is not to be taxed for them, but only in proportion to his rent.

Another obſervation I ſhould make is, that in pariſhes where the rates run very high, as in ſome they do to 3, 4, 6, and even 10*s.* in the pound, in ſuch, the tax is in fact on the landlord, for no tenant will hire land in any pariſh without firſt enquiring what the rates are; and when he finds them ſo high, will give a rent only in proportion to ſuch certain expence; if the rates were to be lowered from 10*s.* to 5*s.* in the pound, the landlord at the expiration of his leaſes would be able to add 5*s.* in the pound to his rents.

Upon the whole, though the poor's-rate, &c. is a direct burthen on the farmers,

yet

yet the amount not being a matter of great consideration, and being laid only on the certain rent, it is not in any respect to be considered as checking the progress and improvement of agriculture: the disputes, litigations and lawsuits, which arise from the quarrels between farmers on some being rated higher or lower than others, and between parishes concerning the settlement of their poor, are in some instances a greater abuse and burthen than the total of what they pay regularly in rates. This is an abuse of freedom, and rather marks the lightness of the burthens laid on our farmers, than their weight.

The tax upon windows bears not particularly upon agriculture; the farmer pays something annually for each window in his house, proportioned to the total number, it is a regular tax, and too inconsiderable to be esteemed a burthen, certainly it has no ill consequences on our husbandry. Were it however, as some authors have advised, to be the only tax, by its absorbing all others, it would be a deadly burthen to the whole kingdom; since no man should pay to the amount of all taxes in proportion as he *possesses*, but in proportion as he *consumes*; but of this more hereafter.

The two great branches of *English* taxes are; the excises and the customs; their

their being burthenſome to agriculture depends entirely on what objects they are laid, and to what extent they are carried; but in general I ſhall remark, that they are much leſs detrimental than commonly imagined. Cuſtoms on the exportation of corn would be ruinous to agriculture: exciſes on wool and leather to ſuch an amount as to leſſen the conſumption and ſink the price in the hands of the farmer, would be evidently miſchievous: ſuch exciſes upon malt as would leſſen the conſumption of beer, and at the ſame time cuſtoms on the export of barley, would greatly hurt the culture of that crop: exciſes laid on butchers for all the beaſts they killed, to ſuch a height as to leſſen the conſumption of meat, would have the ſame effect;—but theſe are caſes of which we have no inſtances in *England*. our cuſtoms and exciſes are not prejudicial to our huſbandry but in very few caſes, the prohibition which is only another word for a very high cuſtom on the export of wool, and raw leather, are certainly heavy burthens laid on agriculture in favour of manufactures, the proof of which, is the price of wool in *England* having fallen half ſince that policy was embraced, which has been a tax of near two ſhillings in the pound additional on land; not that I would

venture

venture to plead in favour of the exportation of wool raw: I ſhall only refer the reader to the arguments of Mr. *Smith*, in his *Memoirs of Wool*, where he will find many extreme curious facts concerning wool and the woollen manufacture.

That cuſtoms and exciſes do not injure in the leaſt the agriculture of *Britain*, we have the cleareſt proof, in their not lowering the prices of any of the farmer's commodities, (wool, &c. excepted, as above;) while they leave them at the price they found or raiſe them, certainly the farmer cannot be injured. When they are carried too far they leſſen conſumption, which in every circumſtance is the great wound the farmer has moſt to fear, becauſe his prices from that moment will fall, but in *England* the conſumption of every commodity has increaſed under every burthen that has been laid on it: this has been uniformly the caſe with malt; nor have we an inſtance of either exciſes or cuſtoms leſſening the conſumption, and conſequently the price of the farmer's products. The excellence of this ſpecies of taxation has been very ably explained by ſeveral writers, who have ſhewn that by the tax being blended with the price, the purchaſer does not feel its weight, and never pays the tax but when he is beſt able to pay it, that is at the moment he makes the

 purchaſe.

purchaſe. If all the taxes of *England* were conſolidated into this general branch *on conſumption*, our ſyſtem would be ſtill more perfect. As to their raiſing prices, it is as I could eaſily ſhew an advantage to every claſs in the ſtate.

From this review of the ſyſtem of taxation in *Britain*, it is clear that the agriculture of the kingdom cannot ſuffer from any part of it, without the amount being carried to a much greater height; but hitherto we have ſeen nothing like even the proſpect of miſchief to our huſbandry from any of our taxes. This muſt ariſe in a great meaſure from their not being laid on improvements—from their being permanent and not varying—from the aſſeſſors, collectors, and receivers being armed with very moderate powers, and with none beyond the mere line of fraud againſt the tax—from their being no reſpectors of perſons, dealing equally with the duke and his little tenant.

SECT. III.

LEASES.

THE improvements which have been wrought in *England* have been almoſt totally owing to the cuſtom of granting leaſes:

leaſes: In thoſe countries where it is unuſual to give them, agriculture yet continues much inferior to what we find it where they are uſual, nor can it flouriſh till this cuſtom is adopted. If the mode and progreſs of country improvements is well conſidered, they will be found utterly inconſiſtent with an occupation without a leaſe. A farmer hires a tract of land in an unimproved or inferior ſtate; he repairs the fences, deepens the ditches—clears away rubbiſh—purchaſes dung—forms composts—drains the wet fields—waters the meadows—adds to the buildings—digs for marle—gets the arable lands into good and clean order; theſe works take him three or four years, during which time he ſacrifices his profits in hopes of being well paid. Now how can any perſon poſſibly ſuppoſe that ſuch a ſyſtem will be executed on his farms, if he will not or does not grant long leaſes? Is it to be expected that a tenant will lay a thouſand pounds out upon improvements, and remain all the time at the mercy of his landlord, to be turned out of the farm as ſoon as the money is expended? The caſe is ſo ſelf-evident that the neceſſity muſt be undeniable; no man of common ſenſe will put ſuch truſt in another.

Nor

Nor is it sufficient that granting leases is a common custom, they must be so guarded by the laws as to give the tenant the most perfect security; he must be sure of his term, and also sure of being safe against any ill designing, malevolent, or insidious attacks of a wealthy landlord, and be as independent while he adheres to the contracts of his lease, as the landlord is of him: all this is the case with the majority of *English* farmers. It is true, there are many tracts of country in which landlords will not grant leases, but then one of two circumstances must exist; either the land is of such a nature that no *improvements* are wanting—or, in consequence of no lease being given, the farms are let much under their value.

In some countries of *Europe* no leases are granted, in others they are very weak guaranties of the tenants security, and in others, the sale of the estate vacates the lease: These are all radical evils which must be cured, or husbandry can never flourish.

SECT. IV.

TYTHE.

THIS is the greateſt burthen that yet remains on the agriculture of this kingdom; and if it was univerſally taken in kind, would be ſufficient to damp all ideas of improvement. Fortunately the ſpirit of our clergy is too liberal in general to live in ſuch a ſtate of warfare with their pariſhioners, as pretty generally is the caſe where they ſubmit to the trouble of gathering for the ſake of the additional profit.

In many pariſhes however, the tythes are gathered, and in them I will venture to pronounce no correct or ſpirited huſbandry will ever be met with —and I may further remark, that in the extenſive journies I have made through this kingdom for the purpoſe of examining its agriculture, I have never met with conſiderable improvements where the tythe was taken in kind; and a very little calculation would ſhew the impoſſibility of it. The reaſon our huſbandry has advanced upon the whole in ſo great a degree, is ſuch a large part of the kingdom not being tythed in kind, but a compoſition *per* acre or *per* pound being taken in lieu, and ſuch a conſiderable portion of it being tythe free, which is every day increaſing by all the new incloſures. The great object at preſent of *Britiſh* agriculture, is to obtain a general exemption from tythe, by giving the clergy ſome ſettled income in lieu of it.

ABOLITION OF TYTHE.

Laſt winter there were ſome reſpectable meetings of gentlemen, for the purpoſe of applying to parliament for an alteration in the tythe-laws: a committee was choſen, and having made one in ſeveral of their meetings, I am able to aſſert that their deſigns are perfectly commendable; having equally in view the benefit of agriculture and the rights of the clergy.

The committee, in the petition they prepared for preſenting to the Houſe of Commons, names no equivalent to be given in lieu of tythe, properly leaving that to the wiſdom of the houſe: It may not, however, be amiſs to make a few obſervations on ſuch as have been thought of.

Firſt, A Pound Rate. The annual value of the living for the laſt ſeven years to be ſtated, and the average to be in future raiſed by a pound rate; not by a fixed ſum, but at ſo much in the pound, conſequently the value of the living will rise with the rise of land and fall of money.

There are two insuperable objections to this scheme. *First*, The difficulty of gaining a fair pound-rate is fully equal to that of abolishing tythes. Three fourths of the kingdom have at times litigated their rates with a view to honest proportions, but in vain; and accordingly the inequalities every where found, and the enormous fallacies, through various reasons, are such as render the plan utterly impracticable. People who have long occupied their own lands, and are rated according to their last lease, though an hundred years old, pay the tythe either in kind or to the value; were it to be paid by rate they would be exempted of three fourths of their just contributions, and the burthen fall on their neighbours, who already pay as much as they ought. For instance, A. B. C. D. and E. are the renters in a parish, and F. and G. farm their own lands. the former contribute to the rates proportionably to their rents; but F. and G. only in proportion to the last rental of their lands: For want of an explicit decision of the value of F. and G's lands, they are unjustly favoured, and the rest of the parish burthened in proportion; is not this inequality sufficient without easing F. and G. of a great part of their

tythe,

tythe, and throwing the weight on A. B. C. D. and E. who are already burthened more than they ought to be? What ſyſtem can be more iniquitous? *Secondly*, If this objection was got over, there is another great one. You want to be eaſed of tythes becauſe of the enormous burthen of a payment proportioned to the crop? How abſurd then would it be to exchange it for a direct ſimilar burthen? The miſchief of tythes, of the taille in *France*, and all taxes proportional to products, valuations, or rents, is the circumſtance of taxing improvements: this monſtrous evil you would not get rid of. If a man buys a farm at 50 *l.* a year, and by excellent management improves it highly, and lets it at 100 *l.* his tenant is at once doubled in the rates—the very evil which has ſo often been complained of in various countries, that groan under taxes varying with rents or valuations. This ſyſtem therefore would be only changing one evil for another: Our poor rates are a tax liable to this great evil; in the name of common ſenſe, therefore, do not quadruple a tax which is open to ſuch objections.

Secondly, It has been propoſed to pay the rector by a corn rent; with the double view of giving him his ſhare of future improvements, and ſecuring his property from finking with the value of money; but this is liable to moft of the objections of the pound-rate. Giving him his fhare of future improvements, is giving him the only thing we want to take away; and if the quantity of corn to be paid per acre is fixed, then you will throw a monftrous oppreffion on all the kingdom below your medium in favour of the part that is above it, which muft appear to every one an infurmountable objection.

Thirdly, It has been propofed that the compofition for tythes fhould be fixed at fo much in the pound rent, throughout the kingdom. This would obviate the objection from the fall of money, but it is open to that of the fecond propofition; and it is alfo open to another, which is the difficulty of fixing a rent to lands long occupied by their owners.

Fourthly, It is propofed to give a value in land—which, upon the whole, is that idea which appears to me open to the feweft objections: It provides for the clergy infinitely upon more favourable and liberal principles than any other mode whatever, infomuch that (which is an object, in the great work of changing tythes, of vaft importance) the clergy themfelves would probably agree to the fcheme upon this footing. It fecures them not only from

fuffering

fuffering by a fall in the value of money, but alfo gives them a property which will rife proportionably to that fall. It is not open to a fingle objection upon the account of fair pound-rates, valuations of rent, or any fuch fources of knavery. It is the fame to the whole kingdom; you will not opprefs one part of it in favour of another. It is but one account; the moment it is fixed there is for ever an end of fquabbles with the clergy, whereas many of the other fchemes would perpetuate them as much as tythes in kind.

That there are objections to this idea is certain, and fome that are very weighty; but I think the whole affair muft depend on overcoming thefe objections; if you cannot do that the bufinefs is impracticable. However, I have yet heard none that are infuperable. An act might direct that the land-owners of every parifh fhould chufe one commiffioner of allotment, and the rector or tythe-owner another, which two to chufe a third, and thefe three commiffioners to be invefted with thofe abfolute powers common in all commiffions of inclofure; they fhould be tied down by the act to afcertain the average value of the living for the laft feven years, including all tythes great and fmall, and to affign, as near as may be, to the parfonage, a portion of land fufficient to yield a rent equal to fuch average value. This would of courfe be done in the ufual method of reducing the whole parifh to money, and then gaining the proportions. That there would be difficulties in fuch a work nobody can doubt, and if acts of inclofure had never paffed, fuch as would be called infurmountable; but we know that no difficulty could arife that has not often been met with, and overcome in inclofures—no variety or complexity of interefts, no difficulty of arranging lands—no more important interefts to be fettled in one cafe than in the other; why not therefore proceed on a fyftem which is put daily in execution in one part of the kingdom or other? I fpeak this under the fuppofition that the lands affigned in lieu of tythes were neceffarily to be in a fpot around the parfonage; if contiguity was not infifted upon, all difficulties would vanifh.

Another objection which has been made to the whole of this idea, is the impropriety of adding to the lands in mortmain, which are already too numerous and extenfive. This may be an impropriety, but are improprieties to weigh down fuch amazing benefits as would refult from the abolition of tythe? Adding to the inconvenience, when no public advantages are to refult from

from it, would be abſurd; but the preſent is a very different caſe. The tenth part of your groſs products is already in mortmain, why not change ſuch a burthenſome payment for an aſſignment of land? This is not in any reſpect a ſimilar caſe with an increaſe by legacies, purchaſe, or donation. But farther; lands in the poſſeſſion of rectors of pariſhes lying around their parſonage houſes, would be ſcarcely open to the uſual objections againſt mortmain: much the greateſt part would neceſſarily be kept in the hands of the reſident rectors, improved juſt as much and as well as the farms of the laity, when in their own hands. I appeal to the knowledge of gentlemen in the country, if the glebes of clergymen, when they lie conveniently for their own houſes, are not as well managed as other lands; unleſs the neceſſary improvements are of a very expenſive nature, and the incumbent very old. And when ſuch lands are let, why are we to ſuppoſe that the rector will not, for his own intereſt, get as great a rent as he can, and if he does, then the greateſt objection to the land being in the hands of the church vaniſhes.

Lands in the poſſeſſion of a dean and chapter, or a biſhop, where the tenure is on lives, and the benefit a fine, or belonging to colleges or hoſpitals, are as entirely different as any two caſes can be. In all theſe caſes, the public ſuffers from the preſent incumbent preferring a preſent advantage of a fine to an annual one in rent; rents therefore are not raiſed, and wherever that is the caſe, all the world knows the public ſuffers from the bad huſbandry exerciſed on ſuch lands. It is the ſame with truſtees for hoſpitals, &c. who never attend to the benefit of the eſtates in the manner they do to their own But in all theſe caſes, the rector of a pariſh would be put on a par with other private gentlemen, having the ſame intereſts, and from the ſituation of the land around his manſion, the ſame inducement to improve for profit and pleaſure. But this reaſoning is upon the ſuppoſition that there were any ſolid objections to the ſcheme, without attending to the advantages; reflect on the evil you get rid of—reflect on the miſchief of tythes to your eſtates—reflect on the improvements made in land tythe free, which can only be made in them—reflect on the riſe of your rents following ſuch a plan—reflect on the ſolid improvement which would reſult from it to the agriculture of the whole kingdom; and then determine if both public and private intereſts do not ſtrongly unite to promote the execution of this plan, the only one by which this enormous tax, MULTIPLIABLE ON ALL IMPROVEMENTS, can ever be aboliſhed.

SECT. V.

FREEDOM FROM PERSONAL SERVICE.

FROM reading ſeveral *French* authors on rural oeconomy, I apprehend their farmers lie under a very conſiderable and irregular burthen in the ſervices performed for their landlords, ſeigneurs of towns, &c. and theſe appear to be of an extenſive nature—at all ſeaſons of the year—and no equivalent or pay returned for them. Of this we have no other traces in *England*, except ſuch articles as are ſometimes inſerted in leaſes, ſuch as carriage of firing, timber, and other materials of building; but theſe are always ſpecified, voluntarily engaged in, and a limitation that they ſhall not exceed a certain number of days work. It can in no caſe be eſteemed a burthen; the exemption from ſuch evils as the *French* writers deſcribe, muſt be eſteemed as a very valuable circumſtance.

SECT. VI.

CORN LAWS.

THE liberty enjoyed by every rank of our people; the eaſe and impartiality of of our taxation—the length of our leases—our freedom from personal service — all these would in vain shed their happy influence, if, for want of good corn laws, foreigners were allowed, in the markets of *Britain*, to rival our own farmers, or if by prohibitory laws our products were kept at a low price; every other advantage under heaven would not make amends for such deficiencies. It is in vain that an hundred encouragements urge the farmer to gain great crops, if when he has gained them he cannot find a ready market and a sufficient price. I have, in several other publications, explained myself so fully upon this head, that at present I have only to make a few observations, which are essential to a clear idea of the dependance which our agriculture has upon the police of corn *.

The

* One argument against the bounty, used by several writers, is the imagination that the *Dutch* buy our corn by means of that premium, and sell it to us again with profit.—Which is much such an objection as was made to Governor *Pownal's* bill, that the bounty would be paid to pretended exporters, who would carry their corn to *Holland* and then ship it back again. But the following table of the expences will shew how well 5s. a quarter would pay for this operation.

Corn-

The firſt great ſtep was to cut off the importation from foreign countries, unleſs when the price at home was very high; this important object preceded another of equal conſequence, the granting a bounty on the exportation when not exceeding certain prices. This was one of the moſt remarkable ſtrokes of policy, and the moſt contrary to the general ideas of all *Europe*, of any that ever were carried into execution.

The deſign was to give a premium to the landed intereſt of the kingdom, in return for the great exertion they had made to place the crown on the head of King *William*. The act declares the price of corn to be too low, and the evident deſign of the

---

	s.	*d.*
Cornfactor's charge of ſhipping, per quarter,	1	6
Commiſſion and inſurance, ſuppoſing wheat at 43*s* - - -	1	6
Freight and primage, - -	1	8
	4	8
The charges from *Holland* are to be eſtimated at 1 *s* more, - -	5	8
	10	4
The charges are the ſame to *Ireland*, but the freight higher to and from, 1 *s* per quarter,	12	4

From which account it is very evident that the 5 *s*. a quarter bounty can have no ſuch effect.

I

the meaſure was to raiſe it. It has, however, been attended with the direct contrary effect, it has ſunk it conſiderably; a point not ſufficiently underſtood by many perſons, who do not take into their account the fall in the value of money, and conſequent riſe in the price of all commodities, corn excepted; if this is calculated, the fall in the price of wheat will be found very conſiderable *. This fall has not been owing to improvements in agriculture, ſince they would have operated equally in lowering the price of meat and other products of the farmers, which has been far enough from the caſe. Here, therefore, remains the paradox, how a meaſure, which has ſunk the price of corn, can have encouraged agriculture?

It has certainly given a greater ſtability to prices, which is an object of conſequence: It is not the farmer's intereſt to have corn three pounds a quarter one year, and five and twenty ſhillings the next. Years in which the price is very low, are the farmers great enemies; in the ſixteen years, from 1741 to 1756, the crops of corn, in this iſland, were ſo uncommonly plentiful, that the price would have ſunk ſo

* In the *Expediency of a Free Exportation of Corn*, 1770, p. 11, I have ſhewn this at large.

ſo low as to have utterly diſcouraged cultivation, had not a remarkably briſk exportation carried off immenſe quantities, and kept the farmers from throwing their wheat to their hogs.—Now had not the bounty effected this, the farmers would not have ſown wheat, and then ſucceſſive years would have riſen ſo high in price, as to have raiſed the general average of the period much higher than before the bounty took place.

In examining the prices before the prohibition of the import of foreign corn, as given in our only record, the *Windſor* Table, we do not ſee the *real* prices, tho' we do ſince that time: They are the prices of corn in that market, which is neceſſarily affected by all the markets around, and by that of *London* in particular, with which it communicates by water.—Now if the *French* or *Dutch* poured in great quantities of corn, it neceſſarily ſunk the price of our own, and probably gave our farmers a low rate when they ought to have had an high one. This operation neceſſarily gave a degree of equality to the prices before that period, which was totally artificial, and not owing to encouragement of our own culture, but the direct contrary. Yet with all this miſchief to our huſbandry, the ſyſtem very poorly anſwered the intent, for the fluc-

fluctuation of prices was, notwithstanding, much greater than it has been since. And when the writers against the bounty speak of the cheapness of corn at former periods, they forget that they are speaking of the cheapness of *French* corn as much as of *English*, since the cheapness they falsely state was effected by importation. This was particularly the case through the reign of *James* I.

The prices since that period are real ones of our own corn, unaffected by foreign imports, and consequently shew the true degree of cheapness.

The cheapness brought on by this measure has indeed in one period been so great, that I do not think our agriculture could have supported it, and continued flourishing, unless the crops had, at the same time, been very abundant. From the year 1730 to 1756, corn was so amazingly cheap in *England*, that this nation ought not to wish ever to see such another period: During the whole of it complaints were incessant, through every part of the kingdom, of the decay and ruin of manufactures: I have a list of above one hundred and forty publications at *London*, in that period, pointing out or complaining of the decline of the woollen and other fabrics: If those complaints had any foundation (which I admit

admit is by no means clear) it certainly was owing to this prodigious cheapneſs of proviſions, which in all countries is ſuch an encourager of idleneſs, that no manufactures can flouriſh under it. From 1741 to 1756, the average price of wheat at the *Windſor* market was 3 *s.* 8 *d.* a buſhel, or 1 *l.* 9 *s.* 4 *d.* per quarter, which is 2 *s.* 7 *d.* per buſhel, or 1 *l* 0 *s.* 6 *d.* per quarter *Wincheſter* meaſure, and average quality. It was impoſſible the farmers ſhould be ſo wealthy as they ought, or even in tolerable circumſtances, with wheat at ſuch a price; —and from the beſt information I have been able to gain, I have reaſon to believe that our huſbandry, in the cheap period from 1730 to 1756, made ſcarcely any advance: I know this was not the caſe in *Norfolk*, but the improvements there were forced by the landlords, who built, incloſed, and marled at their own expence, and then let the land at a fourth of the rent it carries at preſent: Since 1756, that is with a comparative high price of corn, the tenants have done the whole, and made more money in ſixteen years than they did before in ſix and forty.

That the ſyſtem of exporting with a bounty has been of infinite national importance, cannot be doubted: Between 1730 and 1756, the quantity of corn we exported brought in many millions of money to this kingdom, and employed a great quantity of ſhipping, yet the price was very low at home through the whole period, to what purpoſe ſhould we have kept that corn, and loſt that wealth, unleſs to ſink the price, in certain years, ſo low as to ſtop the plough, and conſequently occaſion ſucceſſive ſcarcities. The uniform experience of all nations proves that where the exportation of corn is prohibited, there the price in abundant years falls ſo low that the plough yields no profit to the farmer—it is abandoned, and the lands lie uncultivated—ſcarcity, and even famine, are then never far off. It is not a ſatisfaction to the farmer to tell him, that the immenſe rates of certain years render the general average as high or higher than in other countries. this is no conſolation to a man who has been abſolutely ruined by the low prices of three or four ſucceſſive years. His money, ſtock, and farm are gone, nor can he enter into buſineſs again when the high prices come. To have embraced a ſyſtem directly oppoſite to ſuch a pernicious one, muſt be eſteemed a ſingular felicity in this kingdom.

LATE SYSTEM.

It is here neceſſary to offer a few remarks on the ſyſtem which our legiſlature has purſued ſince the year 1756, becauſe, ſince that period, an almoſt new one has been adopted. In 1757 and 1758, the price aroſe conſiderably, and exportation was prohibited. In the ſix ſucceſſive years the export continued. But from the year 1765, to the preſent time, we have had a perpetual ſhifting policy, in which nothing has been permanent. no regular law; no new arrangement of prices at which export ſhould be allowed or prohibited; every year has produced a temporary act ſuſpending the operation of thoſe laws which had proved of ſuch excellent utility. The legiſlature had almoſt conſtantly been driven into ſuch a pernicious ſyſtem by the riots and complaints of the manufacturing poor, and the *London* mob —and by the fooliſh petitions of ignorant boroughs.

Upon reviewing this period of ſixteen years, from 1757 to 1772, both incluſive, it is remarkable to find that the average of the beſt wheat at *Windſor* has been only 5*s.* 6*d* a buſhel, or 2*l.* 4*s.* a quarter; which, for the average quality and *Winchester* meaſure,

ſure, is only 4 *s.* 4 *d.* a buſhel, or 1 *l.* 14 *s.* 8 *d* a quarter. Now that this has not, upon the whole, been an high price, cannot for a moment be doubted. From 1697 to 1714, throwing out two years in which the export was prohibited, the remainder being alſo a period of ſixteen years, through the whole of which exportation *with the bounty* went on, the average price, in the ſame *Windſor* market, was 2 *l.* 5 *s.*; conſequently the laſt period of ſixteen years, ending 1772, was *cheaper* by 10 *d.* a quarter than the other, during which the bounty was paid! But ſo far from the bounty being paid through this, that it has been ſuſpended during ten of the ſixteen years, and export itſelf prohibited during more than half the period This is ſuch an amazing change of policy, that no ſagacity can diſcover any other reaſons for it than the tranſitory impulſe of riots and complaints.

But let me farther remark, that the late period, which is to be called *dear*, only on compariſon with the ſixteen preceding years, opened with the war, which, during nine years, added ſuch an amazing maſs of bullion and paper to our circulation, and which has, to the preſent time, been every day increaſing rather than diminiſhing, by acquiſitions in the *Indies*, and by a moſt

2 enlarged

enlarged and flouriſhing commerce—that it would have been a moſt aſtoniſhing phenomenon in politics, had not the price of all ſorts of commodities riſen. An increaſe of national debt of ſeventy millions, with the regular circulation of the intereſt—the expenditure, during the war, from twelve to twenty millions a year—and the money brought into the nation the laſt years of the war by a commerce which never was equalled,—a great increaſe of taxes—and a ſtill greater of paper currency of all ſorts, could not fail of having that effect.

But let any perſon reflect on the riſe of all prices during the laſt ſixteen years; let them name one article, in the common courſe of purchaſe and ſale, which has not been conſiderably advanced. All the parts of dreſs, as cloth, linen, ſilk, lace, leather, ornaments, &c. The whole of furniture, your pictures, glaſſes, hangings, carpets, ſopha's, chairs, tables. Your equipage, from the gilded chariot at St. *James's*, to the one horſe chaiſe at *Whitechapel.* All thoſe articles of food which are beyond the purſes of the poor, the whole train of delicacies. Your pleaſures, your diverſions, your education, and your ſtudy. Throughout all this liſt, and that it might be much lengthened every one will agree, can you name a ſingle article the price whereof is not greatly raiſed? We ſee, therefore, by this general riſe, that the cauſes, I juſt mentioned, have taken their natural effect, by raiſing every thing; and it remains to be ſhewn, that wheat ought to riſe with other things. Two words will diſpatch this argument; if the producer of one commodity is proſcribed from ſo general an advantage, while, in every branch of his conſumption, he pays amply to every one elſe—while his rent, his labour, his rates, his tythe compoſition, his wear and tear, and manufactures, all riſe in price upon him, how is he to carry on his culture? He muſt be inevitably ruined. On the contrary, he ought to receive equal encouragement with any other claſs, for exactly in proportion to his encouragement will be the ſpirit and extent of his culture and improvements. Yet, in direct oppoſition to ſuch ideas, do we every day hear complaints of the high prices of proviſions, with inflammatory publications, deſigned to ſhew the too great profits of our farmers, and attributing ſuch prices to falſe cauſes—theſe are vulgar complaints, common in all ages and all places. The capital of the kingdom even petitioned parliament, laſt ſeſſions, to give a bounty on the importation of wheat, and actually gave one itſelf. Let us ſuppoſe the Houſe of Commons had adopted the idea, and offered a bounty ſufficient to have brought in conſiderable quantities of foreign corn—the price before was a juſt one, proportioned to the quantity of money in the nation and the quantity of the preceding crops—conſequently the price was juſt what it ought to be. The import, we may ſuppoſe, lowers it conſiderably; this is the object deſired—but how are the farmers to fare? if proportion demands 7*s.* a buſhel, what is he to do with only 4*s.*? What ſpirit will there be in his culture? What encouragement to raiſe corn? Thus you lay a very heavy tax (for nothing elſe would do in a time of ſuch general ſcarcity) which in the expenditure is to be ruinous to the farmers, in order that corn may be cheap! What a heap of abſurdity and contradiction is ſuch a ſyſtem! Might you not as well cut the manufacturers looms in pieces, and ſet fire to their warehouſes in order to lower the price of cloth? Would not any perſon ſuppoſe that ſuch ideas were found in ſome ſilly pamphlet, inſtead of a petition from a great city to a *Britiſh* Houſe of Commons? From all this we may determine, that our former ſyſtem of corn law was a great encouragement to our agriculture, and ſince thoſe laws were reverſed, the general riſe of prices has operated a ſucceeding good effect.

PERMANENT CORN LAW.

The act which passed last sessions, and which was brought in by Governor *Pownal*, has remedied some of the evils which flowed from the variable shifting policy that had for some years been our disgrace; yet was that bill founded on radical mistakes, since the principles of it supposed that lower export prices ought to be fixed at present than in 1689, instead of which they ought to be *higher*. And the only principle upon which an alteration of the prices could be justly effected, was proving that corn, in the present period, ought to be considerably cheaper than it was in the latter part of the preceding century—which assertion, to be rendered consistent, must be followed by another, that the farmers of this kingdom pay much lower rents than they did; have their labour, implements, furniture, and manufactures at lower prices, and pay much smaller sums in poor rates, at present, than an hundred years ago. What consistency there can be in adopting the *principle* that prices ought to fall, and making it the corner stone of a permanent law, I cannot understand. I do not think that a beneficial system, which had stood the test of many years experience,

should,

ſhould, in its *principles*, be overturned. The act of 1689, declares corn, at that period, to be *too cheap*, and therefore gave a bounty at certain prices. Corn is now much cheaper, and you declare that it is *too dear*, by lowering the bounty rates: In a word, the ideas, which were our guide in 1689, were eſſentially different from thoſe which influence our conduct at preſent.

In anſwer to this, I have not heard any ſatisfactory motives, it is all thrown on the diſcontents of the mob, and the complaints of rioters, who inſiſt on wheat being *cheap*, that they may afford *dear* ſugar, tea, brandy, and ſtrong beer; and be able to conſume four times as much of thoſe commodities, as their more frugal anceſtors did.

As I have declared my opinion of the new act thus far, I ſhall, on the other hand, readily admit, that if the compariſon is not to be drawn with the old policy—but with the abominable ſyſtem that has diſgraced us ſince 1765, Mr. *Pownal*'s act has great merit. *Firſt*, It is a permanent law, which ſingle circumſtance remedies abundance of evils that have perplexed us. *Second*, It preſerves the bounty when corn is very cheap, the very idea of which we were in danger of loſing. *Third*, It gives the bounty whenever exportation goes on, which

which is a plan equally well adapted to a conſtant encouragement both of huſbandry and navigation, and the only means of regaining our loſt corn trade. *Fourth*, The proviſions relative to importation are well imagined, to keep up a *trade* in corn when not wanted for *conſumption*, and obviate the old objection to our laws, that ſhipping in foreign countries could not be ſafely done, when it was an uncertainty whether the price in *England* would allow importation.

Upon the whole, the act has great merit, and will do more good than any other *new* meaſure could have done. and I muſt ſay, that the father of it merits the thanks of every one, as a member who ſacrifices his time and attention to objects of public importance. I have the pleaſure of knowing, from his converſation, that his ideas are perfectly judicious on this point, and that he neceſſarily framed the bill, from a practical knowledge of what would ſucceed *.

VARIATION OF PRODUCTS.

It is amuſing to reflect to what a variety of cauſes the riſe of prices has been attributed—monopoly of farms—incloſures—jobbers—the bounty—horſes—dogs, and all ſorts of abſurdities · others have had judg-

* See Appendix.

judgment enough to reject these idle causes, and acknowledge that there has been a *real* scarcity owing to bad seasons. A late very ingenious author * says, that there has been a failure of crops in general for five years past; and Mess. *Smyth* and *Farrer* at the bar of the house of commons, talked the same language. I cannot, from the most attentive reflection, allow these remarks to be just the average *Windsor* price of six years ending 1772 inclusive, was 2*l.* 3*s.* 6*d.* a quarter, which is, average quality and *Winchester* measure, only 1*l.* 14*s.* 5*d.* Does such a price mark any real scarcity? Compare this price with preceding periods —reflect that it is at a time when all sorts of prices are rising, owing to the cheapness of money, and then tell me if it is possible that wheat should have stood at such a rate, had there been five successive bad, or even indifferent crops! A small deficiency in the markets has always been observed to raise the price beyond the proportion of such deficiency; under which circumstance, a bad crop at a time when every thing is rising in price from the plenty of money, must appear to have a prodigious effect —What therefore must be the effect of

* *Enquiry into size of farms and price of provisions,* p. 51.

of five or six bad crops, causing a scarcity, while the cheapness of money, increase of consumption, waste, luxury, &c. all conspire to raise the price even of good ones? Surely an enormous rate must be the consequence; so that those who attribute the ideal scarcity to bad years, but deceive the people, as there probably will never be better years. It is idle to flatter them in this manner, in my own opinion, the crops for five years past have been not bad, at least; consequently there is no reason to expect corn lower; — an hundred arguments might be brought to prove that it is not high To raise wheat to 1 *l.* 14 *s.* 5 *d.* must so many chimerical reasons be brought! Surely parliament was not very attentive, when she appointed committees to enquire into the causes of wheat getting to so *high* a price!

As to good and bad crops in general, very little dependence is to be placed in the accounts received or given by millers, mealmen, factors, and such people, who depend so much on private intelligence, that they are ever apt to suppose the language of their interested information, that of the kingdom, which is generally a very great error. But five bad crops in succession, when agriculture is highly encouraged! Very suspicious such ideas—I do not believe such a thing

happens

happens in two centuries. Nor do I think it eafy to declare what feafon, wet or dry, beft fuits the production of corn in *England*; the foil is fo various, fuch tracts of fand, fandy loams, gravels, chalks, and other foils, to which a wet year is as fuitable as a dry one to clays. So many tracts of clay and wet loams, to which a dry year is as fuitable as a wet one to fand.—Upon the whole, I am clear that attributing the late prices of wheat (*low* I might fay with more propriety than *high*) to bad feafons, is more rational than to talk of jobbers and poft horfes, but is very far from throwing the matter into its proper light.

I have ventured this remark as an antidote to melancholy accounts of *another bad feafon*—and then we fhall hear of *another*—and another—and another—and the hand of God fuppofed to be chaftifing us for our luxury *, at the very time that he is

* Our political moralifts are ever inveighing againft luxury, I think with very little reafon And I entirely agree with a writer, who gives his opinion in the following paffage. " A clean fhirt and a laced hat are not inconfiftent with piety and virtue, nor ortolans and burgundy with temperance, nor a feather bed with fortitude, nor a p nch of fnuff with fobriety, nor a handfome woman with chaftity. A man may enjoy them all, and yet act up to the dignity of his nature, and conformably to the precepts of religion and

is showering down all the blessings of plenty *.

SECT. VII.

GENERAL WEALTH.

IN proportion to that wealth in a country which is the result not of mines, but of industry, will be the prosperity of agriculture, arts, manufactures, and commerce: Arguments indeed have been used, to shew

---

and morality. Neither, on the other hand, does a man's confining himself to the use of fat bacon, *Lacedæmonian* broth, muddy beer, coarse woollens, a leather doublet, a canvas shirt, and a thatched hovel upon a common, render him the more pious, temperate, sober, chaste, religious and virtuous, for he may confine himself to the use of all these, and yet be a most slovenly sinner and beastly profligate. And it seems that the refined debauchee is the most eligible character of the two." *A Vindication of Commerce and the Arts*, 1758, p. 51.

* Let it not be imagined that I suppose bad crops cannot happen. In 1698 and 1699, the crops are supposed to have been very bad, and the same in 1709 and 1710, in which two years wheat at *Windsor* was 3*l.* 18*s.* a quarter; reckoning the fall of money, this is not far from being equal to 6*l.* 10*s.* or perhaps more. And if we had what really deserved to be called a general bad crop, it is not to be doubted but the price would rise much higher than any thing we have experienced of late years, the prices of which, even 1757 itself, speak not any thing like a great scarcity.

ſhew that the two laſt *may* ſuffer from great wealth, though not, I think, concluſive ones; but I am clear that agriculture muſt always flouriſh in proportion to the general wealth of a country; and I attribute the flouriſhing ſtate of the huſbandry of this kingdom greatly to the quantity of our riches. But as there is a ſyſtem of reaſoning which may be uſed againſt this idea, it will be proper to ſhew upon what grounds the opinion is founded.

Many writers have remarked that agriculture is much encouraged by ſimplicity of manners—that luxury is an enemy to it; that it flouriſhed more among the old *Romans*, with their minute diviſion of the ſoil, when a whole family had but a few acres, than in the more brilliant and wealthy period, the age of *Auguſtus*. But the idea is very falſe for let us grant the fact, that when a family has juſt land enough for its ſubſiſtence, that portion will be well cultivated, what uſeful deductions are to be drawn from it relative to modern policy? Of what uſe in a modern kingdom would be a whole province thus divided, however well cultivated, except for the mere purpoſe of breeding men, which, ſingly taken, is a moſt uſeleſs purpoſe? A province of ſuch farmers would live only to themſelves—they would conſume nothing but the produce of their lands—they would not be able to buy manufactures—and they could pay no taxes without an oppreſſion which would reduce them to indigence and miſery Such a population is of no uſe in a modern ſtate. In the early times of the *Roman* republic they were of great uſe, for the more men the greater the tax paid, *viz* the perſonal ſervice in arms. This diſtinction is ſo ſtrong, that the ſame diviſion of land, which, in one caſe, was a political excellence, is, in the other, a political evil It is of no conſequence to ſay, that the little portion of land is perfectly cultivated, if its perfection is of no benefit to the ſtate Hence ariſes the neceſſity of diſtinguiſhing between the practice of agriculture as a mere means of ſubſiſtence—and practiſing it as a trade. The former is of no benefit to a modern ſtate, the latter of infinite importance.

Now ſimplicity of manners, and a freedom from the effects of luxury, are beſt exhibited in a country portioned into ſuch little properties as are merely ſufficient for ſubſiſtence · Luxury recedes, and ſimplicity advances, as you withdraw from mankind. But that cauſe, which deſtroys a ſimplicity that operates in preventing agriculture being exercifed as a trade, is highly beneficial to a modern ſtate; this is public wealth:

wealth: As money flows in, ſuch little portions of land muſt diſappear *, by becoming united in large parcels, wherein agriculture is exerciſed as a trade—wherein products are raiſed in ſurplus—carried to market—ſold—taxes paid—and the circulation of money active Upon what conſiſtent principles, therefore, can that cauſe be condemned, which works juſt the effects that are eſſentially neceſſary in a modern kingdom?

Now, to quit the period of change from one ſtate of property to another, let us ſee the effects of great national wealth, when the change is effected. Let any perſon conſider the progreſs of every thing in *Britain* during the laſt twenty years. The great improvements we have ſeen in this period, ſuperior to thoſe of any other, are not owing to the conſtitution, to moderate taxation, or to other circumſtances of equal efficacy, ever ſince the Revolution, as the exiſtence of thoſe circumſtances did not before produce equal effects.—The ſuperiority

* Suppoſing the country ſo divided before, as was the caſe at *Rome* The contrary effect happened in the kingdoms portioned out in the feudal ſyſtem; great tracts were reduced, but the principle of the change was the ſame in both; *agriculture for ſubſiſtence*, was in both changed for *agriculture for trade*, and in both the improvement of the national territory was proportioned to this change.

ority has been owing to the quantity of wealth in the nation, which has, in a prodigious degree, facilitated the execution of all great works of improvement.

This idea is, in part, contrary to a common one, that the price of commodities is proportioned to the quantity of money; and consequently that a crown in one age is as effective as a guinea in another; this is very true, but the great difference lies in the superior ease of getting money in the wealthy period When the quantity of money in circulation is very great, it is surprising to see the facility with which all kinds of great works are undertaken and executed the money when raised goes not proportionably farther than a smaller sum in a poorer age; but the greater sum in the wealthier period is gained, acquired, borrowed, raised a thousand times easier than the smaller sum in the poorer one, and this is the circumstance which gives the superiority; and which invigorates to so great a degree the whole range of industry.

In this enquiry no distinction should be made between money and paper, as the effects are exactly similar; and the great figure made in active industry, by this country, has been almost totally owing to the introduction, increase, and support of paper credit. Let thofe who doubt of this fact, reflect on the progrels which agriculture, manufactures, &c. made in a few years in *Scotland*, from the inftitution of land-banks, which threw into actual circulation a large part of the value of the eftates of that kingdom. While the paper of thofe banks circulated in full credit, no undertaking was too great—money was always to be had; and confequently the improvement of lands was rapid — New manufactures, upon the largeft fcale, were every day eftablifhed, and commerce in all her ports increafed. But fince the fhock, which almoft deftroyed that credit, no undertaking of any magnitude has been thought of.—Many that were in action have received fuch a blow, that they expired, and others can fcarcely be faid to exift.

Let us, in the next place, confider, what a ftagnation has, in *England*, been experienced fince the bankruptcy of Mr. *Fordyce*. There is no branch of induftry, whether agriculture, arts, manufactures, or commerce—no public works depending on private fubfcriptions—none carried on by borrowed money, but what have felt the evils of that fhock to credit. If it is faid that credit was carried too far, and the confequences neceffarily mifchievous, I admit it; but this proves nothing againſt my poſition, which is, that the flouriſhing ſtate of agriculture is principally owing to general wealth: this leads at once to the queſtion, whether our public paper is to be ranked in ſtability with the credit of Mr. *Fordyce*, an enquiry which I ſhall leave to itſelf.

Nor do the advantages of which I ſpeak, depend only on the *eaſe of raiſing money*; another circumſtance of great importance, is the increaſe of luxury, which increaſes conſumption. firſt, from increaſing the number of the people. ſecondly, from feeding them better and more plentifully and, thirdly, from waſte.—All theſe circumſtances are but other words for an increaſe of the farmer's market. If the number of the people is increaſed ſince the revolution, of which there can be little doubt, the food they eat yields that increaſe of demand. Of the better living of every claſs, of which no doubt can be entertained, the ſame effect is evident: This better living conſiſts in the people conſuming more food, and of a better ſort; eating wheat inſtead of barley, oats, and rye — and drinking a prodigiouſly greater quantity of beer. This is not the caſe only among the lower claſſes, but in all the middle ranks, and in the kitchens of every family of of fortune in the kingdom. Nor is the article of waſte of leſs importance: if we conſider the number of dogs kept in every houſe, and the profuſion in which people of fortune live, we ſhall be convinced that this article includes no inconſiderable part of our conſumption, and is far greater in a refined and luxurious age, than in a plain and frugal one. It is exactly proportioned to luxury—and is to be eſteemed as much a market to the farmer, as the regular and frugal conſumption at the poor man's board. I have here confined myſelf to wheat—but the remark is yet more ſtriking if we name horſes, which raiſe a vaſt demand for other products of the farmer, and are in numbers exactly proportioned to the general wealth of the nation *.

 Thoſe

* It is incredible that the *French* œconomiſts ſhould ſo far miſtake the very principles of encouragement to agriculture, as to declaim againſt luxury, which they define, l'interverſion de l ordre naturel, eſſentiel des dépenſes nationales qui augmente la maſſe des depenſes non productives au préjudice de celles qui ſervent à la production et en meme tems au prejudice de la production elle meme The expences which flow from luxury not productive! What can be meant by this? The increaſed conſumption and waſte of all the products of the farmer, is not this a market to him? The circulation and riſe of all prices, which, though an attendant, and not the effect of luxury, is a circum-

Thoſe who urge that the ſimplicity of living in frugal times is the moſt beneficial to the culture of the earth, ſhould reflect on the probable circumſtances of a decline in that wealth which they are ſuch enemies to. Let me ſuppoſe that ſuch a declenſion comes — that the people decreaſe — that the reſt eat leſs in quantity, and poorer in quality, than before—that the greater poverty of the times ſtrikes off all waſte. In ſuch a ſituation the farmer finds a great change in his landlord or rich neighbour—inſtead of a profuſion in the conſumption of bread, beer, mutton, and beef, thoſe articles are reduced; the number of ſervants is leſſened — a pointer and a ſpaniel occupy the place of a pack of hounds — a chaiſe and pair inſtead of a coach and ſix—ten horſes kept inſtead of thirty or forty.—All theſe reductions are ſo much taken from the farmer's market; he cannot, from that day, ſell ſo much cattle, corn, hay, and ſtraw as formerly; conſequently will not raiſe

cumſtance of the higheſt conſequence to agriculture and what a contradiction is it to eſteem all expences unproductive, that are not actually employed in cultivation If the luxurious way of ſpending a fortune in this age, was changed for the ſimple manners of three hundred years ago, would agriculture be encouraged thereby? Such ideas are extremely ill founded, and can never be reduced to practice without the moſt miſchievous conſequences

raiſe ſo much. But this is not the only effect; in ſuch a decline he will neceſſarily raiſe more than demanded, the prices will then fall, and *all* his product will be affected by the fall in only a part of his markets: This is the very progreſs to ruin —he can no longer pay the ſame rent, labour or taxes — no longer execute the ſame ſpirited cultivation:—the next ſtep is his land becoming waſte. This degradation is not an opinion—it is an evident fact—a matter of calculation; it is the very train into which ſo many of our writers are deſirous we ſhould fall—ſince it is but another word for a general fall of prices. a more fatal miſtake could never have been adopted. a GENERAL RISE is the great ſignal of national vigour and health; a GENERAL FALL the ſure criterion of decay.

If I am told that an increaſe of general wealth is more favourable to the conſumption of foreign, and other luxuries, than of the products of our ſoil, and that a decreaſe of it would alſo be more felt by them; I reply, that the proportion between their ſufferings is difficult to calculate; but the obſervation has ſome truth in it; but this does not impeach my aſſertion; however the venders of ſuperfluities may ſuffer, yet the farmers will certainly ſuffer with them, for in all the articles I recited above, the rich man muft curtail his expences, and he cannot do that without leffening the farmer's market

It fhould farther be confidered, that the manufacturers and failors with their dependants, who are employed by the confumption of luxuries, form another confiderable branch of market to the hufbandman; and if the decline of national wealth decreafes that confumption, this is a frefh wound to that market.

LUXURY.

A late writer *, for whofe abilities I have the higheft regard, feems to condemn what is called luxury, for the wafte it creates—for the number of domeftic fervants—for horfes—and for the flaughter of calves and lambs, which, he thinks, makes mutton and beef dearer. I am forry I cannot fully agree with him; we both fpeak of thefe matters, not with a view to vifionary ufelefs ideas of the manners of the people, but relative only to the encouragement of agriculture and increafe of plenty. In this light, what difference is there between *wafte*

* *L[illegible], [illegible] Pr[illegible] of P[illegible]fions, and Size of Farms,* p. 4[illegible]. In other paffages, however, he juftly allows lu[illegible] [illegible]ket to the farmer.

waste and *regular consumption?* Between bread eat at my lord's table, and barley consumed by his hounds, or oats by his horses? All these *methods* of consumption are nothing to the farmer—the mere purchase of the commodities is what encourages him, in consequence of which he sets heartily about a farther production of them. And how is the consumption of calves and lambs to lessen the quantity of beef and mutton? The farmer brings these things to market because they are demanded. if instead of demanding ten pounds worth of lamb, you go to market for ten pounds worth of beef, he will bring the beef for you. Here is a given demand for beef; it is supplied. luxury adds another for veal, it is supplied, certainly without taking from the beef—and if luxury doubles that demand, the farmers will answer it, and supply the old one of beef besides. But it is said, there is a given number of calves every year, if the consumption of veal was stopped, so many more would of course come to market as beef, and this additional number would surely make beef more plentiful, and consequently cheaper. Granted. And so you would encourage the farmer to continue this plenty of beef by lowering the price of it!—This is that universal combination which runs through the supply of of all ſorts of markets—the caſe of corn has been pretty well underſtood; but ſtill the remnants of theſe prejudices hang about us in calves, pigs, lambs, and ſo forth. —On the contrary, you ought to act upon the reverſe of theſe principles. Your given fact is the dearneſs of beef, and you want permanently to make it cheaper.—Your only method is to raiſe the price Encourage the ſlaughter of calves, which is ſuch an encouragement to the breeder and grazier, as the export of wheat is to the corn-grower; his prices riſe—he becomes more ſpirited in his buſineſs—he brings more to market. Conſider this train from the beginning—is it poſſible it ſhould have any other conſequence? A century ago, theſe things were ſo ill underſtood, that our anceſtors gave a bounty on the export of corn, *in order to make it dear*: they never dreamt that they were taking the moſt effectual means to make it cheap; and yet it would doubtleſs have been thought a glaring paradox to aſſert, that taking great quantities of corn from our markets, was not a way to raiſe the price. And for what I know, the idea I have juſt dropped, that *in order to make beef cheaper, you muſt make it dearer*, will even in this age be thought another paradox.

I am

I am here aware of an objection which will be made to this: It may be ſaid, that the demand for calves lays a tax on the grazier in the progreſs of his buſineſs, by raiſing the price of what may be called his raw commodity; not ſimilar to the *export* of beef.—I admit this, and am ſenſible that the export of beef would be a better method of effecting it; but let it be conſidered that the way in which export encourages the product of a commodity, is leſſening the quantity in the markets while the demand continues the ſame, and conſequently raiſing the price;—now the objection to killing calves, is, that it raiſes the price of beef. this is what I contend for. It is of little conſequence what does it—if the price is raiſed, the producer of the commodity is encouraged—and in conſequence, will bring forth a proportioned plenty *. Who can ſuppoſe that preventing all the calves of *Eſſex*, *Surry*, and *Hertfordſhire* from coming to market in the ſhape of fat oxen, will

* ———que la ſource des depenſes eſt la dépenſe elle même, que plus on dépenſe pour la production, plus on obtient de produits, que *conſommation* enfin, *eſt mere de la production*. Cette ſource eſt un mèandre; & les anciens peignoient a bon droit la nature, ſous l'embleme d'un ſerpent qui mord ſa queue Mais ne confondons pas la tête & la queue *Elements de la Philoſophie Rurale*

will not be an encouragement to the graziers of *Norfolk* and *Northampton*?—These are my reasons for thinking that luxury does NOT raise the price of provisions, though it will raise the price of whatever can be produced in the markets only in limited quantities, as early strawberries, asparagus, green pease—the works of the fine arts, &c.—Those who doubt this, may consult the prices of common food and *luxuries* at *Rome* in the age of *Augustus* *. At the same time, I do not here mean, that a great increase of wealth will not raise *all* prices: I shall never assert that every thing is now as cheap in *England* as in the fifteenth century. The argument demands it not.

If the principles here laid down are not true, how will the gentlemen who have written so much on the high, exorbitant, monstrous, marvellous price of provisions, account for the low prices of those and other commodities compared with the increase of money. Bread, meat, labour, manufactures, &c. ought in direct proportion to the increase of wealth to have been far higher than they are at present: it is the cause I have now explained that has kept them down. The increase of wealth and luxury has had a gradual tendency to raise

* *Arbuthnot's tables of antient weights and measures.*

raiſe all theſe prices, which, as I before ſtated, has been a gradual encouragement to their production, and conſequently created a regular increaſe of quantity. The operation of this cauſe of plenty in the caſe of proviſions, was as I have already ſhewn; and I have little doubt but the ſame thing has happened with labour.

PRINCIPLES OF POPULATION.

The national wealth increaſed the demand for labour, which had always the effect of raiſing the price; but this riſe encouraged the production of the commodity, that is, of man or labour, call it which you will, and the conſequent increaſe of the commodity ſinks the price. Increaſing the demand for a manufacture does not raiſe the price of the labour, it increaſes the number of labourers in that manufacture, as a greater quantum or regularity of employment, gives that additional value to the ſupply, which creates the new hands. Why have the inhabitants of *Birmingham* increaſed from 23,000 in 1750, to 30,000 in 1770? Certainly becauſe a proportional increaſe of employment has taken place. Wherever there is a demand for hands, there they will abound: this demand is but another word for eafe of fubfiftence, which operates in the fame manner (the healthinefs of one, and the unhealthinefs of the other allowed for) as the plenty of land in the back country of *America*. Marriages abound there, becaufe children are no burthen—they abound in *Birmingham* for the fame reafon, as every child as foon as it can ufe its hands, can maintain itfelf, and the father and mother need never to want employment, that is, income—land—fupport Thus where employment increafes, (*Birmingham*) the people increafe: and where employment does not increafe, (*Colchefter*) the people do not increafe. And if upon an average of the whole kingdom employment has for a century increafed, moft certainly the people have increafed with it.

Go to the fhipping of the kingdom, it will be found the fame; our failors have increafed Why? Becaufe their employment has increafed. As long as the demand for feamen increafes, that demand will be anfwered, let it rife as high as it will.

Nabobs from the *Indies*, planters from *America*, merchants from the exchange, fettle in the counties, they farm, garden, plant, improve—they want men, their demand is anfwered, and was it regular, would

would around every great house found and support a town.

Go to the villages, the same truth will every where be apparent. if husbandry improves, it will demand more labour—that demand is the encouragement of the production of the commodity demanded—and it will be supplied. Who supposes that a county of warrens, heaths, and farming slovens, converted to well tilled fields, does not occasion an increased demand for hands? —And was it ever known that such a demand existed without being supplied?

But the hands, it is said, leave certain villages and go to towns. Why? Because there is not employment in one case, and there is in another—their going to the town, proves that they go to employment —they go to that very circumstance which is to increase their number. They go, because they are demanded; that demand it is true takes, but then it feeds them.

Let any person go to *Glasgow* and its neighbourhood, to *Birmingham*, to *Sheffield*, or to *Manchester*, according to some writers, every cause of depopulation has acted powerfully against such places: how then have they increased their people? Why, by emigrations from [illegible] country. It would be very difficult for any person to shew

ſhew me a depopulation in the country comparable to the increaſe of towns, not to ſpeak of counter tracts in the country that have doubled and trebled their people: But why have not theſe emigrations been to other towns, to *York*, to *Wincheſter*, to *Canterbury*, &c.? Becauſe employment does not abound in thoſe places—and therefore they do not increaſe. Does not this prove that in every light you view it, it is employment which creates population? A poſition impoſſible to be diſproved; and which, if allowed, throws the enquiry concerning the depopulation of the kingdom into an examination of the decline or increaſe of employment.

But ſo much land may be thrown into graſs, and conſequently ſo much employment cut off, that depopulation may enſue. Impoſſible; this cauſe can never operate beyond thoſe lands, more proper by nature for graſs than tillage, for if it did, it would at once counteract itſelf; corn would then riſe to a price beyond the proportion of meat, and of courſe it would be more profitable to *plough*, than to *lay down*. This is a circumſtance that ought to ſhew the enemies of incloſures that they are fighting againſt a chimera—they complain of meat being dearer than corn, in the ſame breath that they ſay the country is depopulated by converting

converting arable to graſs—What a contradiction is this; meat being what they call ſo dear, is a clear proof that a greater proportion of land is not laid to graſs than is broken up for corn, otherwiſe corn inſtead of being cheaper than meat would be dearer.

I ſhall carry this idea yet farther. I have conſidered an increaſed demand, which raiſes the value of a commodity, to be the means of increaſing the quantity of that commodity, by encouraging the production of it; and I have applied it to beef, to mutton, to wheat, and to labour. I remarked that leſſening the quantity in the market while the demand continued the ſame, operated as an encouragement, and preſently ſupplied more than the uſual quantum. It is the ſame with population. You fight off your men by wars—you deſtroy them by great cities—you leſſen them by emigrations — moſt infallible method of increaſing their number—PROVIDED THE DEMAND DOES NOT DECLINE. This is exactly the ſame thing, as rendering beef ſcarcer by the ſlaughter of calves, and wheat by exportation—take a quantity from the market, certainly you add to the value of what remains, and how can you encourage the reproduction of it more powerfully than by adding to its value?

What are the terms of complaint for depopulation in this kingdom?—People ſcarce —labour dear;—would you give a premium for population, could you expreſs it in better terms? The commodity wanted is ſcarce, and the price raiſed; what is this but ſaying, that the value of MAN is raiſed. *Away! my boys—get children, they are worth more than ever they were* What is the characteriſtic of a populous country? *Many people, but labour dear.* What is the mark of a country thinly peopled? *Few people, and labour cheap.* Labour is dearer in *Holland* than in any part of *Europe*, and therefore it is the moſt populous country in *Europe*

Dr. *Price* ſays, that for the laſt 80 years, there has not been one great cauſe of depopulation which has not operated among us *. What is the great encouragement of population? *Eaſe of acquiring income:* It is of no conſequence whether that income ariſes from land, manufacture, or commerce; it is as powerful in the pay of a manu-

* "The humour of blaming the preſent, and admiring the paſt, is ſtrongly rooted in human nature, and has an influence even on perſons endued with the profoundeſt judgment and moſt extenſive learning." *Hume's Eſſay*, 8vo. 1764, vol 1 p 490

manufacturer †, as in the wilds of *America*. What is the great obstacle to population? *Difficulty of acquiring income*. Here then we have a criterion, by which to judge of the population or depopulation of any period. If you view the country and see agriculture under such circumstances that the farmer's products will not pay his usual improvements, and consequently, dismissing the hands he formerly kept. If the manufactures of the kingdom want a market, and the active industry, exerted in them, becomes languid, and decays. If

† I do not here mean that our manufacturing towns increase as fast as the settlements in *America*—I mean only that the *principle* in one case is as powerful as in the other the difference in point of health is one obstacle—but nothing to another, which is manufacturing employment in these towns not keeping full pace with the increase of people In the back settlements plenty of land (*income — employment*) keeps pace with the most rapid increase; whereas, if the manufacturers of *Birmingham* had a demand for all the wares they could make, I suppose it would not be long before they could supply half a dozen worlds—their hands would increase almost as fast as in *America*, their trade would double every twenty years, and their people with it. By the way, I do not think I should be far from the truth, if I asserted, that some of our manufacturing places, particularly *Burslem*, for a certain period increased as fast as any of our colonies, which is nothing more than saying, that employment has kept pace with population

commerce no longer ſupports the ſeamen ſhe was wont to do. If private and public works, inſtead of entering into competition for hands with the manufacturer and the farmer, ſtand ſtill amidſt numbers who cry in vain for work*.—If theſe effects are ſeen, a WANT OF EMPLOYMENT will ſtare you in the face, and that want is the only cauſe of depopulation that can exiſt. Have theſe ſpectacles been common in the eyes of our people ſince the revolution? Are they common at preſent? Does not the great active cauſe, EMPLOYMENT, operate more powerfully than ever? Away then with theſe viſionary ideas, the diſgrace of an enlightened age—the reproach of this great and flouriſhing nation†.

Sir

---

* ———"when labourers are plenty, their wages will be low; by low wages a family is ſupported with difficulty; this difficulty deters many from marriage."—*Obſervations concerning the increaſe of mankind*, ſaid to be by Dr *Franklin*, where more good ſenſe upon theſe ſubjects will be found (mixed with a few thoughts not equally ſtriking) than in half a ſcore of complaining volumes.

† *Davenant* gives the ſigns of a declining nation, which well deſerve conſideration. "Where a nation is impoveriſhed by a bad government, by an ill managed trade, or by any other circumſtance, the intereſt of money will be dear, and the purchaſe of lands cheap. THE PRICE OF LABOUR AND PROVISIONS WILL BE LOW; rents will every where fall; lands

w

Sir *James Stewart* has an obſervation ſimilar to the idea which I am now explaining, that if *Africk*'s ſons were all returned her, who can ſuppoſe ſhe would be the more populous? But he founds this idea on the quantity of food in the country: but I mean to throw the point of food out of the queſtion, taking it always for granted, if a man gains employment which gives him the value of food, that he will never go without it. Increaſe your people as much as you pleaſe, food will increaſe with them Notwithſtanding the increaſe of people which muſt have taken place in this kingdom ſince the revolution, added to the waſte of luxury, and alſo exportation, yet the price of corn has fallen.—Population merely for want of food, will not ſtop till every acre of the territory is improved to the utmoſt.

We are told that ſince the revolution, this country has loſt a million and a half of people: this therefore implies that the cauſes of population were more powerful in the laſt

 than

will be untilled, and farm houſes will go to ruin; the yearly marriages and births will leſſen, and the burials increaſe The ſtock of live cattle muſt apparently diminiſh, and laſtly, the inhabitants will by degrees, and in ſome meaſure, withdraw themſelves from ſuch a declining country." *Davenant's Works*, vol 1. p 358.

than in the preſent century; theſe cauſes, we are told, are ſmall farms, open field lands, and ſimplicity of living; which is not very far from aſſerting, that the leſs employment there is in a country, the more populous it will be. Small farms with their univerſal attendant, *poor farmers*, can never form ſuch a ſyſtem of employ as richer farmers, for this plain reaſon,—they cannot work equal improvements—nor ever were known to do it—and improvements in huſbandry are but another word for increaſe of labour. Beſides, we ſhould reflect, that agriculture in general, by whatever farmers carried on, had not received that improvement in the practice, and operoſe methods of culture which have ſince been introduced; and of which a long catalogue could be given.

A county divided into little farms, with many little eſtates ſupporting little landlords, has certainly the appearance of population: theſe writers ſay, that if the ſmall farms are thrown into large ones, many of the people will diſappear: let us (which we need not do) grant this fact. It is ſaying, that when the country was more populous, its inhabitants eat much more food than at preſent, conſequently could not ſpare ſo much for towns. The people employed in the country in raiſing the fruits of the earth, may be employed with

ſo

ſo little oeconomy as to eat up the whole produce, in which caſe, there can be no towns. Thus the population of the country depends partly on the manners of the age; if it is not the cuſtom to live in towns, there will be little demand for the products of farmers, conſequently they and their dependants will conſume them: but if, as in this age, people gather very much into towns, they demand the products in competition with the uſeleſs hands before ſupported by the land, who, not being able to ſtand that competition, gradually take refuge in towns, as manufacturing employment ariſes. This is a change, advantageous in every reſpect that can be named. You had before a population uſeleſs, becauſe not induſtrious; who, inſtead of adding to the national wealth, only eat up the earth's produce; this population is changed for induſtrious manufacturers, artizans, and ſeamen, who eat the ſame produce, but pay you amply for it. With one population, let it be ever ſo great, you muſt be a poor and a weak nation: with the other, you are a wealthy and powerful one—In this argument, I ſuppoſe huſbandry in the improved period, to raiſe no more products than in the other period, accounting only for the change of thoſe who eat its products. But the contrary is well known to be the caſe, conſequently as there is much more food raiſed, we may ſuppoſe more people who eat it. I have alſo taken for granted, that in the latter period, fewer hands are employed on the ſoil, which would be the caſe if the agriculture was the ſame in both, but improvements far more than ballance the number of farmers, and render the population of the modern period far greater in the country, than that of the remoter one.

Reſpecting open field lands, the quantity of labour in them is not comparable to that of incloſures; for, not to ſpeak of the great numbers of men that in incloſed countries are conſtantly employed in winter in hedging and ditching, what compariſon can there be between the open field ſyſtem of one half or a third of the lands being in fallow, receiving only three ploughings; and the ſame portion now tilled four, five, or ſix times by Midſummer, then ſown with turnips, thoſe hand-hoed twice, and then drawn by hand, and carted to ſtalls for beaſts, or elſe hurdled out in portions for fatting ſheep! What a ſcarcity of employment in one caſe, what a variety in the other! And conſider the vaſt tracts of land in the kingdom (no leſs than the whole upon which turnips are cultivated) that have undergone this change ſince the

laſt

laſt century. I ſhould alſo remind the reader of other ſyſtems of management; beans and peaſe hand-hoed for a fallow—the culture of potatoes—of carrots, of coleſeed, &c.—the hoeing of white corn—with the minuter improvements in every part of the culture of all crops—every article of which is an increaſe of labour. Then he ſhould remember the vaſt tracts of country uncultivated in the laſt century, which have been incloſed and converted into new farms, a much greater tract in 80 years than theſe writers dream of: all this is the effect of incloſures, and conſequently they alſo have yielded a great increaſe of employment.

Laſtly, with reſpect to ſimplicity of living—in what does this conſiſt? Why, it conſiſts in all the claſſes of the people being ſatisfied with a leſs conſumption of all ſorts of commodities than at preſent. Living in ſmaller houſes; with leſs and worſe furniture; fewer carriages; leſs change in theſe articles; wearing fewer cloaths, hats, ſhoes, ſtockings, &c.; uſing, in a word, fewer manufactures of every ſort and kind, and never thinking of a variety, now common in every family. Contented with a worſe and more difficult carriage; no great roads; no navigations; and very few public works; much leſs ſhip building, and fewer of the variety of

fabrics

fabrics which the fitting out a ſhip conſumes—In a word, a ſmaller general conſumption of all ſorts; what is this but LESS EMPLOYMENT *, and of courſe, fewer people? But is it neceſſary to reaſon how theſe cauſes muſt have operated? Does not the knowledge of all old people, and all regiſters, prove the general increaſe of towns? Nay, theſe writers themſelves admit it, and ſpeak of it as the cauſe of depopulation †!

But it is ſaid, that the prices of neceſſaries have riſen ſo much ſince the laſt century, that the eaſe of living has declined, and conſequently depopulation come upon us.

* It is a great income that cauſes a great expence, and it is a great expence that augments population. *Encyclopedie*, vol. ii. Art. *Grain*

† Manufacturers,
Artizans,
Fiſhermen,
Seamen,
Soldiers,
Miners of all ſorts,
Colliers,
Carriers of all ſorts, and navigators of rivers,
Domeſtic ſervants,
Merchants, and their train,
Inkeepers, and their train,
Inhabitants of towns in general,
The claſſes ſupported by the public taxes.

Let theſe ſeveral ſets of men be conſidered, and the moſt inattentive obſerver will at once ſee that all are amazingly increaſed ſince the laſt century: who can imagine that ſuch an increaſe is not ſufficient to anſwer the decline (ſuppoſing there is one, which I do not believe) in the number of farmers.

us. First I say, the fact is certainly false taken in general, though, for what I know, it may be true taken in one particular: in manufactures, I am told that the price of labour has risen very little *; here therefore this observation is partly true; but the pleasant thing is, that manufactures are out of the question, because there cannot be a man so senseless as to suppose as many persons maintained by them in the last age as at present. Dr. *Price* expressly admits this, and throws the depopulation on country parishes. In them the first fact is by no means true, for I have it on good authority in most parts of the kingdom, that husbandry labour has risen greatly. I have shewn the rise of it in very many places, to be much beyond that of provisions; the rise of which has been very little, considering the importance of bread in general consumption, as far as we can judge from registers that are authentic. Very many of the labouring poor are become chargeable to

* At the same time that the nominal pay of manufacturers who work by the day, is not risen equally with that of husbandry labour, yet we should remember that it ought not to have risen equally, as we have it on various authority, that manufacturers had in the last century double the pay of labourers in husbandry.

to their parishes; but this has nothing to do with depopulation; on the contrary, the constantly seeing such vast sums distributed in this way, must be an inducement to marriage among all the idle poor—and certainly has proved so. The reason the rates have increased so much, is the increase of national wealth and the superior ease of the poor. This has enabled them to consume the greater quantity of superfluities, and that consumption (as it always does in all classes) has grown upon them. Let our poor give up tea, sugar, spices, brandy, rum, gin, and ale in immoderate quantities, and they will not feel the high price of provisions, even in manufactures. As to husbandry, they indulge in all those expences, and yet live well *—exceptions there will be, and doubtless, always were, for the nature of man is the same in all ages. Admitting

* Our farms and the cottages of our labourers will stand the test, which *Rousseau* would bring a kingdom to ——C'est en lui que consiste la véritable prospérité d'un pays, la force, & la grandeur qu'un peuple tire de lui-même, qui ne depend en rien des autres nations, qui ne contraint jamais d'attaquer pour se soutenir, & donne les plus sûrs moyens de se deffendre. Quand il est question d'estimer la puissance publique, le bel-esprit visite les palais du prince, ses ports, ses troupes, ses arsenaux, ses villes, le vrai politique parcourt les terres, & va dans la chaumiere du laboureur Le premier voit ce qu'on a fait, & le second ce qu'on peut faire *Jul.*, tome v p 33.

Admitting that the eaſe of living in manufactures was greater—yet the numbers in manufactures are vaſtly increaſed. In villages, the eaſe of living is not a whit leſſened, conſequently there is no reaſon from thence to ſuppoſe a decline. Let us reflect on the different circumſtances of the two periods in another light. In the laſt century, the farms it is ſaid were ſmaller, and conſequently more farmers and their families. But let me aſk what a little farmer or a labourer did with his family? That ſurplus of the population of villages, which in the preſent age finds at all times a refuge in manufactures, commerce, arts, or ſome branch of induſtry, (all which are infinitely increaſed) could not do the ſame then; for they had not ſuch abundance of *employment* to reſort to; and if the villages were better peopled, this muſt have happened at a time when ſuch a reſort was much more wanted. What muſt have been the conſequence of this? Why the little farmers houſes and the cottages muſt have been crouded with people *without employment*, and conſequently *without the means of living*: this might go to a certain point, as far as relations would ſubmit to be burthened, but it would go no farther, and muſt operate as a great diſcouragement to marriage A great family where there is plenty

plenty of employment for all ages, is not a burthen long; but where there is no employment, of what uſe to ſay that proviſions were 15 or 20 *per cent.* cheaper; it muſt have been a monſtrous burthen. Now we have reaſon to think that this was not the caſe, becauſe if it had, the poor's rates would probably have ſhewn it; the inference therefore which I draw, is, that no ſuch population exiſted, that the villages had not more people than to be on a par with manufactures, arts, and commerce, and not near ſo populous as at preſent. Let any unprejudiced reader who has the leaſt conception of the oeconomy and management of a ſmall farm, reflect for a minute on an occupier of from 20 to 50 acres, with a family of 8 or 10 children, moſt of them unable to maintain themſelves from the ſmall progreſs of arts and induſtry. Lowneſs of rents, and a cheapneſs of labour, the conſequence of hands without work, would enable him to ſupport more perhaps than at preſent. but how can any one from ſuch a ſyſtem, deduce the cauſes of population? Here ariſes a freſh reaſon to ſuppoſe the country could not be ſo populous as at preſent, which was labour being dear; if there were ſo many more little farmers and labourers, whoſe children manufactures could not take off, how ſhould labour be dear?

Here Dr. *Price* ſays, " as the number of occupiers of land was greater, and all had more opportunities of working for *themſelves*, it is reaſonable to conclude, that the number of people willing to work *for others*, muſt have been ſmaller, and the price of day labour higher—this is now the caſe in our *American* colonies."—My concluſion is directly the contrary.—Is it to be ſuppoſed that *England* in the laſt century, was in the ſame ſituation as the colonies, every one to incloſe and take land that pleaſed? You ſay the number of occupiers was greater: you admit they had families—here comes the difficulty—*what did they with thoſe families?* Not take freſh farms, for all were full· not take refuge in towns, there was not employment for them; not carry their cultivation by the ſpade and hoe to the higheſt perfection, their huſbandry was miſerable, not a tenth ſo operoſe as at preſent—what therefore could the ſurplus of this great ſyſtem of population do to ſupport itſelf? Nothing but regorge in the cottages—render labour too cheap—become a moſt miſerable burthen on parents—and an effectual check on marriage.—What compariſon can be drawn between this ſituation and *America*, where every child,

child, as ſoon as arrived at man's eſtate, marries, and has a *new* farm immediately.

Mr. *Walace* ſays, " Suppoſe the great body of manufacturers in ſome trading nations that have a large territory, to lay aſide their manufactures, and employ themſelves in agriculture, paſturage, and fiſhing; they would provide a vaſt quantity of food, they would make all the neceſſaries of life cheap, and eaſy to be purchaſed; and it would ſoon become viſible how great a difference there is between agriculture and manufactures in rendering a nation populous * "

I cannot agree entirely to this reaſoning; Mr. *Walace* would give theſe manufacturers ſmall portions of land, ſufficient to yield the neceſſaries of life, and no more. In the ſuppoſition of ſuch a ſmall diviſion of the ſoil, the claſs of farmers eats up all the earth's produce. Now I ſee no difference in point of numbers, between the manufacturers being fed by the farmers, or feeding themſelves: in both caſes they are fed —and they can be no more. But ſuppoſe them turned farmers, every man with his little farm—this ſuppoſes no more increaſe than before. What are their families to do? Are they alſo to marry and turn farmers?

* *Diſſertation on the Numbers of Mankind*, p. 27

mers? If you anſwer in the affirmative, then your obſervation may all be blotted out, and inſtead thereof, you may ſimply ſay, that plenty of land to be had for nothing as in *America*, greatly increaſes the people. Who can doubt it? But this is not the poſition. You are ſuppoſing the manufacturers in a peopled country, which is already property, converted into farmers —I accept your ſuppoſition, and I ſay that then every family, inſtead of being fed by labour in the manufactory, will be fed by the portion of land aſſigned them, but there will be no more increaſe in one caſe than in the other, becauſe the people bred in theſe farms, and alſo in the old ones, (as manufactures are ſuppoſed to be at an end) will have no employment or means of ſupport, conſequently can neither marry nor multiply beyond the fixed number of farms. Nothing can be clearer than this. But there is another conſideration; while the manufacturers formed a diſtinct body, the old farmers had a market, in which their products yielded a value in money, the ſale of theſe muſt neceſſarily enliven their buſineſs, and enable them to improve their culture; and the higher the prices, the more they would be encouraged to work improvements and increaſe the quantum of food, all which cauſes would be at once cut off in the above idea, and of course their effects would vanish. Thus the tendency of the proposition, instead of being favourable to increase, would be prejudicial to it.

Nor can it ever be too much inculcated, that the taking people from towns and spreading them over the country, is attended no farther with *increase*, than in proportion as you have a demand for that increase. A man and woman in *London* do not marry. *Why not?* Because a family, if they had one, would, for want of employment, be a burthen. This is supposing what is the case, that there are people enough in the kingdom to answer all demands for hands. Take the couple into the country, the case will be just the same; a family there, sticking to the cottage, will be just as great a burthen. Such effects are not commonly seen in the country now, because manufactures, arts, &c. take off the surplus of its population; but if these were converted into fresh cottages we should see it every day.

As little reason is there for drawing the causes of depopulation from every refinement that is made upon the simple stages of civilization, which Dr. *Price* says, "favour most the increase and the happiness of mankind. For in these states, agriculture supplies plenty of the means of subsistence; the blessings of a natural and a simple life are

are enjoyed; property is equally divided; the wants of men are few, and ſoon ſatisfied, and families are eaſily provided for: on the contrary, in the refined ſtates of civilization, property is engroſſed.—Our *American* colonies are at preſent in the firſt and the happieſt of the ſtates I have deſcribed."——Relative to the advantages of the preſent *American* ſyſtem, I agree entirely with the author; but I think no uſeful concluſion can be drawn from the fact: what country can poſſibly be produced in any period to which hiſtory goes back, that is a parallel to a new planted colony, with the immenſity of land without any property in it but that of the crown—and ready to be granted to whoever will take it? The young ſociety under the protection of a formidable power, and enjoying the freedom of the nobleſt conſtitution in the univerſe? At what period of our hiſtory was this iſland in ſuch a ſituation? Go back to the ages in which luxury and refinement were out of the queſtion, was not *property engroſſed?* Did a great quarrelſome, fiery, tartar of a baron, give up his eſtate of 900 or 1000 manors to be ſettled by peaſants in property? And had he done it, would propagation in thoſe barbarous ages have gone on as at preſent in *America?* The ſyſtem of which country is ſo peculiar, that a parallel was never to be produced. In any age from *Alfred* to king *William*, landed property in *England* has been decided—no land for thoſe who to take poſſeſſion of it—much greater inequality of eſtates than at preſent—hence therefore depopulation cannot have come upon us from any cauſes the reverſe of thoſe which operate at preſent in *America*, but which did not operate in the laſt century in *England*.

ENGLAND MORE POPULOUS THAN EVER.

It is for theſe reaſons that I ſuppoſe the country at that time could not poſſibly be ſo populous as at preſent, becauſe the population of the villages muſt depend on other cauſes for taking off its ſurplus—it can never advance beyond that point—the moment it produces a greater ſurplus than can be taken off, it counteracts itſelf, and will infallibly leſſen. This production of the village commodity (people) depends on the demand for that commodity occaſioned by manufactures, arts, commerce, wars, &c. This is a univerſal truth in the production of all commodities. And as that demand in the laſt century was not comparable to what it is in the preſent, there thence reſults the

the clearest impossibility of population in the country being equal to what it is at present.

To illustrate the contrary idea, chalk out a line of country; suppose it divided into farms of 20 acres, fix an occupier in each, and force this country to support its own population, that is, cut off the demand of arts and manufactures; there will be a family to every 20 acres. How are the parents to maintain the children? The whole produce of the earth is eaten up, and is insufficient, the children will be the most dreadful burthen imagination can paint—population will destroy itself—the farmers if not starved, will be bankrupts, and nothing can prevent desolation but their either living all unmarried, or else the farms running into one another, and some means taken to reduce the people *. But suppose manufactures, luxury, great cities, and recruiting serjeants to operate, then the farmers may go on getting children as fast as they please, for the very circumstance of the surplus becoming burthensome will drive it away: And without

 supposing

* ———le plus grand produit total n'est pas l'intérêt de l'etat si ce plus grand produit est consommé par de plus grands frais de culture. *Eléments de la philosophie rurale.*

ſuppoſing in one caſe that nothing will leſſen the ſurplus, or in the other, that the whole ſhall be demanded; yet will the effect of the demand be proportioned to it.

Can any thing be more ſimple than this principle? Can any thing prove clearer that the idea of a village population beyond the demand for its ſurplus is chimerical? Is it not evident that demand for hands, that is employment, muſt regulate the numbers of the people? And that if employment in this age is greater than in the former, the total of the people muſt be greater? Ideas of purity and ſimplicity of living in little farms, with the farmers engaged as much in propagation as in culture—the women bringing forth with all poſſible expedition—and every movement in the whole rural machine nothing but increment and multiplication—all theſe notions are fine ſpeculative fancies, equally removed from reaſon and experience. It certainly is the caſe upon the *Ohio*, but for the ſame reaſon that it is not ſo upon the *Thames*

As I have through theſe papers laid it down as a principle that population is proportioned to employment, it neceſſarily follows, that the population of agriculture depends on the employment of agriculture, and the population of manufactures on the employ-

employment of manufacturers—and from hence I give no credit to the reasoning used to convince us that we are less populous than at the revolution, or any remoter period. This principle guides us also in giving credit to or rejecting opinions of any other period. I have been informed, that several of our manufactures have declined since the peace of 1762*, which may indeed easily be conceived from the amazing and unnatural height to which the commerce of this country was carried by the war—being literally erected on the ruins of that of half our neighbours,—such a decline in certain fabrics must be attended with a proportionable depopulation, if others have not made a corresponding advance—And such a depopulation in manufactures, must affect our general numbers, unless the population of agriculture has proportionably increased, which is a matter of opinion, it appears to me that it increases every day.

But why will you reason against facts? Are not the public lists of houses and windows lower than they were in the last century? This is the only apparent *fact* for supposing the people less numerous

Those gentlemen who have taken the trouble to calculate the number of the people, have differed very much in their

 opinions,

* See Appendix.

opinions. Sir *W. Petty* made the number in *England* and *Wales* in 1682, amount to 7,400,000 *.—*Davenant* in 1692, made them 7,000,000 †—but in the fame tract, he makes them 8,000,000—and in 1700, he quotes and approves from Mr. *King* a computation of 5,500,000 ‡.—Sir *M. Decker* fuppofed them in 1742, (from 1,200,000 houfes, at 6 to a houfe) 7,200,000 ‖—Dr. *Mitchel* fays the number is 5,700,000 §—Mr. *Walace*, 8,000,000 ¶—*Templeman* makes it the fame **—Another fuppofes it 6,000,000 ††—Another, 5,480,000 ‡‡—Mr. *Smyth*, 6,000,000 §§—Dr *Brakenridge*, 5,340,000 ‖‖—Another, 8,000,000 *†—Dr. *Price*, 4,500,000 ††.

From

* *Political Arithmetic*, p 15

† *An Effay upon ways and means*, p 136

‡ *An Effay upon the probable method of making a people gainers in the ballance of trade*, p 18.

‖ *Serious Confiderations on feveral high duties*, 8vo 1744, p 15

§ *Prefent State of Great Britain and North America*, p. 113.

¶ *Differtation on the Numbers of mankind*, p. 41.

** *Survey of the Globe* Plate 5

†† *Poftlethwayte's Dictionary of Commerce* Art. *People*.

‡‡ *Confiderations on the Trade and Finances*, &c. 79.

§§ *Three Tracts on Corn Trade*, p. 181.

‖‖ *Phil. Tranf* Vol 49, p 877.

*† *Houghton's Hufbandry*, vol II p 465.

†† *Obfervations on reverfionary payments*, p 184.

From the accounts we have had of former enumerations, there are reaſons to think they were taken with much inaccuracy; but what is deciſive in the compariſon, the laſt public liſts of 1759 and 1766, are known by experiment to be falſe. Catalogues were taken in a variety of pariſhes about *Wentworth Houſe* in *Yorkſhire*, by order of the marquis of *Rockingham*; and ſimilar trials were made elſewhere, in all which, the number EXCEEDED the reports of the ſurveyors; who, in moſt parts of *England*, paid little attention to houſes exempted from the tax: of which the deficiencies I have mentioned, are the moſt ſatisfactory proofs. When the treaſury wants to know the number of cottages exempted from all payment, the receivers general of the land-tax may have orders to direct ſuch a report. But how are they obeyed? Like all ſuch orders in this country, where no penalty to an informer is fixed. The collectors are choſen from among low and illiterate men; ſome may think ſuch an order a preparatory ſtep to a new tax; others are careleſs and forget it; others ſet down what cottages they recollect, and do not take the trouble to ride through their pariſh; an hundred ſuch reaſons may operate in lowering the truth at a time that not a ſingle one can occaſion an exaggeration.

tion However, the circumſtance that cauſes it is not of conſequence—the fact we know is ſo.

In the next place, if you got the number of houſes, you have not that of the people; here the authority is as rotten as elſewhere: in ſome places you have gained the number of people *per family*—but what has that to do with the number *per houſe*? Are not many houſes the habitation of ſeveral families? But farther, from the moſt extraordinary prejudice in the world, you collect the numbers *per* houſe in many places, conſtantly rejecting hoſpitals, priſons, colleges, ſchools, and poor houſes *—you then ſay—there are ſo many houſes in the kingdom—ſuch is the reſult *per* houſe of my enquiries—conſequently you have but ſo many people, MAKING NO ALLOWANCE FOR THE BUILDINGS YOU HAVE OMITTED. Is this a fair way of calculating?

Further, how do we know that a houſe at preſent contains on an average of the kingdom no more ſouls than 80 years ago? I have

* *London* is alſo forgotten, in which *Grant* aſſerted, that among tradeſmen there are 8 to a *family*, in higher ranks 10, and in the pooreſt, near 5 how much more *per houſe* he does not tell At preſent the number *per* houſe is probably 9 or 10, perhaps more.

have little doubt but the population *per* houſe is greater †.

Upon the whole, we may determine that the facts upon which the arguments for our depopulation are founded, are abſolutely falſe: that the conjectures annexed to them are wild and uncertain, and that the concluſions which are drawn from the whole, can abound in nothing but errors and miſtakes.

SIGNS OF DEPOPULATION.

As ideas of depopulation have in all ages been ſo common, and complaints of miſchiefs in the government and policy of ſtate ever annexed to them, and generally without any reaſon; it may not be amiſs to beſtow a few reflections on thoſe ſigns of depopulation, which, whenever they appear, may be ſuppoſed to ſpeak truth. I have ſaid, that populouſneſs in *England* depends on employment, which here operates on the ſame principles as plenty of land in *America*; this offers a very ſimple idea of depopulation—*employment leſſening*. Not leſſening in the pariſh A, while increaſing in the town B; or leſſening in B, while

† See the appendix, for other obſervations on this ſubject.

while increaſing in A, but a general viſible declenſion; ſuch as would take place if the national wealth was to decline, which generally being the effect of *employment*, muſt mark the ſtate of its cauſe. If the ſeamen leſſen and your ſhipping falls away, it is a circumſtance which to this nation would be of the higheſt conſequence, and mark a variety of declenſion—if at the ſame time the great manufactures of the kingdom could no longer find a vent, and conſequently their people without employment, it would be a mark not leſs equivocal—if the cultivated ſoil leſſens—if tracts once valuable, become waſte, and rents fall, it is an unerring ſign of decay—if the prices of labour and commodities in general ſink, it is no leſs to be depended on. Theſe ſigns of national decay need not be multiplied, whenever they are ſeen they muſt mark in proportion to their extent, the declenſion of our proſperity.

Decreaſe of ſhipping—decline of manufactures—decline of agriculture—a general fall of prices.

It appears to me that theſe are circumſtances which involve every other cauſe of national declenſion; they mark a loſs of wealth—A DECREASE OF EMPLOYMENT, which muſt univerſally bring down population with it.

Whenever therefore we heat of other caufes of depopulation, fuch as engroffing farms, inclofures, laying arable to grafs, high prices of provifions, great cities, luxury, celibacy, debauchery, wars, emigrations, &c. we may very fafely refolve them into a ftring of vulgar errors, and reft affured that they can have no ill effect, while the five great caufes mentioned above, do not fubfift.

LAW OF SETTLEMENTS.

Having ventured thus far on the activity of the caufes of the population of *England*, which I think far fuperior in power to any tendency there can be found to the contrary, I fhall very freely acknowledge there is one caufe of depopulation among us, however it is in general overcome by favourable circumftances; this is the *law of fettlements*, the moft falfe, mifchievous, and pernicious fyftem that ever barbarifm devifed. By forcing every parifh to maintain not the refident, but the fettled poor; and by difenabling the poor from fettling where they pleafe, you give a ftrong and effective motive to very many people to do every thing in their power againft population, by raifing an open war againft cottages. The landlord and the

the farmer have almoſt equal motives to reduce the number of poor in their pariſhes: marriages are very frequently obſtructed; the couple muſt, if they marry, ſtay at home; the overſeers of the poor will grant no certificates; if they marry therefore, where are they to live? No cottage is empty—they muſt live with their fathers and mothers, or lodge; the poor abhor both as much as their betters, and certainly in many caſes, run into licentious amours, merely for want of a cottage or a certificate. The whole ſyſtem of our poor laws is ſo miſchievous, that it muſt be attended with this effect. Suppoſe an unmarried labourer applies to the lord of a manor for leave to build a cottage on the waſte—*No*, ſays the gentleman, *the cottage when built, will be a neſt of beggars, and we ſhall have them all on the pariſh*. Can you wonder at ſuch language from a man who probably can let land worth 20 *s.* an acre, for no more than 14 *s.* on account of high poor rates? It would be amazing if he acted otherwiſe.

Dr. *Price* quotes with applauſe, an obſervation of Lord *Bacon*, in praiſe of the act of *Henry* VII. which prohibited all new cottages with leſs than 4 acres, but what tendency had this but the evil I have now deſcribed? If a poor man buys half a rood of land to build on, he cannot do it; he

muſt

muſt buy four acres!—This is the very circumſtance that now gives the power of reſtraining the erection of cottages.

Our policy is weak beyond all doubt, becauſe it conſiſts of prohibiting the natural courſe of things: all reſtrictive forcible meaſures in domeſtic policy are bad; population ſhould not be expreſsly encouraged, but it is ridiculous to throw wanton reſtrictions on it: It ought certainly to be left to its own courſe; people will not multiply beyond the demand for the ſurplus of their increaſe, but thus far they ought to be allowed; and to prohibit cottages, which when built, would be filled with induſtrious inhabitants, is a violent and a miſchievous ſyſtem. It is true, the cauſes of population in this kingdom are ſo powerful, that they overcome theſe obſtacles; but this is no reaſon againſt remedying them. The firſt effectual cure is to annul the law of ſettlements, and allow every man to ſettle where he pleaſes: the ſecond, to repeal the act which allows no cottage with leſs than 4 acres. This would do a great deal; but a great cauſe of the evil would ſtill remain, for as long as the poor are ſupported by the pariſh, it will be the intereſt of every landlord and farmer to oppoſe their increaſe; but this would be much remedied by breaking the laws of ſettlement, ſince

any

any couples who wanted to marry and settle, if refused at home, or if no habitation could be found for them, might then go settle where a cottage and employment were easiest had.

POPULATION IN NORFOLK.

Since the preceding observations were written, the second edition of Dr. *Price's Appeal to the Public on the National Debt* came to hand. Annexed to it is a very sensible and well written memoir on the decline of population in the county of *Norfolk*; in which many appearances and reasons are set forth, to prove that the people of that county are much decreased. If this is really the case, the principles which I have advanced, if not false, will at least have received a wound; for a county which has been improved more than most others, to have fallen off in population, would be an exception to all rules. But the gentleman who has examined this matter, carries back the period of superior populousness to the reformation, not acknowledging any such effect since the revolution, which is a declaration extremely counter to the whole argument of Dr. *Price*.

But what causes more favourable to population could have existed before the reformation,

mation, which have not exifted fince the revolution? This will be very difficult to fhew: I fhall attend not to churches, manor houfes, names of fields, gateways, and foot paths, but to firft principles—living effective principles. Was liberty in that age clearer and more explicitly defined? Was it practically better among the lower claffes? Were farmers and peafants more independent of the nobility, lords of manors, &c.? Was there more employment for the poor in a more correct hufbandry—more flourifhing manufactures, or more extenfive commerce? Were other demands for the furplus of the country population more powerful?——What, but an abfolute negative, is to be the anfwer to all thefe queries? And fhall we then believe numbers under thofe circumftances to have exceeded the prefent!

If none of thefe circumftances operated, pray what were thofe which did caufe fuch an effect? I know not what can be mentioned, unlefs it be the charity of the monafteries—that charity I can conceive to have maintained numbers of idle poor, but that it could poffibly equal the reverfe of the circumftances I juft now mentioned, appears to me utterly incredible. For fuppofing very confiderable revenues fpent in the fupport of the attendants on monks and friars, and thereby to have been a parallel to a part of modern labour, this must then be considered as the *employment* of those people, who since have turned labourers; but what demand for the surplus of their population? What parallel to modern manufactures, arts and commerce? The class supported by charity, must have multiplied like other lower classes, without an outlet for their surplus, which, wherever wanting, is poison to population, and the mark of a system utterly inconsistent with it. If it is said that charity was the parallel, not of modern labour, but manufactures, &c. then I say, you suppose agriculture in that age to have been as good and operose as at present—and if on that proposition you will rest your argument, nothing farther can be made of it.

The truth is, there was not in that age an employment for the people comparable to what there is at present, how therefore could there be as many people? Let their maintenance be pointed out. But it is amusing to see the faculty men will have of complaining of present times, and lamenting the past; we are not satisfied with our numbers, but assert that *England* was better peopled in *Henry* VIII's time; and nothing was so common in that age as the same complaint, as we learn even from the statute

tute books. To what period I wonder did the croakers of that age refer? To that of the desolation I suppose which flowed from the quarrels of the roses—or the tumults of the barons of King *John*.

Compare the supposition before us with every possible cause of it, and the result will be, that no such effect could ever take place. But let us examine into the foundations of the idea.

Large churches are found where the people are not numerous enough to fill a single aile; and some to a single family. This gentleman admits, that churches were often built more for ostentation than use. If in those bigotted times, legacies were left for church building where none were wanted, what could the pious executors of such testaments do, but raise useless edifices? No satisfactory way of accounting for the fact—but if ostentation was their motive to one degree of folly, why not to another. Besides, most of the *Gothic* religious buildings in the kingdom, wherever money enough was to be had, were conspicuous for this extravagance: what idea of utility could be the guide in constructing many of the cathedrals? While this species of expence was the fashion of the times, and while we every day see proofs that the mere idea of religious magnificence and little thought of utility, was the motive of ſuch works, why ſhould we now think of meaſuring the population of that age by the edifices of ſacred ſhew?

Proper names, diſtinguiſhing fields, incloſures, roads, trees, gateways, &c. now almoſt forgotten. This I think is but a very ſlight preſumption of a ſuperior population, we cannot know what were the original cauſes of ſuch names, whether the reſidence of a proprietor, or the wantonneſs of ſtraggling ſhepherds and warreners: it is poſſible to have been, as the writer mentions; it is very poſſible not to have been ſo.

Roads and foot paths at preſent altogether needleſs. This is an argument which proving too much, proves nothing. We have them common in this country (*Hertfordſhire*) within leſs than 20 miles of *London*, and in great numbers; if they are a proof that *Norfolk* was better peopled above 200 years ago, they are alſo a proof that this county was the ſame, which was ſimply impoſſible. But the original reaſons for marking all the roads we now ſee, is ſo difficult an enquiry that it cannot be brought to prove any thing; chance probably, and unnoticed uſe, were the fathers of numbers, and as ſome became common, others were neglected, without population having any thing to do in it.

Houſes

Houses appearing in ruins—villages on the sea coast scenes of desolation. This is positive evidence, and more deserving attention than any of the other reasons. What does it prove? It proves depopulation in the parishes of A, B, and C. But have not D, E, and F, increased? This we are not told, but if it is not known, what proof can be fixed in the opposite facts? Can the writer imagine that *Lynn* 200 years ago was what it is now? *Wells* he acknowledges to be almost a new town. *Norwich* certainly was not what it is. There are no appearances to make one suppose *Yarmouth* more populous two centuries ago, and the same observation might be made on many others. But among the villages, probably many of them have much increased:—at least, thus much we may venture, that if the contrary is not proved, no proof arises of general depopulation from some being in ruins.

When it is considered that so large a part of this county was sheep walks, which is now under an excellent corn culture, it is incredible that it should have declined in population: since to have done so, employment of the people must have been pernicious to their increase, and the inhabitants most numerous when they had the fewest means of living.

While I am writing this, I have the pleasure of the company of some *Norfolk* gentlemen in my house: I made enquiries of them; they confirmed part of this gentleman's account, in such a place the cottages in ruins.—*The farmers then do not cultivate the lands?* Yes they do, better than ever. *Where do the men come from then?* From other places —This is the general round; it is a circle; depopulation here; population there.—They named many parishes which they knew to be considerably increased.

But I think I can account in a very plain manner for the most important of all the reasons assigned by this gentleman—that of so many villages being in ruins —When a whole parish becomes one farm, under one landlord, the power over both the poor and their habitations will center in such landlord and tenant. The tenant pays the poor-rates, and perhaps as a part of his agreement, repairs the cottages; here therefore are two strong reasons why he should drive the people away, and let their houses go to ruin, or perhaps advise his landlord to pull them down; first, he eases himself of rates, and secondly, he gets rid of repairs. As to his labour, he hires men from parishes not in the same predicament, of whose population, as he does not pay to it, he regards not. This may also be the case where a parish

parish consists of two or three farms, provided the farmers agree. This is certainly an evil, but it is owing to the absurdity of our poor laws, not to great farms: however, the amount of it is by no means of consequence, and for this reason. The farmer's want of hands when he has destroyed population in his own parish, is directly to its amount, a premium upon the population of the neighbouring parishes; upon the principle of *demand* which I have before explained. It is then impossible but the people in them must proportionably increase. Thus the very existence of the evil in one place is a demonstration that there must be a cure for it somewhere else; for this county is not one whose farms are laid to grass; the depopulation complained of, is in the midst of tillage.

The great leading fact is admitted by every one — the rural employment has not declined; on the contrary, it has much increased; for every one knows, that inclosing, marling, dunging, ploughing, turnip-hoeing, &c. are in this respect very different from sheep and rabbit feeding. As *the work is done*, it must be done by somebody; and whether that somebody lives in one parish or another, has nothing to do in the enquiry. Much of the harvest is got in by *Scotch* itinerants. There is nothing to object to in this; where the people come from is not the enquiry; all I look to is, that from somewhere they must come. This supply of *Scotchmen*, however, is only in harvest; the works of the rest of the year are sufficient to establish the truth of my observation. *Irishmen* do most of the reaping in *Hertfordshire*; this is so little a proof of depopulation, that great tracts of our county (most of it) are almost a continued village.

Upon the whole, I cannot, upon the most attentive reflection, on the cases brought by Dr. *Price*'s very ingenious correspondent, find any reason to consider them as exceptions to the general principles I before laid down. They certainly carry the appearance of depopulation, perhaps an undeceiving appearance; but we must never form conclusions from such particular instances.

POPULATION IN FRANCE.

The most particular registers of population that I have met with, are those of *M. Messance*, in his *Recherches sur la Population*, printed at *Paris* in 1766. This gentleman gives the progress of population in several of the provinces of *France*. The following extracts will shew the increase of people in those provinces.

Auvergne, 162 pariſhes.

Births from 1747 to 1757,		68,934
1690 to 1700 *,		56,814
Ditto, 38 pariſhes.		
1747 to 1757,	-	13,547
1700 to 1710,	-	11,146
Ditto, 119 pariſhes.		
1747 to 1757,	-	20,611
1710 to 1720,	-	17,953
Ditto, 61 pariſhes.		
1747 to 1757,	-	23,047
1720 to 1730,	-	21,258

Lyon †, 133 pariſhes.

1749 to 1759,	-	40,126
1690 to 1700,	-	35,228
Ditto, 118 pariſhes.		
1749 to 1759,	-	32,014
1701 to 1711,	-	25,318
Ditto, 72 pariſhes.		
1749 to 1759,	-	40,145
1710 to 1720,	-	30,380
Ditto, 109 pariſhes.		
1749 to 1759,	-	30,968
1720 to 1730,	-	26,532

Rouen ‡, 541 pariſhes.

1752 to 1761,	-	123,037
1690 to 1699,	-	120,691

And in general he finds the preſent population

* Page 18. † Page 35. ‡ Page 77.

lation of the three generalities of *Auvergne*, *Lyon*, and *Rouen*, to be to the population of 1700, as 1456 to 1350*.

Provence, *Auch*, *Pau*, *Burgundy*, &c.	1752 to 1763 †, -	426,035
	1690 to 1701, -	390,375

General View.

Comparison between the present population of *France*, and 60 years ago.

		BIRTHS	
	Parishes	*First period*	*Second period*
Auvergne, -	162	5681	6893
Lyon, - -	133	3523	4012
Rouen, - -	541	12069	12303
Lyon City, -	——	3775	4137
Rouen, - -	——	2449	2271
Paris, - -	——	16988	19221
Marseille,	——	3465	3218
Toulon, - -	——	1416	1073
Aix, - -	——	989	822
Montaban, -	——	607	602
Sezanne, - -	——	185	160
Vaison, - -	38	1023	1183
Carcassonne, -	——	495	523
Valence, - -	——	259	266
Vitry, - -	——	416	250
Burgundy, Provence, &c.	1278	32531	35503
		‡ 85871	92437

* Page 128 † Page 268. ‡ Page 272.

From the whole of *M. Meſſance*'s examinations, it appears that the people of *France* have increaſed in the laſt 60 years. I cannot but quote this fact for the opportunity of aſking the *Engliſh* complainants, if the cauſes of depopulation have not been *almoſt* as ſtrong in that kingdom as in *England*? If under thoſe circumſtances, *France* has increaſed her people, may we not liſten to the voice of reaſon, which tells us that *England* has done it in a much greater degree? It is true, complaints of depopulation have been as common in that kingdom as with us; and I ſuppoſe there never was a period or a country where ſuch complaints were not in the mouths of many *.

* In the courſe of theſe papers I took occaſion to quote a paſſage from Mr. *Hume*, not omitting to pay that tribute to his political ſagacity which I ſhould ſuppoſe every one muſt acknowledge I ſhall now tranſcribe an obſervation from another writer, whoſe admirable talents enlighten every ſubject he pleaſes to undertake. A man who deſcribes with pleaſure the proſperity of his country

——" to make ſettlements in the moſt diſtant parts of the globe, and by a wiſe and happy conjunction of our labours both there and in *Britain*, at once extended our wealth and power without the leaſt diminution of our people, contrary to the effects of plantations made from other countries, which have ſuffered at home by aggrandizing themſelves abroad, whereas

IMPORTANCE OF WEALTH.

It is upon these principles that I reckon wealth but another word for consumption, and esteem it as the soul of agriculture had

---

whereas our domestic power is constantly augmented in proportion to the advantages derived from our settlements abroad, and to this circulation of our commerce it is in reality owing that our strength is so much greater, our lands so much more valuable, and our intrinsic wealth so much increased, as it is since that time, and this in spite of long wars and other intervening accidents, not at all favourable to our interests.

This may look like a paradox to some, and there may be others who perhaps will regard it as a thing taken upon trust. But in reality, the facts are absolutely certain, and it is to the wonderful growth of our plantations that we owe the strength and populousness of this island, which could never otherwise have attained its present condition. A very little attention will make this plain. The commodities and manufactures of any country, have a certain limit, beyond which, it is impossible they should extend, without an alteration of circumstances, that is to say, when they are carried so high, as that no new markets are to be found, domestic industry can proceed no farther. Now it is owing to our colonies that hitherto we have not been very sensible of this truth, for the people settled there from a variety of causes, into which I have not room to enter at present, take off much greater quantities of our commodities and manufactures than if they had remained at home. So that one of our countrymen established in *America*, finds

had not very ingenious men held a direct contrary opinion, I should have thought my time as ill spent in explaining it, as in demonstrating that 2 and 2 make 4. Those princes and states therefore who would wish to have the agriculture of their dominions flourish, should wish to see the general wealth of their subjects increase, and encourage every branch

---

finds full employment for several hands here, and AS FULL EMPLOYMENT WILL ALWAYS DRAW PEOPLE, it plainly follows from thence, that our settlements abroad must increase the number of people at home. As this method of arguing shews the reason of the thing, so the truth of it may be likewise demonstrated from experience It is certain that the number of people in the city of *London* is about five times as great as at the death of Queen *Elizabeth*, and though it cannot be supposed that the number of people in this island hath increased in the same proportion, yet it is certain that they have very much increased, as is apparent from the growth of other great cities, the swelling of small villages into large towns, and the raising on our coasts of many new sea ports It may indeed be objected, that if people remove out of the country into great towns, this augments the number of their inhabitants, but not that of the nation, but then the fact must be proved, which is a thing impossible, for such as dwell in great towns consume a larger quantity of provisions and all other necessaries than such as live scattered up and down the country, they must consequently be supplied with these, and therefore *the growth of towns must increase the number of people in the country about them.* Thus the farther we trace this matter, the clearer and the more certain it appears, and therefore what is deduced from it cannot be rationally called in question." *Present State of Europe*, 3d edit p 508

branch of industry that can render their people rich—they should remember that when they exhaust a country by ill devised taxes, or otherwise, they as effectually ruin husbandry as if they burnt all the ploughs in their territories, and prohibited the future use of them: destroying the farmer's market is, in effect, doing this.

It is also destroying it for no good purpose, since a cheapness of provisions is not attended with the least advantage to any class or order of a state *. Nor let him in the

---

* A writer in the last century has a very good observation on this "It is the dearness of corn that encourages the farmer, not only to pay his rent well and give good prices, but also to live high, and improve all his unimproved land within his reach, which will still increase trade and revenue, and the necessity will make the manufactors work harder, and that will increase manufacture, and that will make us sell cheaper, till we have gotten so many new, or so improved our old customers, as that our quantities will not serve *Anno* 1683, I offered to make it appear, that this kingdom will thrive more, and the manufactors live better when provisions are dear than cheap: There I shewed that plenty or cheapness caused laziness, *that* dearness, *that* industry, and *that* plenty; and also, 'TWAS GOOD TO ENCOURAGE THE PEOPLE TO A HIGH LIVING, and the conveniences of it That if the manufactors cannot live as they use to do, by three days in a week working, they must work four, or find some quicker way, and that will produce a fourth part of more manufacture, which must

the right progreſs of his policy be turned aſide by erroneous ideas concerning the luxury that flows from this wealth; let him equally diſregard the gloomy notions of depopulation, ſecure in the idea that if he gives wealth to his people, he gives employment, and of courſe they will multiply.

PRICES

---

muſt cauſe it to be ſold cheaper. I there alſo ſhewed how 'twas the king's intereſt to give money for exporting corn, and our intereſt to have the exciſe higher, and a duty not only on brewers but on all that brew" *Houghton's Collection of Huſbandry and Trade*, vol ii p. 266. The idea of encouraging the people to live high, is a very bold, but I believe a juſt one. In another place he ſays, "If corn was ſold at 12*s* the buſhel, and beef 6*d*. the pound, by means of an encouragement for their exportation, or double conſumption, I ſhould not be ſorry." Vol. iv. p 91. At page 382, he enlarges the idea It is not only in *England* that proviſions ſhould be dear—the inconveniences of cheapneſs are the ſame all the world over It is ſo in *Aſia* Dr *Campbell* deſcribing the great plenty in the *Maldives*, ſays, "The natives it's true, don't grow rich, and that I take to proceed from their cheap and eaſy living, which encourages them to negligence and idleneſs" *Harris's Voyages*, vol. i. p 706 And of *Siam* he ſays, "The peaſants lead a miſerable life, by reaſon that proviſions are ſo cheap here, that they cannot get any thing by their labour." p 782.

PRICES DEPEND ON QUANTITY OF MONEY.

Here it is proper to remark that the importance which I give to general wealth is founded on the same principle with that laid down by *Montesquieu* and Mr. *Hume*, *that the price of commodities is proportioned to the quantity of specie.* But as Sir *James Steuart* has opposed this idea, and endeavoured to establish another in its room, it is necessary to say a word or two upon his arguments; because if they are just, my observations on the consequence of national wealth to agriculture, must be erroneous, or at least but indifferently founded. There may be (according to Sir *James*'s idea) a great influx of wealth, and yet no rise of prices, and consequently no benefit accruing to the farmer: The passages I mean are the following:

" I have laid it down as a principle that it is the complicated operations of demand and competition, which determines the standard price of every thing. If there be many labourers and little demand, work will be cheap. If the increase of riches therefore have the effect of *raising* demand, work will increase in its value, because *there* competition is implied; but if it has only

only the effect of *augmenting* demand, prices will stand as formerly."—"Let the specie of a country therefore be augmented or diminished in ever so great a proportion, commodities will still rise and fall according to the principles of demand and competition, and these will constantly depend upon the inclinations of those who have *property* or any kind of *equivalent* whatsoever to give, but never upon the quantity of *coin* they are possessed of."

There is an obscurity in the distinction between *raising* and *augmenting* demand, which is not at first to be [illegible], but the point principally to be attended to, is another distinction, which I humbly apprehend may be without a difference, *viz.* that between *specie* and *demand.* I never understood either M. de *Montesquieu* or Mr. *Hume* to assert or mean, that very great variations would not be frequent, independantly of the quantity of money. Nobody could suppose they were so short-sighted as to form such ideas. If there is much corn brought to market this week, and few buyers, prices will certainly be higher than in another week, when there is little corn brought, but many buyers: Mackarel are

I certainly

* *Enquiry into the Principles of Pol. Oeconomy,* vol. i. p. 400.

certainly cheaper when many boats arrive than when but few come: If any commodity in general and regular demand, is brought to market at a particular season in much greater plenty than at any other season, who can doubt but the price will be low? All such variations are perfectly consistent with the idea that the price of commodities will depend on the quantity of specie; because this idea is not relative to certain days, weeks, months, or markets, but to general periods in which money has increased or decreased; one century compared with another;—one 50 years with another 50; twenty years since a peace with twenty before it, &c. In such a comparison, and neither the *French* writer nor Mr. *Hume* could have any other in view, the idea of demand and competition, is absolutely lost in that of specie, because they are in fact the same thing. Sir *James* will keep close to the circumstance, that the quantity of money has nothing to do in the case, if a man will not *spend* when he *possesses*: but this appears to me to be taken for granted: relative to a market day, or other point of competition, I admit of it; but I think it should be rejected in application to *a period*. Suppose foreign commerce increases from a war or other reasons, so as to add immensely to the national

national wealth; an additional income is added to the fortunes of many men, these men will in general increase their expences, and consequently demand. I have no idea of a great increase of national wealth any where without an increase of the expences of individuals following; there certainly may be such cases, but they must carry rather the appearance of exceptions, than the ground of new principles. Why did land sell in the last century for 15 years purchase? Because there was so little specie that there was no comparative demand, people who have not MONEY do not add to *demand.* Why is land at present so much higher? Because a greater plenty of specie has given a greater demand. Demand and competition appear to be *effects*; money the *cause.*

Sir *James* supposes it remarked—"that articles of indispensable necessity must remain constantly in proportion to the mass of riches. This I cannot by any means admit to be just. Let me take the example of grain, which is the most familiar. Is it not plain from what we have said above, that the proportion of wealth found in the hands of the lowest class of the people constantly regulates the price of it; consequently let the rich be ever so wealthy, the price of subsistence can never rise above the faculties of the poor."—In answer to this it may be obſerved, that the price has riſen far beyond what the faculties of the poor in former times could purchaſe, and they would now all be ſtarved, if *quantity of wealth*, that is *demand for labour*, had not riſen the price of it, as well as of wheat — Through whatever political mazes we are carried, we ſhall find that an increaſe in the national wealth will be only another word for increaſe of demand, ſo as to be ſcarcely poſſible for one to ſubſiſt without the other.

From various of the inſtances quoted by Sir *James*, there is reaſon to believe he principally draws his argument from the demand and competition at certain times, for certain commodities, at a market for corn, at ancient *Rome* for a mullet; prices in *January* 1759, &c. and what is remarkable, he ſays nothing of the increaſe of money from the diſcovery of *America*, on which *Monteſquieu* founds his idea; and it is from a gradual increaſe of wealth from induſtry that Mr *Hume* ſupports his And yet Sir *James* aſſerts, that the money in *Europe might* be increaſed to ten times the preſent quantity, without the prices of commodities being affected —Upon the whole, the matter turns principally on the proportion which holds between money and demand—throughout this eſſay I have ſup-poſed

posed them the same thing; because I see, whichever way I look, the expences of all ranks of people increase, with an increase of their incomes, and luxury spreading through countries in proportion to their wealth. now luxury is wealth—is demand—is competition for the thing desired, and prices rise in proportion to expences, that is to money. If this is not true, how are we to account for the prices of a thousand things before the discovery of *America*, compared with the present prices of the same commodities;—or, without going so far back—for those in the last century, not only of rarities, but almost every commodity that can be named, provisions, labour, manufactures, land, &c. Why is labour, provisions, house-rent, land, and commodities in general, except foreign manufactures, cheaper in *Sweden* or *Norway* than in *England* or *Holland*?—Surely it is because those countries are not equally wealthy. You may, if you please, add the consequence, that there is not an equal demand. Further, let us take Sir *James*'s supposition, suppose our national wealth to be increased to ten times the present amount; how would it be possible for the prices of commodities not to rise immensely, unless every man became a hoarder, which I shall never suppose? Thus every man

 possessing

possessing ten times his present wealth and income, immediately increases his expences; increases his servants, equipages, labourers, builders, artizans; his house-keeping expences multiply; more is eaten, drank, and wasted; all this forms a fresh demand for every article; and as the wealth of others has the same effect with them, here is competition, if prices in consequence of this demand and competition should not rise, surely it would be miraculous? This was the idea of Messrs. *Montesquieu* and *Hume*, who, from seeing an universal effect regularly following a visible cause, justly attributed the former to the latter; they saw that a great increase of national wealth always caused a great rise in prices; and that in poor countries commodities were cheaper than in rich ones; hence they deduced their reasoning; and what we have since seen and felt in this country, would, if any proof was wanting, confirm their doctrine.

This I think is the direct and plain way of attributing the effect in question to its proper cause. But here I readily admit a partial exception; an exception which Sir *James* seems to have wrought into a complete hypothesis: I admit that to an unknown degree, an increase of wealth increasing the demand for certain manufactures,

tures, will increase the quantity brought to market, and prices stand as they were: For instance, send a gradual increase of orders to the manufacturers of *Manchester*, *Norwich*, *Birmingham*, &c. and they will answer the increased demand for perhaps a long time, without an increase of prices; because the people will increase with their industry, and a want of hands will not be felt. This is the strongest exception that can be put to the rule of Mr. *Hume*, yet is it not of importance enough to overturn his idea, since the word *commodities* includes such a variety of things besides certain manufactures, that his expression may be deemed sufficiently accurate: land, houses, labour, provisions, &c. are all clearly within his rule, not to speak of a variety even of manufactures, not wrought in great manufacturing towns.

But even in this great exception of Sir *James*'s, there are some circumstances which favour Mr. *Hume*'s hypothesis: Why are not all manufactures cheaper now than they were 300 years ago? If the argument urged by Sir *James* is just, they ought to be cheaper, or at least not dearer; but if the difference of the periods be considered relative to favouring manufactures of every kind, they ought now to be produced 500 *per cent.* cheaper. Yet in 1460, good cloth, such as was to serve the best Doctor at *Oxford*, was sold at 3*s* 7*d* a yard, but as there were 30 shillings in the pound at that time, we must call this near 7*s* 6*d*. whereas now the proper cloth for such a person would cost 18*s*. In *William* the Conqueror's time the serjeant of an infirmary had a coat for 4*s*. I instance these only to shew, that in periods very distant, the prices of manufactures depend on the quantity of money, and if their rates in the last century be examined and compared with what they are at present, it will be found that scarce an instance is to be produced in which there has not been a considerable rise; which must be owing to the increase of money.

In any one period of no great extent, the increase of demand from the increase of wealth, may not be found to operate its natural effect; but in a longer period a change happens from a gradual and almost imperceptible progress; and then manufactures as well as all other commodities get up to a proportion with the quantity of money. That this must be the case during a long period cannot be doubted, when we consider that the price of labour has much more than doubled in a century, and that several articles of raw materials in many fabricks have risen equally with labour;

2 and

and if we take a larger ſcope, and go back to the period when proviſions, labour, and every other article were not a fourth of the preſent price, how are we to conceive that manufactures could be as dear as we pay for them? And to what cauſe is it poſſible to attribute the change but to the ſuperior quantity of ſpecie?

I have been led into this diſquiſition from its intimate connection with my ſubject, as I cannot but eſteem great national wealth as one of the moſt important circumſtances in the encouragement of agriculture; and if the reaſoning laid down by Sir *James Steuart* is juſt, as I underſtand it, this wealth muſt be of little importance, and my reaſoning fallacious. It is with diffidence I venture an opinion, contrary to the ideas of a writer of ſuch diſtinguiſhed abilities; and who has given ſuch uncommon attention to every part of the ſcience of political œconomy. nor perhaps would this apology be deemed ſufficient, had not Sir *James* taken the ſame liberty with the illuſtrious *Monteſquieu* and the ſagacious *Hume*.

SECT. VIII.

INCLOSURES.

THE next article I ſhall mention is the circumſtance of ſo large a part of the kingdom being incloſed, and the policy in the legiſlature of conſtantly increaſing incloſures.—To enter into a detail of their advantages here, would be a uſeleſs undertaking—the prejudices of ſome of our writers, who have even to the preſent day declaimed againſt them, are to be reckoned among thoſe abſurdities that never die—they are to be found in every branch of philoſophy, literature, and art. I ſhall here reply to one aſſertion thrown out by the enemies of incloſures—They ſay that rich lands after incloſing, are laid down to graſs, and the kingdom thereby depopulated. Suppoſing the caſe in the firſt inſtance, yet I have a great doubt whether the huſbandman converting his farm to that uſe for which the ſoil is moſt adapted, which pays him beſt, and conſequently adds moſt to the national wealth, can depopulate the country:—it may depopulate one pariſh, but probably others will gain beyond the proportion by it. However, granting the poſition, which is more than there is occaſion to do, yet I think

think population is but a fecondary object The foil ought to be applied to that ufe in which it will pay moft, without any idea of population. A farmer ought not to be tied down to bad hufbandry, whatever may become of population. Population, which, inftead of adding wealth to the ftate, is a burthen to the ftate, is a pernicious population—and will be found fo in every country where the national ftrength does not depend on troops ferving without pay. As to attributing to inclofures the many evils, moft of them imaginary, which fome writers have laid to their charge, they are merely ideal.

That many abfurd opinions fhould be commonly embraced concerning *new* meafures, is natural enough, but that we fhould fee the fame errors relative to matters of which we have had long experience, is certainly remarkable. The complaints againft inclofures are of a very long date; we have had them between two and three hundred years, and they never appeared without receiving the moft folid and fatiffactory refutation. One of the moft remarkable inftances is in the reign of *Elizabeth*; the following extract from a very curious tract will fet this matter in a clear light.

A Compendious, or briefe Examination of certayne ordinary complaints of divers of our countrymen in theſe our days. By W. S. (*ſuppoſed to be* Wm. Shakeſpeare) 1581.

Huſbandman] Many for theſe incloſures doe undoe us all, for they make us pay dearer for our lande that we occupy, and cauſes that we can have no lande in manner for our money to put to tyllage, all is taken up in paſture. I have known of late a dozen ploughs within leſs compaſs than ſix miles about me, layd down within theſe ſeven years, and where threeſcore perſons or upwards had their livings, now one man with his cattel has all, which is not the leaſt cauſe of former uproires for by theſe incloſers many doe lack lyvings and be idle; moreover all things are ſo deere that by their day wages they are not able to lyve *.

Capper.] I have well the experience thereof, for I am faine to give my journeymen two-pence in a day more than I was wont to doe, and yet they ſay they cannot ſufficiently lyve thereof.

Merchaunt] Moſt parte of all the towns of *England*, *London* only except, are ſore decayed in their houſes, &c. whereof it is long,

* One would have thought, without ſeeing the title, that this had been a tranſcript of the common complaints of the present time.

long, I cannot well tell, for there is such a general dearth of all things, as before 20 or 30 years hath not bene the like, not only of things growing within this realm, but of all other merchaundize that we buy from beyond the sea, as sylkes, wines, &c. then all kind of vittayle are as deere or deere agayne, and no cause of God's part thereof as far as I can perceive; for I never saw more plentie of corn, grasse, and cattle of all sorte than we have at this present, and have had (as ye know) all these 20 yeares passed continually.

Knight] Since ye have plentie of all things, of corne and cattel (as ye say) then it should not seem this dearth should be long of these inclosers, for it is not for scarceness of corne, that ye have this dearth, for (thanked be God) corne is good cheap, and so hath been these many years past. Then it cannot be the occasion of the dearth of cattle, for inclosure is the thing that nourisheth most of any other*. yet I confess there is a wonderful dearth of all things; and that doe I, and all men of my sorte feel most grief in, which have no way to sell, nor occupation to lyve by, but only our lands For you all with other artificers may save yourselves meetly well. Forasmuch

* An admirable reply to the croakers of the present [illegible]

much as yee, as all things are dearer, do aryse in the pryce of your wares and occupations accordingly.

Husbandman.] Yee rayse the pryce of your lands, and ye take farms alſo, and paſtures to your hands, which was wont to be poor men's lyvings ſuch as I am.

Merchaunt.] On my ſoul yee ſay truth.

Knight.] Syr, as I know it is true that yee complayne not without cauſe, ſo it is as true, that I and my ſorte, I mean all gentlemen, have as great, yea, and far greater cauſe to complayne; the pryces of things are ſo riſen on all hands, we are forced either to miniſh the third part of our houſehold, or rayſe the third part of our revenues; and for that we cannot ſo doe of our own landes, that is already in the hands of other men, many of us are enforced to keep peeces of our own landes, when they fall in our own poſſeſſion, or to purchaſe ſome farme of other men's landes, and to ſtore it with ſheep, &c.

Huſbandman.] Yea, thoſe ſheep is the cauſe of all theſe miſchieves.

Doctour.] I perceive by you all, that there is none of you but have juſt cauſe to complayn.

Knight.] I marvel much, maiſter doctour, what ſhould be the cauſe of this dearth, ſeeing all things are ſo plentiful.

Doctour.]

Doctour.] Syr, it is no doubt a thing to be mused upon. *Quere*, Whether if the husbandman were forced to abate the pryces of his stuff, this dearth would be amended; if he should be commanded to sell his wheat (for instance) at 8*d* the bushel, rye at 6*d.* barley at 4*d.* his pig and goose at 4*d.* his hen at 1*d. ob.* his wool at a marke a tod, the landlord to return to his old rent, &c. would goods in that case from beyond seas be brought as good cheap after the same rate? A man would think yes. For example, if they now sell a yard of velvet for 20*s.* or 22*s.* and pay that for a tod of wool, were it not as good for them to sell their velvet for a marke a yard, so they had a tod of wool for a marke*?"

In another part he says, "that in 20 or 30 years before 1581, commodities had in general risen 50 *per cent.*; some more. Cannot you neighbour remember, says he, that within these 30 years I could in this town

* *Memoirs of Wool*, vol. I. p. 113. I transcribe this extract from Mr *Smith*, not having been able to procure the original. He tells us, that the *Doctour* resolves the general dearness into the greater plenty of money from increase of trade, and accounts for wool being dearer in comparison than corn, from the former being allowed to be exported, and the latter too much restrained in that respect, but that by giving an equal liberty to both, notwithstanding inclosures, the ballance would be preserved by the farmer shifting from sheep to corn, and *vice versa*.

town buy the beſt pig or gooſe I could lay my hands on, for four-pence, which now coſteth twelve-pence, a good capon for three-pence or four-pence, a chicken for a penny, a hen for two-pence." P. 35.—Yet the price of ordinary labour was then 8 *d.* a day, p. 31 *.

As a commentary on theſe extracts I ſhall give the price of wheat through the 16th century, in the coin of the preſent ſtandard †.

		£.	s.	d.
1500,	Wheat the quarter, -	0	6	7
1504,	—— ——	0	8	9
1514,	—— ——	0	5	6
1519,	—— ——	0	5	6
	Average of 20 years,	0	6	7
1521,	—— ——	1	7	7
	—— ——	1	15	10
1527,	—— ——	0	19	9
	Average of 7 years, —	1	7	8
1532,	—— ——	0	8	10
1550,	—— ——	0	5	1¾
1551,	—— ——	0	1	9

* *Mr Hume's History of England*, vol [illegible] p 484.
† This I take from *Combrune's Enquiry*, folio.

			£.	s.	d.
1552,	——	——	0	2	4
1553,	——	——	0	8	2
1554,	——	——	0	8	2
1555,	——	——	0	8	2
1556,	——	——	0	6	4
1557,	——	——	1	2	6
1558,	——	——	0	11	2½
1559,	——	——	0	8	2
1560,	——	——	0	8	2
1561,	——	——	0	8	3
1562,	——	——	0	8	3
Average of 31 years,		-	0	8	3½
1573,	——	——	2	1	2½
1574,	——	——	2	1	2½
1575,	——	——	1	4	9
Average of 3 years,		—	1	15	8
1586,	——	——	2	18	8
1587,	——	——	3	6	6
1588,	——	——	0	6	5
1592,	——	——	0	19	6½
1594,	——	——	3	2	10
1595,	——	——	2	3	6
1596,	——	——	1	17	4
1597,	——	——	2	14	6
1598,	——	——	2	4	2

	£.	s.	d.
1599, — —	1	10	6
Average of 14 years *, -	2	2	4

It is upon record that the riſe of price in 1573, was not owing to any natural ſcarcity; and it is farther known, that in 1561, a free export was allowed and continued for ſome years. It has been aſſerted that the ſucceeding high prices were owing to that freedom of exportation. The whole of this table ſhews the contrary; exportation, whenever it raiſes prices, raiſes them immediately; for inſtance, in a few weeks inſtead of years; yet the price in 1561 and 1562 continued low.

But it appears from the dialogue quoted above, that from 20 to 30 years preceding 1581, prices had riſen 50 *per cent.* It is plain that this had nothing to do with wheat, which continued at a tolerably ſteady

* This table, as I mentioned before, is taken from the *Enquiry into the Prices of Wheat, Malt*, &c. folio; but I must remark the authority not much to be depended on. The author aſſerts his having reduced the prices to the preſent ſtandard, but biſhop *Fleetwood* gives 5*l* 4*s.* the price of 1507, and 4*l* that of 1596. I have taken this fallible guide, because I conſider here merely the comparison of the periods. I have before ſhewn what little dependance is to be placed on a man who makes the profit of arable land in fallow, wheat, barley, 78 *per cent.*

ſteady price till 1573, and then aroſe for many years more than 50 *per cent.* The author of the dialogue writes in 1581, and in it incloſures are much arraigned for converting arable into graſs for ſheep; but mark, that this complaint followed 31 years, the average price of which was 8 *s.* 3 *d.* ½, and we are told that the labouring poor could not live, whoſe wages were 8 *d.* a day! Such are the prepoſterous and abſurd complaints, which, like thoſe of depopulation, are, as Mr. *Hume* moſt juſtly remarks, *a vulgar complaint in all places and all ages* *. We have Sir *W. Petty*'s poſitive authority that day labour was 8 *d.* a day a century after this period; and at preſent it is 16 *d.* on an average.

But how could incloſures act againſt the plenty of corn, while wheat for 31 years ſtood at 8 *s.* 3 *d.* ½ preſent money? Does not this palpable contradiction ſhew the folly of ſuch an idea: Does it not ſhew, what we have ſo often remarked, that any operation which has a tendency (like throwing arable to graſs) to raiſe the price of any particular product—has in its very nature a tendency to the direct contrary effect. Throw ſo much arable to graſs as to raiſe the price of corn, and you encourage the

* *Hiſt. Eng.* vol. v. p 482.

corn farmers so much, that an increase of culture immediately follows. Every very high period in the preceding table is surely followed by a low one, until wheat came to 3 *l* 6 *s*. 6 *d*.; the highest price of all: what followed? Why 6 *s* 5 *d*. a quarter the very next year; such an encouragement to the farmer was the former price that it at once produced the latter. The same remark is just in every table of prices that has been published throughout *Europe*. And the low price being an equal discouragement, it must at once produce an high one.

Is it not evident therefore that the *Knight* in the dialogue has reason to say that it could not be owing to inclosures that corn was dear; nor could they make cattle dear, for inclosures cause plenty of cattle. This is the very mirrour of the present state of *England*: Inclosures are condemned for raising prices How do they raise prices? Why they raise wheat to 2 *l*. 3 *s*. 6 *d*. a quarter for 7 years *, and they make beef and mutton dear by infinitely increasing the number of fat sheep and oxen!—When shall we see an end to these absurdities?

The author of the dialogue tells us, that in the 20 or 30 years preceding 1581, commodities in general had risen 50 *per cent*.

* *Observations on Reversionary Payments*, 3d Edit p. 383

cent. and ſome more · and the ſhort-ſighted good people of thoſe days attributed this evil to ſheep, incloſures, graſs, and great farms, they would not look at the right cauſe with *Shakeſpeare*, the increaſe of money. it is the nature of the vulgar, great and ſmall, in all ages, to attribute evils to ſuch a cauſe as may be changed; becauſe the malignity of man loves an opportunity to quarrel with government. If ſheep are the cauſe; prohibit, ſay they, great flocks; if horſes, tax them; if great farms, divide them: ſuch cauſes admit of remedies, which if not applied, give an opportunity of clamour: but attribute them to an increaſe and conſequent cheapneſs of money—to publick wealth—to national proſperity—the proſpect is too brilliant for a jaundiced eye, that can look with pleaſure only on ideal evil and chimerical declenſion.

Among the preſent complaints of the high prices of proviſions, we are told by ſome writers that it is not the rates of wheat that oppreſs the people, but thoſe of meat. Among theſe, Dr. *Price* is pleaſed to rank himſelf · he ſays that it is the ſuperior price of fleſh that hurts the poor, as it forces them to conſume bread only, conſequently they could before live better when wheat was high, than they can now while it is comparatively low. I cannot ſubſcribe to

 this

this obſervation, for the reaſons I am going to produce, nor do I put much faith in the regiſtered prices of meat, from their being ſo uncertain and deſultory; we have them not (except at the victualling-office) in the ſame regular manner as the *Windſor* prices of wheat and malt. In Mr *Combrune*'s table of prices, who ſupports the ſame general argument as Dr. *Price*, we have the following minutes:

		£	*s.*	*d.*		£	*s.*	*d.*
1309,	Wheat,	1	1	11	An ox,	2	14	0
1314,	—	3	1	2	—	3	13	6
1315,	—	3	1	2	—	7	6	9
1336,	—	0	6	1½	—	1	0	4½
1349,	—	0	5	6	—	0	18	4
1444,	—	0	9	0	—	3	4	9
1532,	—	0	8	10	—	1	16	6
1550,	—	0	5	1¾	—	0	18	0
	Averages,	1	2	4	—	2	14	0

Hence it appears that a fat ox in thoſe days was worth as much as 20 buſhels of wheat. If we call the preſent price of wheat 6 *s.* 6 *d.* a buſhel, it is for 20, 6 *l.* 10 *s.*; then if we conſider that the improvements in huſbandry for two centuries have contributed more to improve the food and ſize of cattle than any other article; we ſhall have great reaſon to think that ſuch an ox as in that period yielded a price equivalent to 6*l.* 10*s.* would not at preſent yield more. If the total want of turnips, and thoſe other means of winter fatting, long ſince diſcovered, be conſidered —and that hay ſold as well or better than at preſent, and conſequently muſt be ſparingly uſed, we may conjecture to what ſize their cattle aroſe; and then judge if they were probably better than the *Scotch* black cattle bred on mountains with little winter food, which ſell fat from 5*l.* to 10*l.* at preſent.

		£.	s.	d.		£.	s.	d.
1309,	Wheat,	1	1	11	Sheep,	0	9	1
1314,	—	3	1	2	—	0	3	7
1336,	—	0	6	1½	—	0	2	0½
1310,	—	0	17	9	—	0	3	9
1448,	—	0	13	0	—	0	5	0
1531,	—	0	8	10	—	0	3	10¾
1532,	—	0	8	10	—	0	5	6½
1558,	—	0	11	2½	—	0	3	6
	Averages,	1	0	0		0	4	6

The value of a ſheep therefore was equal to 1 buſhel 3 pecks and ⅓ of wheat: this at preſent would be at 6*s.* 6*d.* a buſhel, 12*s.* 2*d.* for more than which I do not apprehend one of the ſheep of thoſe days

 would

would ſell, for the ſame reaſons I before mentioned in reſpect to oxen *.

In 1532, when wheat was 8 *s.* 10 *d.* a *fat* ſheep is 5 *s.* 6 *d.* ½; this is equal to 5 buſhels, a much higher price than they yield now; and difference of breed conſidered, probably double.

But Dr. *Price* gives, from a manuſcript of the Duke of *Northumberland*'s, the following particular: "In 1512, the price of wheat was 6 *s.* 2 *d.* a quarter, that of a fat ox, 13 *s.* 4 *d.*; the price of wheat therefore, ſays he, was about a ſeventh of its preſent price; that of meat, only a fifteenth." Here therefore we find the Doctor fixes the preſent price of the fat ox at 10 *l.*. But on what poſſible authority can he ſuppoſe, ſuch oxen as were fed in *Yorkſhire* 150 years ago, to be of a ſize that would now yield that ſum. if the conſiderations I before urged are admitted, I ſhould rather ſuppoſe the oxen of thoſe days no better than *Scotch* runts at preſent. At beſt therefore it is only one ſuppoſition in ſupport of another ſuppoſition; an uncertainty

* I muſt remark on both theſe articles that it is uncertain whether the oxen and ſheep were fat or lean, but in all probability both, as they are ſometimes called an ox *fat*, a ſheep *fat*, if all were ſo, it would not be ſpecified ſo in particular years, and not all.

tainty that muſt run through all accounts of the price of cattle, which vary ſo prodigiouſly, that 20*l.* may be very cheap for an ox, and 5*l.* very dear. Further, a wether (not ſaid if fat or lean) is 1*s.* 8*d.* or equal to 2 buſhels 1 peck of wheat. That quantity of wheat at 6*s.* 6*d.* is 14*s.* 7*d.* a very good price for a wether at preſent through the North of *England*; and in ſome parts of the North, an high one: the ſame obſervation is applicable to the hog at 2*s.*

The Doctor next quotes from *Maitland* another proportion. Wheat, 12*s.* An ox, 1*l.* 18*s.* A wether, 3*s.* Butter, ¾ and 1*d.* a pound. Cheeſe, ½*d.* Theſe are,

The ox, — 26 buſhels of wheat.
The wether, - 2 ditto.
Butter the pound, 2 quarts ditto.
Cheeſe ditto, - 1 quart ditto.

The prices of theſe commodities at preſent would be (wheat at 6*s.* 6*d.*)

		£.	s.	d.
The ox,	—	8	9	0
— wether,	—	0	13	0
— butter *per* pound,	-	0	0	4¾
— cheeſe,	—	0	0	2½

From theſe prices I muſt draw very contrary concluſions from the Doctor: the ox and the wether are probably as cheap now as before, but what amazes me is the article of butter; which he prints in italicks, that it may be remarked. Salt butter is frequently

quently in the present period 6 *d.* a pound, and butter in 1549, so high as 4 *d.* ¾! Is this produced to shew the disproportion of the products of cattle to wheat? Twenty years ago butter in *London* was cheaper than 200 years ago. If the butter is supposed to be fresh, the price is high, but why may we not think it all salt so soon after an age that had no mutton in winter but what was salted?

No idea on these subjects is more mistaken than the supposition that butter in this age is dearer than formerly: very many instances might be produced of the contrary. Instead of being dearer, it has not advanced near so much as most other commodities. In *June* 1695, *Houghton* expressly says, fresh butter *in the country* 70 miles from *London* sold at 6 *d.* a pound, and he mentions it as a common price *. Cheese is low, but unless we knew what cheese it was, we can found no conclusions: In *Norfolk* and *Suffolk*, cheese is at this time but 3 *d.* ½, and some under that. But let us quit such uncertain conjectures founded on accidental circumstances—the prices of single years—of particular purchasers, which can give us no more knowledge than we at present reap from hearing that *Nokes* bought beef last *Saturday*

* *Collection for Improving of Husbandry and Trade,* vol 1 p. 390.

day at 2*d.* a pound, or *Stiles* butter for 11*d.* What was the quality? Was the market day high or low? Did others buy so? Such insulated circumstances scraped out of dusty libraries and records are not worth transcribing for such general uses as are too often made of them. The only register of the prices of meat that carries with it the least degree of authenticity is the records of the victualling-office, the prices of which are always cheaper than the common ones in the market, but this is not of consequence, when one period is compared with another, as that circumstance operates equally in all. The following table of the *London* prices of beef and pork, will shew us how much these commodities are advanced.

Years.		*Beef per Cwt.*			*Pork per Cwt.*	
		s.	*d.*		*s.*	*d.*
1683,	- -	18	8	—	25	1$\frac{1}{2}$
1684,	- -	20	0	—	26	0
1685,	- -	20	0	—	26	6
1686,	- -	17	0	—	26	0
1687,	- -	20	0$\frac{1}{3}$	—	25	3
1688,	- -	20	6	—	23	9
1689,	- -	20	10	—	31	8
1690,	- -	20	4	—	25	0
1691,	- -	19	3	—	24	2
1692,	- -	18	6	—	24	11

Years.		*Beef per Cwt.* s.	d.		*Pork per Cwt.* s.	d.
1693,	- -	22	0	—	29	6
1694,	- -	23	4	—	32	6
1695,	- -	26	0	—	32	3
1696,	- -	25	2	—	29	6
1697,	- -	25	0	—	31	0
1698,	- -	26	0	—	32	6
1699,	- -	21	9	—	33	10
1700,	- -	25	0	—	33	10
1701,	- -	24	6	—	32	4½
1702,	- -	27	3	—	33	7½
1703,	- -	22	6	—	27	6
1704,	- -	21	2	—	24	0
1705,	- -	25	7	—	27	10½
1706,	- -	21	5	—	27	5
1707,	- -	19	0	—	25	7½
1708,	- -	20	6	—	28	4½
1709,	- -	26	0	—	30	7½
1710,	-	31	0	—	45	7½
1711,	- -	39	6	—	58	6
1712,	- -	23	10	—	31	9
1713,	- -	23	1	—	30	9
1714,	- -	21	10	—	29	10
1715,	- -	23	3	—	28	0
1716,	- -	23	9	—	31	3
1717,	- -	22	0	—	30	9
1718,	- -	23	0	—	29	10½
1719,	- -	24	7½	—	27	6
1720,	- -	29	3	—	37	9
1721,	- -	21	9	—	43	3

Years.		*Beef per Cwt.* s.	d.		*Pork per Cwt.* s.	d.
1722,	- -	26	9	—	31	0
1723,	- -	18	0	—	24	0
1724,	- -	21	6	—	31	0
1725,	- -	20	8	—	34	6
1726,	- -	26	1½	—	37	6
1727,	- -	21	9	—	35	6
1728,	- -	19	7½	—	32	0
1729,	- -	26	0	—	40	6
1730,	- -	18	6	—	29	3
1731,	- -	18	3	—	24	5
1732,	- -	16	9	—	19	0
1733,	- -	16	1	—	25	0
1734,	- -	16	5	—	23	5½
1735,	- -	13	3	—	21	2½
1736,	- -	13	7	—	23	11
1737,	- -	13	5	—	22	6
1738,	- -	18	7	—	30	1
1739,	- -	18	1½	—	25	9½
1740,	- -	23	7¾	—	31	0½
1741,	- -	24	9½	—	36	3¼
1742,	- -	24	4	—	32	9
1743,	- -	19	2½	—	27	2¼
1744,	- -	18	3½	—	22	5¼
1745,	- -	18	9½	—	21	9¼
1746,	- -	21	3⅜	—	24	8¼
1747,	- -	19	4¼	—	24	0½
1767,	- -	25	5½	—	none b[t].	
1768,	- -	25	3½	—	ditto.	
1769,	- -	22	9	—	33	0

2

Years.	Beef per Cwt. s.	d.		Pork per Cwt. s.	d.
1770, - -	22	2¼	—	41	5
1771, - -	22	6	—	43	5½
Average of the last 5 years, -	23	7	—	39	3
Average of the 17 years of the last century, - -	21	5	—	28	1
Former dearer by - - - - -	2	2	—	11	2
Average of the years 1709, 10, 11, 12, - - - - -	30	1	—	41	7
Last 5 years,	23	7	—	39	3
Former dearer by - - - - -	6	6	—	2	4

If the 17 years ending 1771 were known, the average would probably be lower, or at least as low as the 17 of the last century. I think this is upon the whole, a reply to the observation of Dr. *Price* *, that the exportation, which in 1697,

* Page 383. The uncertainty which attends the antient registers of prices (except those of wheat and malt

1697, went on without clamour, though at 3*l.* a quarter, was becauſe meat was ſo reaſonable as to enable the poor to live on that: On the contrary in 1697, beef was 2*s.*

---

malt at *Windſor)* is ſo great, that I ſhould never have thought of making uſe of them had not others given them an importance which they do not deſerve. While it is ſo difficult to know theſe prices at preſent, how can we ſuppoſe it ſo eaſy to know thoſe of the 15th century? Before the late act of parliament for publiſhing the prices of corn, how did any perſon know what was the price even of wheat? *I bought at 5s* *Nay*—ſays another, *I gave 7s 6d* A third in company (from a place where the meaſure is 11 gallons) 9*s* A fourth, who bought the worſt wheat he could find in the market, 3*s.* 6*d.* A fifth, who looked for the fineſt, 8*s.* If any one of them happened to make a minute in a book which is found 300 years afterwards, the price minuted is aſſerted to be that of the period. We find in theſe old regiſters wheat, *ſo much*, oats, *ſo much*, an ox, 1*l* 16*s.* Very pretty regiſters truly! How came the gentleman who made ſuch a minute, to know what the price of an ox was? He might buy an ox, and minute the price of it—and ſo may I now go into *Smithfield* and buy one worth thirty guineas, or I may buy one worth 5*l.* 10*s*, but am I in either caſe to ſay for the information of poſterity, *ſuch is the price of an ox*? It is the ſame with calves, ſheep, pigs, and geeſe, any of which may be dear or cheap, without conveying the leaſt information if all the cauſes are not explained. I have mentioned above the price of labour being 8*d.* a day in 1581, and the ſame in 1681, on the authority of *Shakeſpeare* and Sir *W* *Petty* but muſt it not ſtrike every one, that neither of theſe writers could know any thing of the matter? They ſpeak of 8*d* being

2*s.* 6*d.* *per* cwt. dearer than in 1771, and pork only 2*s.* a cwt. cheaper than in 1769. Let me alſo remark, that for this fact I have not only publick contracts to quote, but alſo private prices In 1682, the common price of beef was 3*d.* *per* pound*. And

being the common price of a day's labour. Where was it the common price, at *London*, or in the mountains of *Yorkſhire?* Was it the price in hay, in harveſt, or in winter? Thus Mr. *Combrune* tells us that in 1351, the price of labour was 2*d.* ¾ a day, but reapers had 4*d.* ½, threſhers 7*d* and mowing graſs, 1*s.* 1*d.* ¾ *per* acre or day, I know not which, but either is an abſurdity, for no ſuch proportions could poſſibly exiſt in any age. There is an extreme difficulty in knowing what the price of labour is at preſent in any place, for in many, there are three or four prices *per diem* in the year, ſome with board, others excluſive of it; beſides which, there are many ſorts of work generally done by the piece, inſomuch that a man whoſe nominal pay ſhall be 1*s.* a day, ſhall on an average of the year, earn 1*s.* 4*d.* From all which conſiderations it is ſurprizing that writers, very acute in other matters, ſhould readily accept any information which tends to ſhew prices in former times, while they muſt know it to be ſo difficult to gain thoſe even of the preſent. And this conſideration ought to make us value the regiſters on real authority much the more, ſuch as the *Windſor* prices—the regiſter act—and the prices of meat laid before parliament by the victualling-office, all of which, though not infallible, are far more deſerving of notice than the goſſiping tittle tattle of converſation, in which every man remembers juſt thoſe prices that ſuit his argument, and quotes purchaſes that have about as much authority here, as they have in the Moon.

* *Houghton*'s *Huſbandry*, vol. ii p. 91.

And in 1768, I ſhewed, that on an average of a great part of the kingdom it was 3*d.* and even at *London* only 3*d.* ½ † How upon the whole is it poſſible for any perſon to aſſert, that the export of corn—monopoly of farms—or incloſures, have raiſed the price of beef and pork ſo as to exclude thoſe poor from eating them now, who in the laſt century eat them on wages of 8*d.* a day?

All theſe ideas are contrary to the nature of things; we alſo find them contrary to the few facts that can be gained. As little reaſon is there to think that the proportion between the prices of bread and meat has varied in any degree ſufficient to be the leaſt oppreſſive.—none of theſe circumſtances, nor any others that can be named, are comparable to the riſe of huſbandry labour and poor-rates throughout the kingdom.

But the ſame writer, whoſe accurate inveſtigation of other ſubjects makes his opinions on this point the more to be lamented, has other arguments againſt incloſures, which muſt not be overlooked. He ſays, the increaſe of tillage is now at an end, and adds, " I have lately received an account of a large common field in *Leiceſterſhire*, which uſed to produce annually 800

L quarters

† *Six Months Tour*, vol. iv. p. 278.

quarters of corn, besides maintaining 200 cattle, but which now, in consequence of being inclosed and getting into few hands, produces little or no corn, and maintains no more cattle than before, though the rents are considerably advanced *." If the Doctor had formed his tables of Observations on no better authority than this, they would not have been very famous. *Rents raised—corn disappeared—cattle not increased* † !—What are we to think of such facts? I travelled through *Leicestershire* and *Northamptonshire*, and not I think without attention I saw great tracts of country inclosed, and laid from arable to grass; but I saw throughout the graziers fields, such herds of fat sheep and oxen, as delighted

---

* *Observations on reversionary Payments*, p 388

† "We shall only observe, that it seems more the national interest of *England* to employ its land to the breeding and feeding of cattle, than to the produce of corn, for, as Mr *Fortrey* has well noted, "the profit of one acre of pasture in the flesh, hide, and tallow of an ox, or in the flesh, wool and tallow of a sheep, or in the carcase of a horse, is of so much greater value abroad, than the like yield of the earth would be in corn, that the exportation of this nation might be at least double to what it is, if rightly disposed" *Davenant's Works*, vol. ii p. 229 Sir *Thomas Moore* says, that a shepherd and his dog will eat up townships, but will not the wool and skins produced by an acre of pasture, make greater employment than the tillage of such an acre can? I question it not." *Houghton's Husbandry*, vol i p 49.

delighted the eye—the generality of theſe lands are ſtocked at the rate of a large ox, and 2 ½ ſheep to every two acres; and the ſoil does ſo well in graſs that they fat large ſheep the winter through.—Before the incloſure, thoſe lands were managed in the courſe,

1. Fallow,
2. Wheat,
3. Spring corn.

How in the name of wonder were fat oxen and ſheep kept before? Upon the fallows? Or upon ſtraw? That the corn diſappears is moſt certain; but that it is amply made up in beef and mutton is as certain.

The ſyſtem of incloſing arable lands and laying them down to graſs, leſſens the quantity of corn—yet does the Doctor admit that corn in the preſent period is cheap: This ſyſtem increaſes greatly (as *Shakeſpeare* well obſerved) beef and mutton; yet the Doctor complains of thoſe commodities being dear, and *owing to incloſures.* What is this but in other words ſaying, that we leſſen the quantity of beef by increaſing the number of oxen:—and render mutton extremely dear, by making ſheep more plentiful! But theſe marvellous effects take place at a time when, according to the ſame writer, depopulation operates like a pestilence: here, therefore, is a fresh reason why meat is dear—the mouths that eat it being daily lessened!

The fact is this, in the central counties of the kingdom, particularly *Northamptonshire*, *Leicestershire*, and parts of *Warwic*, *Huntingdon* and *Buckinghamshires*, there have been within 30 years large tracts of the open field arable under that vile course, 1 fallow, 2 wheat, 3 spring corn, inclosed and laid down to grass, being much more suited to the wetness of the soil than corn; and yields in beef, mutton, hides and wool, beyond comparison a greater neat produce than when under corn. At that time, the horses that tilled the land eat up the few grass inclosures near the farm houses, and a considerable part of the spring corn, whereas at present, many farms of from 500 to 1000 acres have not more than two or three nags on them for the farmers, to ride and see their stock. Thus the land yields a greater neat produce in food for mankind—the landlord doubles his income, which enables him to employ so many more manufacturers and artizans—the farmer increases his income, by means of which he also does the same—the hides and wool are a creation of so much employment for other manufacturers

—How any one from ſuch a ſyſtem can deduce the melancholy proſpects of depopulation, famine and diſtreſs, is to me amazing.

But further; Dr *Price* and the other writers who aſſure us we ſhould throw down our hedges, and waſte one third of our farms in a barren fallow by way of making beef and mutton cheap, will confine themſelves to the incloſures which have converted arable to graſs What ſay they to thoſe which have changed graſs to arable? They chuſe to be ſilent. I do not comprehend the amuſement that is found in conſtantly looking at thoſe objects which are ſuppoſed to be gloomy—and in regularly lamenting the evils that ſurround us, though they flow from cauſes which ſhower down much ſuperior bleſſings. When I look around me in this country, I think I every where ſee ſo great and animating a proſpect that the ſmall ſpecks which may be diſcerned in the hemiſphere, are loſt in the brilliancy that ſurrounds them. I cannot ſpread a curtain over the illumin'd ſcene, and leave nothing to view but the mere ſhades of ſo ſplendid a piece *.

* A *French* writer has a very good obſervation on the diſtempered imaginations of our croaking politicians "L'Angleterre ſe trouve dans l'etat d'un homme qui ſe porte bien, qui jouit d'une ſante brillante, qui a la

What will these gentlemen say to the inclosures in *Norfolk*, *Suffolk*, *Nottinghamshire*, *Derbyshire*, *Lincolnshire*, *Yorkshire*, and all the northern counties? What say they to the sands of *Norfolk*, *Suffolk* and *Nottinghamshire*, which yield corn and mutton and beef from *the force of* INCLOSURE *alone*? What say they to the wolds of *York* and *Lincoln*, which from barren heaths, at 1*s*. per acre, are *by* INCLOSURE *alone* rendered profitable farms? Ask Sir *Cecil Wray* if without INCLOSURE he could advance his heaths by sainfoine from 1*s*. to 20*s*. an acre.—What say they to the vast tracts in the peak of *Derby*, which *by* INCLOSURE *alone* are changed from black regions of ling to fertile fields covered with cattle? What say they to the improvements of moors in the northern counties, where INCLOSURES alone have made those countries smile with culture which before were dreary as night?—What have these gentlemen to say to these instances? Cannot they manage to assure us the prospect is delusive? They can.

a la respiration libre, mais qui ne connoît pas assez l'anatomie pour sentir quels sont les principes de la santé dont il jouit, si quelqu'un lui dit que son embonpoint pourroit bien être le principe masque d'une maladie, il craint, il s'allarme, il se trouble, l'inquietude le gagne." *Traité de la Circulation et du Credit*, 1771. p 44.

can. Hear how they are characterized.— " Inclosures of waste lands and commons " *would* be useful *if* divided into *small al-* " *lotments*, and *given up* to be occupied at " moderate rent, by the poor. But *if* besides " lessening the produce of fine wool *, they

L 4 " bear

* How far the produce of wool is declined, may partly be gathered from the rates at which it has been sold in different times, being now as cheap as it was centuries ago, while the value of money has sunk so much, that most other commodities have greatly risen in price.

Years.			*Price per Tod in present Money.* l.	s	d.
1198, Wool,	—	—	0	15	0
1337, ——— the best,	—	—	1	8	0
1339, Wool,	—	—	1	10	3
1353, Wool,	—	—	1	10	4
1390, —(the sale restricted to certain places)			0	10	11
1425, Wool,	—	—	0	17	5
Average,	—	—	1	1	11
1533, ——— the best cloathing,		—	0	13	4
1581, Wool,	—	—	0	18	5
1622, Wool,	—	—	1	3	8
1641, Wool,	—	—	1	4	0
1647, Romney Marsh,		—	1	17	6
1648, Ditto,	—	—	2	0	0
1651, Ordinary,	—	—	1	8	0
Civil War,	—	—	1	19	8
1656, Wool,	—	—	2	1	3
Average, from the beginning of the civil War to the Restoration,			1	15	0

" bear hard on the poor, by depriving them " of a part of their subsistance, and *only* " go

			l	s	d.
1660, Wool,	—	—	1	19	8
1670,	—	—	1	8	0
1677,	—	—	0	14	0
1694,	—	—	1	8	0
1698,	—	—	1	1	0
Average, from the Restoration to the end of the Century,			1	6	1
1706, Wool,	—	—	0	17	6
1707,	—	—	0	16	6
1712,	—	—	0	15	0
1713,	—	—	0	18	0
1717,	—	—	1	5	0
1737,	—	—	0	11	0
1739,	—	—	0	13	0
1742,	—	—	0	14	0
1743,	—	—	1	0	2
Average,	—	—	0	16	8

Smith's *Memoirs of Wool*, Vol ii. p 507 The writer justly observes, that when wheat was 8*d* a bushel, the goose 4*d.* and the hen 1*d.* wool was a mark a tod, and that the fall in price was a great burthen upon the landed interest And manufacturers clamoured so much about the year 1737, upon account of the decay of our woollen trade, that much was written on it, and parliament busied with their complaints, they brought the low price of wool as a proof of this, but all was false, for at that very time the export of woollen goods amounted to 4,158,643*l.* 17*s.* 0*d* which was twice what it was in 1698 Thus the author of the *British Woollen Manufacturers* *to*

" go towards increasing farms already too " large, the advantages attending them " may

---

to the Members of Parliament, 1737 · " Your honours are fully apprized, even by your tenants, that the effects of a declining trade are now generally felt: and no general cause can be ascribed but the great decay of our woollen exportation trade " The author of the *Observations on British Wool*, 1738, says, " Our trade is considerably decreased, and even the landholder finds the inconvenience thereof by the present low price of wool " And the author of the *Essay on the Causes of the Decline of foreign Trade*, 1739, (from whose fallacious accounts the *French* writers have borrowed so much) says, " That the foreign trade of *Britain* declines, will appear by the following symptoms, viz *the low price of wool* I appeal, says he, to the experience of every honest man conversant in trade, whether it does not decline, year after year, especially *our woollen trade* " And Mr *Webber* — " The present low price of wool shews the great decay of our trade Hence it is evident, that we have not one THIRD PART of the quantity of goods carried to *foreign markets* which we formerly had " And Mr *Lowndes* intitles his Scheme, printed 1745, by order of the house of commons, " *A Scheme*— in order to RE-ESTABLISH the woollen manufacture of *England* "

I have inserted these long accounts to shew the disposition that is so common of seeing imaginary evils, and magnifying them as much as possible.—these writers, and some others, alarmed the nation at the *decline* of what was then FLOURISHING; and it is the same with our present complainants of luxury and depopulation.—From the above table, Dr. *Price* may collect how much reason there is for thinking the quantity of our fine wool lessened, for after 1743, the price

"may not much exceed the diſadvan-
"tages * " Hence therefore we find all theſe improvements very equivocal—Before it is allowed that converting ling to corn is beneficial, it muſt previouſly be aſked if the im-

price continued for many years low, for ſome years laſt paſt it is riſen to about 20*s* or a guinea, but that price is nothing (the value of money conſidered) to what it was from the Reſtoration to 1699, viz. 1*l* 6*s* 1*d* equal now to double that ſum

* *Obſervations on Reverſionary Payments*, p. 390. While our own writers, in the uſual manner of depreciating every thing in their own country and their own age, would fain make out the miſery of this kingdom, foreigners are ſtruck with a very different idea. S'il exiſte une nation qui, ſans etre tres nombreuſe, poſſede une grande quantité de terres bien cultivees, ſi cette nation augmente journellement ſon agriculture et ſon commerce, ſans que ſa population augmente en pareille proportion, en fin, ſi elle fait naître beaucoup plus de ſubſiſtances ſans nourrir plus d'habitans, je dis, *Il faut que cette nation conſomme* ſpécifiquement plus que les autres, il faut que le tarif de la vie humaine y ſoit plus haut. Et c'eſt la l'INDICE LE PLUS CERTAIN DE LA FELICITE DES HOMMES Tel eſt le cas où ſe trouve l'Angleterre *Felicité Publique*, tom ii p 141 And again, ſpeaking of our great national debt, the great evil of which he thinks has been not expending the money in the improvement of the waſtes of *Scotland* and *Ireland*, he ſays, " J'avoue que je trouverois difficilement d'autres objets que la guerre ait fait négliger, car *cette heureuſe contrée offre par tout* L'IMAGE DE LA PROSPERITE. Population, agriculture, manufactures, grands chemins, établiſſemens magnifiques, rien ne paroît y manquer, et c'eſt un argument terrible entre les mains des ſceptiques en politique." *Ib* tom ii p. 190.

improvement is wrought by that ghoſtly object of dread and terror—a great farmer: before it is acknowledged right to make that ſand which would not feed rabbits, produce beef and mutton, we muſt know whether the poor were deprived of a part of their ſubſiſtence:—before you will ſubmit to change the heaths of *Lincoln* to fertile fields of ſainfoine, you muſt demand, *Were the allotments ſmall?* I muſt own, it is with aſtoniſhment that I thus ſee ſuperior minds ſtooping to prejudices ſo unworthy of their abilities.

How, in the name of common ſenſe, were ſuch improvements to be wrought by little or even moderate farmers! Can ſuch incloſe waſtes at a vaſt expence—cover them with an hundred loads an acre of marle—or ſix or eight hundred buſhels of lime—keep ſufficient flocks of ſheep for folding—and conduct thoſe (for the lower claſſes) mighty operations eſſential to new improvements? No. It is to GREAT FARMERS you owe theſe. Without GREAT FARMS you never would have ſeen theſe improvements—much I ſuppoſe to the ſatiſfaction of thoſe who declare themſelves ſo indiſcriminately their enemies *.

* I muſt beg leave to tranſcribe from Mr. *Hume*, whoſe political ideas have an acumen that diſtinguiſhes him in an uncommon manner, a paſſage or two which highly

SECT. IX.

CONSUMPTION OF MEAT.

THESE points are the great foundation of *Britain's* agriculture; but there is another circumstance which though not of equal

---

highly deserve attention, and are indeed the best reply to most of the advice given by Dr *Price* on great farms, inclosures, luxury and depopulation.

Encouragement by Exportation

"It was prohibited to export horses, as if that exportation did not encourage the breed, and render them more plentiful in the kingdom" *Hist. of Eng* Vol. iii. p. 401

Freedom of Prices

"Prices were affixed to woollen cloth *, to caps, and hats †. and the wages of labourers were regulated by law ‡ It is evident, that these matters ought always to be left free, and be entrusted to the common course of business and commerce." *Ib.* p. 402.

Rise of Prices

"Labour and commodities have certainly risen since the discovery of the *West-Indies*, but not so much in every particular as is generally imagined The greater industry of the present times, has encreased the number of tradesmen and labourers, so as to keep wages nearer a par than could be expected from the great increase of gold and silver. And the additional art employed in the finer manufactures, has even made some of these commodities fall below their former value Not to mention that merchants and dealers being contented with less profit than formerly, affords

* 4 H. 7. c 8. † *Ib.* c. c ‡ 11 H. 7. c. 22

equal consequence, should not be forgotten — It is the custom of eating such quantities

---

afford the goods cheaper to their customers" *Ib.* p. 402 —And again—"There seems to have been two periods in which prices rose remarkably in *England*, namely, that in Queen *Elizabeth*'s reign, when they are computed to have doubled, and that in the present age. Between the two, there seems to have been a stagnation It would appear, that industry during that intermediate period encreased as fast as gold and silver, and kept commodities nearly on a par with money." *Ib* Vol. v p 484 —This is an excellent idea, and accounts in one word for the effect which other writers attribute to engrossing farms, enclosures, and all the nonsense we meet with in so many volumes.

Enclosures, Farms, and Population.

"The absurd limitations of manufactures proceeded from a desire of promoting husbandry, which however is never more effectually encouraged than by the encrease of manufactures For a like reason, the law enacted against inclosures, and for the keeping up of farm-houses, scarcely deserves the high praises bestowed on it by Lord *Bacon.* If husbandmen understand agriculture, and have a ready vent for their commodities, *we need not dread a diminution of the people* employed in the country. All methods of supporting populousness, except by the interests of the proprietors, are violent and ineffectual During a century and half after this period, there was a frequent renewal of laws and edicts against depopulation, whence we may infer, that none of them were ever executed The natural course of improvement at last provided a remedy." *Ib.* Vol. III. p. 404.

quantities of meat in this country, and, on comparison with others, so little bread. —It is true, a very able writer draws from this a direct contrary conclusion from what I shall, and as his authority is too good in general not to demand a proper deference, I shall offer what I have to observe on this subject only as doubts that I have conceived.

Whatever a people principally consumes for their subsistence, must be the great object of the husbandman in his culture: thus in *France*, where bread, I apprehend, forms 19 parts in 20 of their food, corn, and especially wheat, is the only great object of cultivation; vines answering to our barley. In *England*, on the contrary, the quantity of meat, butter and cheese, consumed by all ranks of the people, is immense—to a much greater value, I should suppose, than that of wheat; hence cattle to our farmers is an object as important as corn: Thus the husbandmen in *France* keep scarcely any cattle, addicting themselves almost entirely to corn —in *England* vast quantities of cattle are kept. This circumstance I should apprehend would, if every thing else was equal, give a prodigious general superiority to the *English* agriculture. Let us consider on what principles the farmers of the two countries

countries muſt neceſſarily manage their lands. In *England*, they keep ſuch part of their farms in meadow and paſture as are by the nature of the ſoil ſo adapted; they throw their arable land into ſuch courſes of crops, that ſeveral are introduced which are either ſummer or winter food for cattle: thus the beſt cultivated parts of the kingdom adopt the following courſe.

1. Turneps.
2. Barley or oats.
3. Clover.
4. Wheat.

In which courſe, there is as much food for cattle raiſed, as corn; and as a large part of the ſecond year's produce, which is barley and oats, alſo goes to the cattle, above half the period is applied to their ſupport, and wheat occupies only a fourth. After the wheat many farmers add,

5. Peaſe or beans.

Which is another year given for cattle. This courſe is that of very good huſbandry; but where the culture is not ſo good, more crops are taken, but the addition generally oats. Now upon this ſyſtem, a conſiderable part of the whole farm or meadow, and a large portion of the arable are employed for cattle—the quantity of dung raiſed is very great, which being ſpread,

as

as it usually is on the arable fields, insures good crops—so much better than if such stocks of cattle were not kept, that I question if three acres are not quite as productive as five would be. Nay, I have in this point no doubt but the barley and wheat in a farm thrown into the course abovementioned, with a due proportion besides of meadow, yield a greater value than the corn in general would if one year was fallow, and the three following ones were wheat and barley—of such great consequence is this system of manuring.

Now let us turn to the *Frenchmen*, their two most general courses are,

1. Fallow,
2. Wheat.

And,

1. Fallow,
2. Wheat,
3. Barley or oats.

Much the greatest part of the farm arable—the meadow and pasture being very trivial, except in spots that cannot be otherwise applied, and near great towns. Thus very little cattle can be kept, except for tillage; in very many farms no other. Here we find manuring in any degree is cut off at once, consequently the crops must be poor, besides this, one half or one third of the land is fallow, at a mere barren expence: A ſyſtem which we know from the experience of our open fields is miſerable, and not to be compared for profit to thoſe in which crops for cattle are made the preparation for corn.

Wheat being in *France* the great object, all the expence is applied to that: A year's fallow is given, and what little dung they raiſe is all ſpread on it; this produces a middling, perhaps a good crop; an effect we experience in our own open fields, and when the farmer reaps his wheat he often finds himſelf out of pocket, and has to depend for his profit on a poor crop of ſpring corn. Thus the little demand for meat, butter and cheeſe, neceſſitates him to apply all his land to corn—the conſequences of which are, he purſues a bad courſe of crops—he has no dung—his products are ſmall—his profit comparatively nothing.

It muſt ſurely be evident to every one, that there is a great advantage to the *Engliſh* farmer from corn and cattle being in equal demand; ſince he is thereby enabled to apply all his lands to thoſe productions only to which they are beſt adapted—and at the ſame time the one is conſtantly a means of increaſing the product of the other.

Nor is this advantage by any means confined to the huſbandman;—the ſtate is intimately concerned. A much greater value is drawn from the earth; of this we have proof in the open lands in *England.* A crop of wheat in the courſe, 1. turnips, 2. barley, 3. clover, 4 wheat, on an incloſed farm, with a part meadow, yields acre for acre, from one quarter to two more than in the courſe, 1. fallow, 2. wheat, 3. barley, on an open field farm: And barley in the former ſucceeding turnips, yields on an average, nearly, if not quite double what it does in the latter ſucceeding wheat: But ſuppoſing the one 2½ quarters, and the other 4, it is giving as little ſuperiority as can be admitted. A ſlight calculation will ſhew this point clearly.

Open field.

	£.	s.	d.
Wheat after fallow, 2½ quarters an acre, at 50*s.* -	6	5	0
Barley after wheat, 2½ quarters, at 30*s.* - - -	3	15	0
In three years, - - - -	10	0	0
Per acre *per ann.* - - - -	3	6	8

Inclosure.

	£.	s.	d.
Turnips, - - - - -	1	15	0
Barley, 4 quarters, at 30*s.* -	6	0	0
Clover, - - - - -	4	0	0
Wheat, 3 quarters, at 50*s.* -	7	10	0
In four years, - - -	19	5	0
Per acre *per ann.* - -	4	16	3
	3	6	8
Superiority *per* acre *per ann.*	1	9	7

This every practical farmer will allow me is as little superiority as can be admitted;—yet are the national consequences prodigious; for there is a much greater deduction from the open field produce for expences, than from the product of the inclosure, where a proper part of the farm is grass. Thus more in proportion is the farmer's profit, consequently he is wealthier, and more able to work improvements—and at the same time to pay his landlord a greater rent · points of vast importance to the national interest. But if the superiority of one course to the other was only 1*l.* 9*s.* *per* acre on all the arable

 land,

land, it would prove of a magnitude extremely deserving attention.

The author abovementioned therefore thinking we should be more populous if we lived as much on bread as the *French*, is an idea that seems doubtful. It is a strange position at best, that bad husbandry should add to our population—that losing 1*l.* 9*s.* 7*d.* an acre on our arable lands should increase the people. This is fairly stating the case, for if the demand for meat is changed to an increased one for wheat, the farmers must either change their good course to the bad one of the *French*, or the wheat must be imported; as the latter can in no country be depended on, the former must inevitably be the case. and the moment the sale of meat stops, those crops which best prepare for corn must disappear, when there would be no choice left the farmer but the old husbandry of fallow and wheat—unless new refinements were introduced, which we cannot speak of here with propriety.

But this comparison of population depends on another enquiry: Which yields most food for man, 1. fallow, 2. wheat, 3. barley, or 1. turnips, 2. barley, 3. clover, 4. wheat? The abovementioned author I apprehend, supposes the country of bread eaters the most populous, because a given tract of land applied to yielding bread, will feed

feed more than if applied to bread and meat: If this is *not* his reaſon, I cannot conjecture what *is*. But I ſhould ſuppoſe that the latter courſe yields far more food than the former.

The part of a farm when properly arranged, that is under graſs, is the part more applicable to graſs than corn—ſo that when all is converted to corn, the produce of the whole muſt not be ſuppoſed upon a par with the part which is beſt for corn. And ſurely an acre of graſs in three years will yield beef and mutton to ſupport a man, as long as one acre of wheat; for the ſecond crop in corn countries is oats for the team. But ſuch proportions can only be taken in the value of the crops in money: in the compariſon I gave of the two courſes above, the ſuperiority of 1 *l.* 9 *s.* 7 *d.* *per* acre, is what ſhould decide it, with this additional point relative to food, that it is gained by a courſe which gives three crops in four years as food for man; *viz.* the wheat, and the turnips and clover fed by cattle, to ſay nothing of the barley; whereas in the other courſe, only one in three is to be reckoned, *viz.* the wheat. This ſuperiority will more than anſwer the inferiority (ſuppoſing it ſuch) of a part of the farm being meadow and paſture; but it is not clear that good paſture does not yield as much food for man as corn land without the aſſiſtance of graſs.

Unite both objects as they ought to be, ſo as to have the farms from one third to half of meadow and paſture, and the other two thirds or half thrown into a proper courſe for the winter ſupport of the cattle, and ſuch a farm will, I apprehend, be found to feed more men than if it is all ploughed up, and as much wheat raiſed as is poſſible upon the *French* ſyſtem.

Perhaps it may be ſaid, that there is not ſuch a connection between the cuſtom of the people in their food, and the courſes of the farmers, as I have ſtated, ſince what is not in demand at home might be ſold abroad. But this reaſoning I do not think is juſt; if a ſurplus of corn is raiſed, it may, generally ſpeaking, be exported—though not always: But as to meat, butter and cheeſe, there is no dependance of that ſort, the foreign demand is too various and uncertain Nothing can uniformly encourage the farmer to keep ſufficient ſtocks, but a great home conſumption.

SECT. X.

INFERIOR OBJECTS, AND DEFICIENCES IN BRITISH HUSBANDRY.

I BEFORE remarked that it is utterly vain to recommend minute improvements in the practice of agriculture to any people who feel the want of those essential and capital articles of encouragement, with which I began this dissertation: but at the same time it is necessary to observe, that when a country like *England* is happy enough to enjoy such encouragement, then it is wise and prudent to give much attention to inferior objects, such as the culture of waste lands, the introduction of new branches of culture, the improvement of old ones, alterations in methods, and abundance of other articles to which it is very necessary to attend, if we would have our agriculture generally good. It is therefore upon very wise and liberal principles that the society established at *London* for the encouragement of arts, manufactures, and commerce, offers premiums for such improvements, and gives bounties to such farmers and mechanics as excel or invent any thing valuable.

It is very ſurprizing to think of the general advantages enjoyed by this nation, and yet to ſee what large tracts (much the greateſt part of the kingdom) are under a culture infinitely inferior to that of other parts. After viewing the huſbandry of *Norfolk*, *Suffolk*, *Eſſex*, and *Kent*, to obſerve the miſerable management of ſo many other counties, muſt convince every ſpectator of the importance of ſpreading the knowledge of what is good:—of letting the unenlightened parts of the kingdom know what is done elſewhere—and of explaining to them the principles and practice which give wealth to one ſet of farmers, mediocrity of fortune to others. This idea urged me to undertake the tours I made through a part of the kingdom, the regiſters of which are before the public.

The improvements which are much wanting in ſo many parts of *England*, are particularly the ſpreading the knowledge of good courſes of crops, ſo as utterly to baniſh fallows; a practice purſued very generally in the counties I have named above; and which is effected by the introduction of turnips, beans, peaſe, tares, clover, &c. as preparations for white corn—covered drains—manuring with marle, chalk, and clay—watering meadows—the culture of carrots, cabbages, potatoes, ſainfoine, and

lucerne

lucerne—performing works of tillage with no more cattle than neceſſary—the uſe of oxen in harneſs—an almoſt general reform in implements—the introduction of the drill huſbandry for beans—the culture of madder, woad, liquorice, hemp and flax, on ſuch lands as are ſuitable—with ſeveral other points too tedious to mention.

Every one of theſe articles, excepting cabbages and lucerne, are already *commonly* practiſed by tenants in ſome part or other of the kingdom; and all of them in the lands of gentlemen, with great ſucceſs: the ſpreading the knowledge of ſuch uſeful practices, is therefore of the higheſt conſequence to the general welfare of Britiſh agriculture.

But above theſe and all other circumſtances is to be named, the bringing into culture our waſte lands; which form ſo large a proportion of the territory, that I much queſtion if we have not eight or ten millions of acres waſte in *England*, and a great deal more in *Scotland*. The want of public ſpirit in the generality of their proprietors is truly amazing—and no leſs is it ſurprizing that they ſhould be equally inattentive to the advantages of themſelves and families. Where would be the mighty exertion in one of our great owners of moors to ſay to a ſpirited practical man,

You

You have the knowledge necessary for making a trial of my moors, but not the money. I have the money, but not the knowledge: fix upon what spot you please in my estate, and I will supply you with a thousand pounds a year for ten years to come at common interest, and all the security I ask is being convinced that the money is spent upon the land? Where would be the hazard in such a case? for such a person would have the best security for his money of all others, his own estate; and he would certainly have double interest; the common, and the advantage of all the improvements at the end of the term of years agreed for.

That there are many active practical persons, no visionary theorists, who would settle the moors upon such conditions, I have no doubt; and that the great moor-possessors in general, proceeding on such principles, would in no long term cover them with cultivation, I have as little doubt: how much this would add to the nation's wealth I need not say. Such undertakings increase the classes of the people, that form real POPULATION.

Nor is it only to private landlords that these observations are applicable, it appears to me surprizing, that the legislature should never have thought it worth their pains to attempt something in favour of cultivation on thofe immenfe waftes: A private expenditure of between twenty and thirty thoufand pounds would not make any great figure in the national expences, yet might it be fo managed as to have confiderable effects. I enlarged pretty much on this idea in a pamphlet I publifhed about a year ago *; I explained the practicability and the advantages of fuch an undertaking; but among the infinite fums expended by our government, fuch works poffefs a moft contemptible fhare †.

I have endeavoured to fhew, that as this kingdom enjoys moft of the great fupports of a flourifhing agriculture, that therefore it is right to attend to thefe fmaller circumftances, and the *London* Society judicious in fo doing; but at the fame time I muft remark that they carry their attention too far to the minutiæ of management, and too little to the more important objects: they offer more premiums about drilling and horfe-hoeing, than for the improvement of wafte lands: and as their gold medal is the higheft premium that can be gained, there being but two, the gold and filver one; this *higheft* declaration of merit is often given

---

* *Obfervations on the prefent State of the Wafte Lands of Great-Britain*, 8vo. 1772.

† See Appendix, No. IV.

given to very inferior objects, for want of a better scale of reward Hence comes their practice, which totally destroys the great ideal value of the medal, of offering *twenty pounds, or the gold medal.—Thirty pounds, or the gold medal.* Thus the importance of the premium is explained by the sum given if the medal should be rejected, or if the claimant should be a member *. Hence arises a necessity of classing objects in the same light, which are of infinitely different merit; and as gentlemen are more desirous of honorary premiums than pecuniary ones, there ought to be some higher reward devised than the gold medal, which having been given to inferior objects, is no longer a reward for capital ones.

Suppose a gentleman has improved five hundred, or even one hundred acres of moor; and did it in various methods, in order to discover the most effectual—he has built a house, barns, stables, and all the buildings requisite for a farm; inclosed, planted, manured, and reduced a desart tract to be a fertile farm; such a gentleman, that his experience may be useful to others, sends an account of his operations to the society: What do they decree?—They give him their

* Members can receive only the honorary premium.

their gold medal: that is, they rank his merit in the ſame claſs as a man who fats hogs, plants coleſeed, drills turnips, and horſe-hoes wheat. Can this be right? If a ſociety inſtituted for rewarding merit, confounds all ideas of merit, ſurely the end of their inſtitution is wretchedly anſwered.

They ſhould offer an ornamental model of a plough in gold or ſilver, ſo curiouſly wrought, as to be an object of beauty and *ſhew*; and on the mould-board the inſcription. A man would place ſuch a thing in a glaſs caſe, and ſet it where it might be ſeen: but a medal, unleſs a hole is drilled through it, and you wear it pendant from a button hole, is ſeen by no one—a man muſt be put to the bluſh to bring out his medal and ſhew it. A ſilver or gold cup with the inſcription, which paſſing round the table, would promote converſation on huſbandry, and raiſe emulation in every one preſent to gain the like, would alſo be a good expedient. In a word, vanity is very prevalent in this age, and I ſee no reaſon why we ſhould not render the paſſions of mankind ſubſervient to the good of agriculture.

Perhaps the ſpirited endeavours of this excellent ſociety in the encouragement of huſbandry, may have been partly the reafon why his prefent Majefty, who has fo munificently protected the fine arts and literature, fhould not have given more attention to the means of advancing the agriculture of his kingdoms, as I am informed that he has founded feveral eftablifhments with this view in his electoral dominions. The fmall progrefs however, which has been made by that fociety in the great article, the culture of wafte lands, fhews that a more effective encouragement is wanting. But as I have ventured to make this obfervation, I fhall not refufe myfelf the pleafure of remarking with how much judgment even the amufements of the young princes are made conducive to juft ideas of the importance of hufbandry. Nor will the lover of that art fail to congratulate himfelf on the hands in which the future hope of *Britain* is placed, when I relate an anecdote, which to fome may perhaps feem trifling, but appears to me pregnant with excellent confequences.

A fpot of ground in the garden at *Kew* was dug by their royal highneffes the prince of *Wales* and bifhop of *Ofnabrug*; they fowed it with wheat; they attended the growth of their little crop, weeded, reaped, and harvefted it. They threfhed out the corn, and feparated it from the chaff. And at this period of their labour, were taught to

reflect

reflect from their own experience, on the various labour and attention of the farmer. Nor did this admirable lesson stop here. The princes not only raised the crop; they also ground it; and having parted the bran from the meal, attended to the whole process of making it into bread. This bread it may be imagined was eaten with no slight relish: the King and Queen partook of the philosophical repast, and beheld with pleasure the very amusements of their children rendered the source of useful knowledge—An instance, and no trifling one, that a great nobleman from having attended to agriculture, is so much the better qualified to superintend the education of a prince—and that lord *Holdernesse* has attended to agriculture both as a philosopher and a man of practice, I have on another occasion, given the world sufficient proof *.

This

* The instance I have now inserted justifies me as a farmer, for saying that this country has reason to be happy at the princes' education being committed to this nobleman, since it is by such a conduct that they will best become acquainted with the importance of husbandry Not that I would have it supposed I confine the merit of the governor to points of this sort those who know him best, would best be able to refute such an idea. Nor let his lordship's recommendation of Mr *Smelt* for an assistant in his important office, be forgotten—a man whose general knowledge

This pleasing idea, I hope, will be a prelude to a farm, in some of the royal gardens, parks, or chases, where our amiable young princes may have a farther opportunity of learning the theory and practice of agriculture:—where they might see a course of rational experiments, and gain not a mere mechanical idea of what that useful class of the people the farmers perform, but a political acquaintance with the connection between the expenditure and the products of husbandry:—they would learn the necessity of the farmer being secure in the possession of that harvest his industry prepared;—the dependance of all the orders of the state on the soil—the population that flows from a good culture—in a word, they would see that well tilled fields were the source of armies, of navies, of conquests, of splendid courts, and magnificent expences. They might set their hands to the plough, and remember that its good progress was the test of a nation's happiness and a monarch's glory; and from hence, never forget the maxim of the wise sovereign, THE KING'S FAVOUR in matters of

---

knowledge and amiable manners, rendered him the delight of an extensive neighbourhood, a character formed rather to give lustre than to receive it from a court.—And let me also add with pleasure, an excellent farmer.

of agriculture, IS AS DEW UPON THE GRASS.

An experiment from whence ſuch inſtruction might flow, is ſurely worth the trial.

* * * *

Thus far I have proceeded in endeavouring to point out the miſtakes that may eaſily be made by adopting in one country the policy of another. Before I conclude, I ſhall ſuppoſe that things will continue much in the ſame train in moſt countries; and in caſe it ſhould be ſo, I ſhall recommend an experiment that might very eaſily be tried by the legiſlature of any country; —I mean the

SYSTEM OF ENGLAND

in matters of huſbandry and taxation. Suppoſe in *France*, *Spain*, or parts of *Germany*, individuals were backward to engage in it; it might eaſily be executed in the ſovereign's demeſne. What I mean is, to eaſe, in a certain number of pariſhes, the farmers from all ſorts of taxes which are laid any ways in proportion to their wealth, induſtry or products; in lieu of them, raiſe the ſame ſum of money partly by a permanent land-tax, exactly in the manner of that of *England*, not ſubject to variations, to the amount of about 2 *s.* 6 *d.* in the pound rent, and this, as in *England*, ſhould be charged by the tenants to the account of the landlords. Thus the farmers would be exempted from all taxes except tythe, and thoſe general ones on conſumption, which equally affect every claſs Let all the diſtrict be incloſed in fields proportioned to the ſize of the farms Let leaſes of 21 years be given to every farmer at a rent per acre equal, (all national circumſtances, rates and prices conſidered) to what ſimilar land lets for in the beſt cultivated parts of *England.* Exempt them abſolutely from all perſonal ſervice, and as to the price of their corn, in order to anſwer the effect of the corn-laws of *England,* eſtabliſh near this diſtrict a magazine where their corn may always be carried when they chuſe to ſell at or under a given price, but from thence to be carried immediately to the neareſt port, and ſent where the conſumption of it cannot poſſibly affect the price of the diſtrict in queſtion. After theſe regulations, let the farmers purſue their huſbandry in quiet, in whatever manner they think proper.

In the next place, form out of this experimental diſtrict a farm of 1000 acres, to be cultivated entirely in the *Engliſh* manner, under the direction of a perſon perfectly acquainted with the beſt huſbandry of *Britain*. Let the arable part of it, which ſhould not be leſs than 800 acres, be divided into four parts, of each 200 acres: one-fourth to be conſtantly under turnips, cabbages, carrots, and potatoes; another under ſpring corn; another under clover; and the laſt under wheat: by means of theſe articles being thus arranged, and perfectly well cultivated, the ſuperiority of this ſyſtem to that of a fallow would ſoon appear. The ſtock of cattle on this farm ſhould be ſufficient for the conſumption of 200 acres of graſs, ſainfoine or lucerne (according to the ſoil) and 200 of winter food; 200 of clover; and 400 of ſtraw.

Beſides theſe circumſtances, the teams of horſes and oxen (the latter the moſt numerous) ſhould be large and able beaſts, a pair of either ſufficient to plough an *Engliſh* acre in a day. All the harneſs and implements of every kind to be *Engliſh*, and of the beſt ſort. The buildings compoſing the farm-yard to be complete, and in every reſpect ſufficient for conducting the farm in winter on the *Engliſh* ſyſtem, with a view to raiſing manure. If ſuch a plan was executed completely, the expence of ſtocking and ſupporting ſuch a farm would be 7*l.* an acre, or 7000*l.* for 1000 acres.

Now I conceive that the regulations here propoſed, would yield two very important pieces of intelligence firſt, they would ſhew the ſuperiority of the *Engliſh* mode of taxation over that of *France*; and this in reſpect, not only to the welfare of the farmer, but alſo to the wealth of the landlord, who ſhould calculate the difference of his neat receipts at two different periods, one under the old management, and the other under the new. Secondly, it would ſhew what improvements practiſed in *England*, are wanting in the country where the experiment was tried; this would evidently appear by comparing the management of the farmers after being eaſed in taxes, &c. with that of the *Engliſh* farm on the ſame ſoil, and under the ſame circumſtances: and I ſhould add, that the eſtabliſhment and regular conduct of ſuch a farm would be a conſtant ſource of information to every perſon in the country who was deſirous of improving the practice of huſbandry. Among other very ſpirited plans carrying into execution for the benefit of agriculture in his majeſty's *German* dominions, I ſhould preſume ſomething of this ſort might prove equally beneficial with any other ſcheme hitherto deviſed.

2

CHAP. II.

REMOVAL OF OBSTACLES.

HAVING explained the principal causes of the agriculture of this nation being so flourishing, I shall pursue my design by remarking, that other countries that would enjoy the same advantages, should follow the same maxims: it is a little surprizing in this case, that other nations should shew the greatest eagerness to advance their husbandry, manifesting clear ideas of its importance, and yet in most of their plans beginning at the wrong end: if the principles are well understood which prove favourable to agriculture in one country, what should prevent others from adopting those principles as far as climate, government and manners will allow; instead of which we see volumes written on modes of culture, where political principles should alone be attended to.

We must not, however, suppose that in every country where plans are laid for the improvement of agriculture, that such an admirable constitution as that of *Britain* must first be established, since in disquisitions of this nature, little utility can reſult if we are not practical. Thus, under the article government, if its nature is unfavourable to induſtry, the buſineſs of the ſtateſman is to molify its ſeverity; and as the principles of it are miſchievous, to ſoften them by a gentle and equitable adminiſtration.

In the articles above examined, on which principally depends the proſperity of *Engliſh* agriculture, other countries that would wiſh to imitate the example, ſhould firſt remove ſuch circumſtances as militate moſt againſt them. That this is the right way of proceeding, can hardly be doubted; to think of making improvements in the modes of culture—in manuring, fencing, tillage, horſe-hoeing, or introducing new vegetables, while the farmers are oppreſſed by taxes, ſlavery, perſonal ſervice, or a want of leaſes; or where bad corn-laws, defeat every purpoſe for which they were intended; or where a want of general wealth leaves him a poor market, is to labour againſt the ſtream: ſuch a conduct, inſtead of giving any radical cure, can only make a ſhew of little temporary local palliatives; of no conſequence in themſelves, and diſgraceful to the ſtateſman who uſes them. But let us proceed to inſtances of great obſtacles, which ought firſt to be eradicated.

SECT. I.

TAILLE.

IN the article taxation, I ſhall mention the *French* land-tax, the *taille*, which is laid on the renters and occupiers of all lands, who are not called noble, that is, what we call the gentry are exempted: there is nothing hurtful in ſuch an idea, as the exemption is very fair, the tax being laid on in lieu of the perſonal military ſervices which were peculiar to the lower claſſes: the great evil lies in the method of laying it.

The miniſtry having determined the ſum to be raiſed by the taille, decides the proportion to be paid by every diſtrict. This is ſent to the intendant, who makes the diſtribution upon all the pariſhes in his diviſion, and the ſum is raiſed by collectors in each pariſh, who impoſe it on individuals by rules ſent them by the intendant. The expreſſion of a well-informed writer is, that theſe rules of taxing are on—"every ſpecies of income, every emolument of induſtry, even every animal in the poſſeſſion of thoſe who are ſubject to this tax. This proportion is calculated to carry the moſt ſcrupulous attention to every man's gain upon all effects belonging to him, and upon every possibility of making profit by industry *." If the first assessment does not bring in the total demanded, second and even third assessments are made upon the rules of the first, till the total sum comes in. Here, therefore, we find the taille is in fact a tythe only the full value of the proportion taken instead of the product itself, and consequently has all the mischievous effects of that most pernicious tax. A farmer is taxed in proportion to his industry and improvements, let the tax be ever so justly laid on: but the aggravating circumstance is, that a shew of improvement is taken as a sign of wealth, and a burthen laid in proportion not perhaps to the fact, but the idea of the collector—herein it is worse than a tythe. Now how is it possible that a man can carry on any spirited husbandry if his tax is augmented proportionably for every improvement—for every good crop he gains—for every increase of his cattle—for a good dunghill—better implements of husbandry than common—in a word, to be burthened in every instance in proportion to his merit. Would it not be very ridiculous to tell one of these farmers that he should sow beans in

* *Stewart's Political Oeconomy*, Vol. ii p 566.

in drills, that he ſhould hoe turneps, cut drains, and manure ſo and ſo—would he not in reply ſay, *for whom am I to do this?* NOT FOR MYSELF.

At the ſame time that the principles of this tax are ſo contrary to the intereſt of agriculture, the height to which it is carried exceeds any thing we know in *England:* We learn from *Duprè de St. Maur* * that in *Sologne*, the occupier of a little farm, let for 20*l.* 11*s.* 3*d.* pays 9*l.* 10*s.* 9*d.* taille, beſides 2*l.* 4*s.* 7*d.* capitation. In another farm, let for 11*l.* 7*s.* 6*d.* the farmer pays 5*l.* 5*s.* 0*d.* and 1*l.* 12*s.* 6*d.* capitation.

It is amazing that a people ſo clear-ſighted in various inſtances ſhould remain ſo blind in this!—Surely it would be eaſy to change ſomewhat the nature of this tax by levying it as a proportion of the rent of a farm: in the firſt place to direct, that all farms ſhould be held by leaſe, though only for a year; ſecondly, that all leaſes ſhould be regiſtered; thirdly, to aſſeſs the tax at ſo much in the pound on the rent; and if it fell ſhort, to have freſh aſſeſſments to make up the deficiencies, as the intendants now make freſh diſtributions on that account; and as in *England* the pariſh-officers make

* *Eſſai des Monnoies*, p. 26.

make fresh rates to levy the deficiencies of former ones Let all exempted from the taille be exempted from this tax: the only object is to make the assessment depend on a certain criterion, which is rent; and not to be increased because of improvements. If a man hires a farm at the rent of 1000 livres, let this taille be levied in proportion to that rent without the intendant's having any thing to do with his crops, stock, or circumstances; the farmer then would not fear working improvements; and their husbandry would soon wear a new face. I see some objections which I should suppose a *French* minister might start; but none that have any solidity.

There is no necessity of extending instances of improper taxes relative to the husbandry of a country; they may, in any case, be understood by considering the principles upon which they are framed; it is impossible agriculture should flourish, if they are made proportional to the wealth, stocks, improvements or industry of the cultivators.

SECT. II.

WANT OF LEASES.

IN the next place, concerning the tenures on which the tenants hold their farms. If the legiſlature of a country would have agriculture flouriſh, encouragement of every kind muſt be given to letting land on long leaſes. If a landlord would have his eſtate well cultivated, he muſt adopt the ſame principles: The endeavours uſed by many of the conſiderable nobility and gentry in *Scotland* to improve their agriculture, will meet with ſucceſs only where this eſſential principle is purſued. How can any man be ſo blind as to ſuppoſe that farmers will enter into a correct and ſpirited huſbandry, which is but another name for great expences, if they have not abſolute ſecurity of a term ſufficient to repay them with a competent profit.

Conſider the common wants of the *Scotch* agriculture; waſtes to be incloſed and converted to corn and graſs; bogs and marſhes to be drained; turneps, and clover to be introduced; good fences to be promoted; and expenſive manuring to be wrought; experienced labourers in ſeveral articles of management, procured from

from *England*. Where is the farmer from whom any of these articles are to be expected while a tenant at will, or under a lease of no more than seven or nine years? When I hear the gentlemen of *Scotland* talking of their improved husbandry, and understand that they grant no leases, or short ones, I guess what the improvements are, and how durable they will prove: At the same time, however, it is right to observe, that there are some among them who have just ideas of this point; and for the sake of giving this solid encouragement to the husbandry of their country, give up the vanity of having their tenants in a state of dependance, and readily grant leases of 21 and even 32 years where they are well deserved.

In *Ireland* the custom of granting leases of a proper length is coming fast into practice, yet is it introduced in a manner well calculated for destroying much of the good which naturally attends the measure. Lands are let in very great tracts by auction, with a liberty of re-letting to others; thus the overgrown tenant, who is probably no farmer, has that security which the cultivator of the land should have, who, on the contrary, is often only tenant at will: in this pernicious system, long leases are prac-

practised without one good effect flowing from them.

We have lately heard much in the public papers of great emigrations from *Scotland* and *Ireland* to *America*, not only of poor inhabitants of towns, and country labourers, but even of farmers; if this is true, it must be owing very much to the mischievous obstinacy of their landlords in not giving them sufficient security in their tenures; for under fair and proper leases, it is impossible that farmers should dream of leaving their country. It is greatly to be wished that the landlords of those kingdoms in their ideas of improving agriculture would attend to this policy of first removing the great obstacles to their success; this will prove more beneficial than introducing horse-hoes, or planting cabbages.

Leases are granted in *France*, and often of considerable length, but there it is not a matter of great consequence; for the taille so effectually crushes all spirited husbandry, that it leaves little mischief for a want of this sort to perform.

In *Spain* and *Italy* the sale of an estate vacates the lease. This is not an evil that operates in common, therefore is not of a general bad consequence; but it deserves attention, and should be put an end to.

SECT. III.

TYTHE GATHERED.

AS to the obſtacles that ariſe from tythes, they are great in proportion to their frequency of being taken in kind. Every government deſirous of carrying agriculture to perfection, ought to take every poſſible meaſure for ſubſtituting ſome other method of paying the clergy.

SECT. IV.

PERSONAL SERVICE.

BUT in the article of perſonal ſervice, the caſe is different in this there are no difficulties that might not be overcome almoſt without trouble. In *England* the farmers were moſt miſerably oppreſſed by purveyance, while the crown had that prerogative; in which the ſervice of themſelves and teams were demanded, and little or nothing returned, beſides proviſions being taken of them, at one-tenth of their value —and ſometimes for no value at all. But in *France* there are great remains of the antient perſonal ſervice, which was very important before money was plentiful: their

their *corvees* have been much complained of by the modern *French* writers on political œconomy: they are perſonal ſervices performed by all the labouring claſſes in carrying on all ſorts of works, ſuch as roads, cauſeways, navigations, &c. The value of them reduced to money by compoſition is not calculated to exceed 60,000*l.* through all *France*, and yet the diſtreſs brought on huſbandry by means of the oppreſſion, is probably more than a million ſterling: Nothing can exceed the miſerable policy of ſuffering a people to be fleeced for ſo inconſiderable an advantage: The farmers teams are driven to a great diſtance—their cattle jaded, and often deſtroyed—their carts broken—themſelves ill-uſed—and this very often, and at all ſeaſons of the year. Where the labour and carriage of all public works are thus performed, the evil muſt be of a moſt extenſive and dangerous nature,—and one that is very well adapted to depreſs the agriculture of any country. But there is in *Germany*, *Denmark*, and in ſome parts of *France* (where the peaſants are free) another ſort of perſonal ſervice, which is that of performing all the labour and carriage of the landlord's houſehold and farm; which is often a conſiderable part of his eſtate: all his ploughing, carting, dunging, harveſt, hay, and, in a word, all the work of a farm. Whatever such little tyrants may suppose, we may depend on it that these seeming advantages are in reality heavy taxes on themselves—their farmers cannot, under such burthens, pay them near the rent that is paid in other countries—if they would absolutely release them from such services, the increase of rent would far more than enable them to do the whole by their servants. We may guess what would be the countenance of an *English* farmer, if his landlord demanded all his teams in the middle of seed time.

The small real value of personal service we experience in the last remnant of it in *England:* The six days duty in the highways. It is done so miserably, and so much time is necessarily lost by going to a distance, that nobody can doubt but any new road or considerable work might be made by a private man, or an appointed surveyor, with teams on purpose, for one-tenth of the sum which it would cost if performed by parish work. Not having substituted a tax universally instead of these services in a country so enlightened as this, is a very great reflection on our police.

SECT. V.

CORN LAWS.

THE obſtacles to good huſbandry, which are found in bad corn laws, have been very much diſcuſſed of late years—yet there are readers remaining who will not acknowledge the juſtice of the innovations recommended. The countries in which very bad regulations have moſtly prevailed are, *France*, *Spain* and *Naples*; in thoſe and others no tranſportation of corn from one province to another was for a long time allowed, which is yet the law in ſome parts of *Spain*: It is but very lately that any exportation was allowed in *France*, even when corn was the cheapeſt; and all exportation has been regularly forbid to this day in *Spain*, *Portugal*, and ſeveral other parts of *Italy*. I do not apprehend it is poſſible, under ſuch a ſyſtem, to have a flouriſhing corn huſbandry—prices will be too fluctuating—ſome years will be ſo cheap, that the farmers will be ruined—and others ſo dear, that the people will be ſtarved. Long experience muſt convince us, that this is not only reaſoning, but fact. Famines never appear in countries that admit a free exportation;

but in all above named, where a contrary policy has been purſued, they have appeared frequently and ſeverely.

The variations in the earth's products owing to ſeaſons, though not ſo great as ſome have imagined where the huſbandry is good, yet where it is indifferent muſt neceſſarily be conſiderable: Let us lay down one maxim, which can hardly be contradicted, *the good of huſbandry requires that the price of corn ſhould be proportioned to the product.* Let us then ſuppoſe the common conſumption of a nation to be 5,000,000 of quarters of bread corn. the proportion between the common product and the common conſumption muſt vibrate according to various circumſtances.—Suppoſe a crop of 6,000,000 of quarters, and no exportation, what muſt be the conſequence? There is the ſurplus of a 6th in the markets, conſequently the price is brought down much lower than that proportion: Here lies the misfortune. If corn in ſuch a year yielded a price proportioned only to the plenty, the misfortune would not be great—but the addition in the markets of a ſixth ſinks the price probably a third, and perhaps more.—Mr. *King*, the political arithmetician, calculated the proportion; but as it is impoſſible to attain any accuracy in ſuch a calculation, it is ſufficient to ſuppoſe the

the difference very considerable. To continue the case, we may suppose another good crop with a new surplus of a sixth or seventh; this coming upon graneries full of a part of the former surplus, sinks the price yet lower; and then the farmers are not only discouraged, as several writers have observed, from sowing another crop, but what is as bad, they are impoverished so much, that they cannot plough, harrow, dung, drain, ditch, fence, or do any thing with proper spirit. These two circumstances, inability in future to act well, and discouragement from sowing again, can hardly fail of occasioning in future years a scarcity, or probably a famine. Then the farmers reap of course a thin crop from their former inability, and that too over only a part of the land usually sown; in such a case, corn must be very high to recompence the farmer—probably so high, that the government of the country is alarmed, and imports corn from wherever they can get it, then the price falls, when he again suffers. Thus a great crop or a bad one operates equally against him, and nothing can support him at all but such a product as pretty exactly answers the annual consumption. There is no balance preserved in the measures, exportation is prohibited, yet importation is allowed; so that it is impossible the price should with any regularity be such as can encourage good husbandry.

On the contrary, if the policy of the state admits exportation, the surplus of a large crop being sent away, keeps the price at home from falling too low: this is an encouragement to the farmer acting two ways; first, by enriching him, he is able the better to improve all his culture; secondly, he is induced to sow as much corn as possible, for every man, whatever be his trade, is desirous of increasing that commodity which sells best at market. The bounty on exportation given in *England* was a refinement on the policy I am now recommending—it was given in order that corn might rise in price, as an encouragement to the country gentlemen; yet, contrary to the expectation of those times, it has made corn much cheaper, by being so great an inducement to sow it.

In such countries as will adhere to so destructive a system as that of restraining the export of corn, it is not of much consequence what other advantages are given to husbandry, since all others united, that can be named or thought of, will not make amends to the farmer for the want of a market: it is of no consequence to enable him to raise noble crops, if, when he has

got

got them, he cannot ſell at a proper price; his plentiful harveſts tend only to his ruin. It would be endleſs to anſwer the objections of thoſe who have written againſt the beneficial meaſures adopted in the laſt century by *England*; they inſiſt on miſchief having ariſen to manufactures and the poor from exportation making corn dearer: they aſſert a fact which is contrary to record, and on that they build the falſeſt hypotheſis that ever was diſplayed, the great end of which is to prove, that in order to advance the intereſt of a people, their agriculture muſt be depreſſed;—and, to make corn cheap, the culture of it is to be diſcouraged!

SECT. VI.

NATIONAL POVERTY.

IN the next place, in relation to the inconveniences ariſing to agriculture from the want of general wealth, we are not to ſpeak with ſuch certainty as in other caſes; for although laws and regulations are within the power of a legiſlature, yet is not this the caſe in the great point of rendering a nation wealthy. It is true, that a uniform encouragement of manufactures, commerce, and every branch of national induſtry, will as long as it is carried on tend powerfully to that end, but as the busineſs requires unremitting attention, and is a long time effecting, we cannot ſay to a ſtateſman, *Make your people rich*, as lightly as we can adviſe him to repeal an ill-judged law.

However, this caſe is not without a remedy. if the evil lies in the want of general wealth, the farmer will find himſelf moſt oppreſſed by a want of a good market. the ſtateſman ſhould in that caſe, beſides taking the uſual methods of encouraging agriculture, endeavour by every means to make the prices of all commodities riſe, and reſpecting the farmers products, he ought to give a bounty on the exportation, as this remedy bears immediately at the evil, by providing the huſbandman with that market abroad which he cannot get at home —this I think is in ſuch a caſe the moſt political conduct he can purſue.

SECT. VII.

OPEN FIELDS.

AS to the article *incloſures*, he has much more in his power. In this inſtance, he ſhould lay it down as a maxim, that without incloſures there can be no good huſbandry: while a country is laid out in open

open field lands, every good farmer tied down to the husbandry of his slovenly neighbour, it is simply impossible that agriculture should flourish. Of what consequence is it that in all the preceding articles the farmer is favoured, if he lies under the weight of this evil? Let taxes be fair, equal and unoppressive; leases long; tythe not gathered;—no personal service; good corn laws, and general wealth in the nation to provide a market. Let all these points be established, yet of what consequence if the husbandman cannot pursue the plans which he knows to be right: if he is tied down to a system, which, with all possible advantages, cannot be made to equal inferior modes in inclosed countries? It is also a happy circumstance that this capital obstacle to good husbandry requires nothing but resolution to be destroyed The tenderness to liberty, which is so commendable in the *British* legislature, prevents their interfering in these cases, except when requested by the parties concerned: this makes the business much slower here than it need be in other countries; where a less proportion of owners applying for the measure might be made to bind the whole. When the proprietors have the absolute and free choice of the commissioners who are to order the division, there cannot be any objections of importance to facilitating the measure.

Inclosures, like the export of corn, have engaged the attention of many writers, who declare against them. But if no measures favourable to agriculture are to be embraced until such are discovered as shall meet with universal approbation, we may safely venture to pronounce that nothing great or good can ever be performed. I do not at present recollect any cases which ought to be pleaded as exceptions: Doubtless there are many *Spaniards* that would be vehement against them on the principle of their destroying the immense walks assumed by their shepherds from one part of the kingdom to another. and granting that the inclosure of open dry country, is prejudicial to the fineness of wool; yet is nothing to be considered but wool? Is not five hundred pounds in corn as good as one hundred pounds in wool? Besides, the boasted fineness of the *Spanish* wool is like their *American* mines, of much greater benefit to foreigners than to themselves. In all disputes of this sort, the statesman should enquire what application of the lands brings in the greatest product valued in money, and then universally adhere to that party who satisfies him of the superiority, without paying any regard to the contrary pre-

judices

judices—always providing that he lays no prohibitions, no reſtrictions on their antagoniſts. If one party adheres to ſheep, let them ſtick to ſheep, without controul; and whenever he would favour any branch of culture, let it be by ſuch encouragements as ſhall not depreſs another. What! ſays one, would you, for inſtance, encourage corn in *England* to the extirpation of wool for manufacturers? I reply, the caſe is impoſſible. Suppoſe any meaſures were adopted to encreaſe the corn culture to the moſt immenſe extent—ſuppoſing farther, that ſheep ſuffered—yet the very progreſs of ſuch an effect remedies itſelf; for the increaſing price of wool would counteract your encouragements of the corn culture, and make the one as profitable as the other. Such fears, therefore, are groundleſs: while prohibitions and reſtrictions keep their diſtance, and every man is left to do what he pleaſes with his land, a general level will be obſerved among all common products *.

* It is remarkable, that ſome of the *French* writers, in deſcribing our agriculture, overlook this great point, incloſing.

As an inſtance, among many others, we may turn to M. BUTRE's *Obſervations diverſes ſur la grand et la petite Culture*. In which he entitles one of his ſections, *Grande culture opulente d'Angleterre*. Which great and opulent culture we call a miſerable exploded ſyſtem.

SECT. VIII.

SLAVERY.

BESIDES these grand obstacles to the improvement of agriculture, there are others which are not to be properly classed under the heads with which I set out. among these let me name, first, the absolute slavery of the peasants in some parts of *Germany*, in *Denmark*, in *Poland*, and in *Russia*, in all which countries, they were lately considered as cattle, and transferred from master to master with the estate on which they live. In this system the landlord farms all his estate by means of these slaves,

system. But he says, it is faite avec splendeur, one plough cultivating 150 arpents, having six horses (two for ploughing and four for carting) and the farm is in three divisions, one of fallow, another wheat, and the third spring corn! Surely Mr *Butré* might among our husbandry writings have found out that this is the course of crops peculiar to our old open fields, where the farmers can practise no other, but that the moment they are inclosed, they reject so vile a system for many others They then lay aside fallows, and sow turnips and clover instead of fallows, or some other ameliorating or hoeing crops—this is our splendid and opulent husbandry that quoted by Mr. *Butré* is a miserable and beggarly culture †

† Ephemerides du Citoyen [illegible] Vol. xii p. 75

ſlaves, except the ſmall portions left for their own ſubſiſtence. It would be raſh to aſſert that this ſyſtem is inconſiſtent with good huſbandry; for if the landlords enjoy the advantages which I have ſtated before, they may certainly carry on any culture, and in whatſoever manner they pleaſe; but this can only be on a certain extent of land, no greater than can be well overſeen by the landlord himſelf; the appointment of ſtewards and overſeers for diſtinct eſtates will not do, ſince when once the extent is too great for one perſon to overlook, he muſt neceſſarily truſt entirely to others, which is always the common huſbandry of the country, how bad ſoever it may be: improvements are then introduced with great difficulty. Yet this is the ſyſtem in theſe countries, of whatever ſize the eſtate, all is in the hands of the owner, and the peaſants aſſigned in diſtricts to the ſtewards and overſeers, by whom a very miſerable agriculture is uſually carried on, and with all the oppreſſion and cruelty ariſing from the ſpirit of ſlavery.

It will not admit of a moment's doubt, but that ſuch landlords would increaſe their income prodigiouſly if they would overturn this ſyſtem, by declaring their peaſants free, and let them farms according to their abilities of ſtocking and cultivating them:

many advantages would flow from such a conduct, the landlord would receive his rents with very little trouble, one steward would do the business of twenty overseers and bailiffs; frauds and impositions would in a great measure vanish; the population of the estate would much increase, and as this increase of people would arise from an increase of wealth and industry, it would bring a new market without any disadvantages attending it. As the farmers grew richer, they would keep greater stocks of cattle, and cultivate their lands better; and of that the landlord might take his advantage without any oppression, by raising his rents with judgment on the renewal of the leases. I am sensible there are many who will laugh at my talking of freeing peasants, and giving leases in *Poland*: but so far from there being any thing idle or extravagant in this idea, that I aver the thing has been done, and with great success, on a part of the estate of the Prince de *Massalski*, as I was assured by himself.

SECT. IX.

HUNTING.

BEFORE I quit these remarks on great obstacles to the improvement of husbandry, I must mention the excess to which hunting is carried in some countries by the sovereign. I recollect a remarkable instance given by Mr *Hanway* in his travels, that of *Saxony* under King *Augustus*, who not allowing his deer, &c. to be any where destroyed, they multiplied all over the electorate to such a degree, that the miserable *Saxons* offered readily an addition to the army of 6000 men, only for liberty to reduce the deer to half their number; but were refused with contempt. If such a thing was not well authenticated, it would be difficult to give credit to so excessive folly. Wherever hunting and other rural sports are carried to any such excess, it must be almost to the ruin of agriculture. I have seen hares in *England* in so great abundance, as very much to injure the husbandmen. If the crops when gained, are to be devoured by game, we may easily conceive that all the encouragement in the world, and the removing of every other obstacle would

would all be in vain.—Let it ever be laid down as a maxim, that if the farmer is not to reap, he will not sow.

SECT. X

RECAPITULATION.

THERE are abundance of other circumstances which are real obstacles to husbandry, but which I think do not demand a particular attention here; because I conceive that such are not radical evils; if a right system of encouragement is adopted, they would disappear, without any particular attack.

The articles I have dwelt upon, are obstacles so mischievous, that enterprizing spirits among the nobility and gentry who are desirous of promoting the good cause, should direct their utmost endeavours to remove them. Princes, statesmen, and the legislature of every country desirous of a flourishing agriculture, should attend to these objects, and let me further remark, that it is a vain work for individuals to attempt the introduction of new improvements in farming: to talk of turnips, cabbages, carrots, lucerne, clover, and other articles of husbandry cultivated with such success in *England*, to tenants that have

no

no leafes, to men who pay a taille, to farmers who pay every tenth cabbage, and every tenth lamb and pig to the parfon; to people expofed to all the oppreffions of perfonal fervice; to the hufbandmen of a country where the exportation of their products is forbidden, yet importation allowed, or of a territory fo poor that they cannot find a market for the crops when raifed:—what can fuch recommendations be efteemed, but a frivolous infult upon common fenfe? Gentlemen who act in this manner may mean well, and they have as much merit as people can have who begin at the wrong end—but no general or lafting good can ever flow from their moft ftrenuous endeavours.

CHAP. III.

EXAMINATION OF FALSE PROPOSITIONS.

HAVING explained the principles upon which the happy ſtate of agriculture in *England* principally depends, and endeavoured to point out the capital obſtacles which in various countries, oppoſe themſelves to the buſineſs of adopting thoſe principles, I ſhall in the next place touch upon certain new ſyſtems that have been recommended to the world, which it is probable may attract the attention of a ſtateſman in the great work of improving the agriculture of his country. If many ſchemes of public conduct are recommended by different writers of reputation, it may without uncommon attention be difficult to pronounce which plan is beſt. In the caſe before us there have been ſome propoſitions laid before the world with a view to encouraging agriculture, which appear to me to have a very bad tendency; and of courſe it is neceſſary to explain the reaſons for my differing in opinion from gentlemen for whoſe abilities I have not leſs reſpect than others.

SECT. I.

UNION OF TAXES ON LAND.

WITHIN these twenty years there have been an amazing number of publications in *France*, *Holland*, and *Germany*, on the means of promoting agriculture; and, as might well be expected, most of the writers became ideal financiers: The evils of the taille could not but strike every eye, and new modes of taxation were called for with all possible vehemence. System upon system was framed, and their authors looked upon themselves as the founders of a new science; the *oeconomical science*, or, as they termed it, *Physiocratie*. At the head of these writers appear *Quesnay*, the *Marquis de Mirabeau*, and *du Pont* *, who agree in the great outlines of their

* The number of writers who have published on this subject in *France* is very great; among the many works on the branches of this pretended new science, the following may be consulted

Encyclopedie, Art *Fermier Grain*, &c.

Les Eléments de la Philosophie Rurale, par Mirabeau, 12mo. 1767

L'Ordre naturel et essentiel des Sociétés politiques, 4to. & 12mo 1767

their plan, which is to abolish all the long list of *French* taxes, and substitute a single one upon land; no idea of their own, but which is borrowed from *English* writers, from *Locke*, *Decker*, &c. They agree to it for the same reasons as are advanced by our writers, particularly the capital principle, that all taxes fall ultimately on the land; and as they build so much on this, it will be necessary to say a few words on it.

That the maxim is false and founded on nothing but absurdity, has been very clearly, though

---

La Physiocratie, ou Constitution naturelle du Gouvernement le plus avantageux au genre humain, par Quesnay, 2 tom 8vo 1767

De L'Origine et des Progrès d'une science nouvelle, 8vo. 1767, par Dupont

Lettres d'un Citoyen a un Magistrat, sur les vingtiemes & les autres impots, par M. l'Abbe Baudeau, 12mo. 1768

Doutes adressés aux Philosophes économistes sur l'ordre naturel & essentiel des Sociétés politiques, 12mo par M l'Abbé Mably, 1768

Précis de l'Ordre Légal, 12mo par Marquis de Mirabeau, 1768.

Mémoire sur les effets de l'Impot indirect, par Saint P[illegible], 1768

L'[illegible] H[illegible], par le M de Mirabeau, 7 tom. 1757

T[illegible] O[illegible], a[illegible] s[illegible] explication, 4to. par [illegible], 1758

[illegible], par le M de Mirabeau, 12mo 1760.

[illegible]

[illegible]

though elaborately proved by Sir *James Steuart*; but as it is too important a link in the preſent argument to be paſſed over merely with a reference to another book, I ſhall add a few obſervations to make it plain to every one.

The argument of Mr. *Locke*, *Decker*, and the *French* writers is, that exciſes and other taxes on conſumption are blended by every artizan, &c. with the price of his work, which accumulating as they advance, render every thing dearer except to people in trade who draw back the accumulation, ſo that the landed intereſt not being in trade, receives the weight at laſt with the progreſſive profits of the whole train. This ſtate of the matter has many fallacies in it: the tradeſman who advances the taxes, can draw back only a part of them; the other part he *pays* as much as the landlord does his land tax. The exciſes he pays on the goods he manufactures, he draws back completely; but thoſe upon the luxuries he conſumes, he cannot draw back. The brewer is repaid the taxes on malt, beer, and hops, by the conſumer, but he is not repaid for the chintzes with which he hangs his rooms, the ſtamps on papers and plate, the duty on his coach wheels, the cuſtoms on his wines, brandies, and fruit, and in a word, every article out of the line of his

 trade.

trade. The ſhoemaker is refunded his tax on leather; but let him go to the alehouſe and drink porter; let his wife be extravagant as ſhe pleaſes in tea, ſugar, and ſpices, he pays the taxes on all thoſe commodities, but moſt aſſuredly he will never be able to charge them on his cuſtomers.

But, ſays Sir *Matthew Decker*, taxes make all articles of houſekeeping ſo dear, that tradeſmen are obliged to charge the higher prices in order to enable them to ſupport the expence, and others doing the ſame, it comes at laſt to the landlord. Nothing is farther from the truth; they cannot raiſe their price on any account that does not equally fall on all their brethren: the taxes on leather fall equally on all ſhoemakers, and conſequently all may raiſe their prices proportioned to the taxes; but as to *dearneſs of living*, it affects them merely in proportion as they chuſe to be expenſive: if ſome are for *living well*, conſuming much wine, punch, porter, tea, ſugar, and other ſuperfluities, and in proportion to THIS *dearneſs of living*, raiſe the price of their ſhoes; their trade will ſpeedily be gone to others who are content with pork, cabbage and ale. What can be more idle than to ſuppoſe I am to pay in my ſhoes an increaſed price, becauſe my ſhoemaker drinks wine inſtead of porter?

ter? In the name of common ſenſe, will he not be underſold by his neighbour, who ſticks to porter, and if the porter drinker has raiſed his price becauſe malt is taxed, will he not be underſold by the poorer man who is contented with ſmall beer?

It is in this manner that the people in trade are able to draw back nothing more than the amount of the tax they pay, with ſuch a profit on it, as all their brethren unite in, but as to a brewer's ſelling his beer dearer on account of the high price of candles, and the tallow-chandler on account of the high price of ſhoes, and the ſhoemaker on account of the high price of tea and ſugar, as *Decker* would perſuade us, it is ſelf-evidently an error.

The fact is, that all taxes on conſumption, ſuch as exciſes of every denomination—cuſtoms and other duties, are all paid by the conſumers of the commodity taxed; which ſo far from being the poſſeſſors of land alone, includes every rank of the people; the tradeſman when he is extravagant as much as the duke; and in proportion to the wealth acquired by tradeſmen, who often are enriched by taxes, is the landed and other idle intereſts eaſed, becauſe that very wealth is ſpent in taxed commodities, and conſequently contributes in proportion to itſelf to the wants of the ſtate.

Thus are taxes on consumption the fairest and most equal, and the least burthensome of all others; every class of the people, every individual in the nation bears his share, and that a *voluntary* share, because if he forbears consuming he pays no tax, never advancing a penny unless he buys a taxed commodity, and his very purchase implies an ability to pay; whereas taxes on property, like land taxes, and on houses, which was Sir *M. Decker*'s favourite scheme, force a man to pay not because he *consumes* but because he *possesses*; the one is a proof he is able to pay, the other no proof at all of it.

As this is the case, let any impartial person judge of the consequences of throwing the whole weight of taxes upon land, under the preposterous idea of favouring it. A pretty figure our landed interest would make if the ideas of these gentlemen were realized in this kingdom; let us state the supposition

	£	*s.*	*d.*
The land tax to raise 2,000,000*l.* is in the pound, -	0	4	0
The customs bring in 2,000,000*l.* this is - -	0	4	0
The excise 4,600,000*l.* this requires in the pound, -	0	9	2
Carry over, - -	0	17	2

	£.	s.	d.
Brought over, -	0	17	2
The inland duties, 1,000,000, or	0	2	0
The malt tax 600,000*l.* or in the pound, - -	0	1	2
£.	1	0	4

So that for our land tax to abſorb all our other taxes, it muſt be laid at 20*s.* 4*d.* in the pound*; and then we are perſuaded by theſe gentlemen that the landlords would

grow

* La Hollande eſt la preuve la démonſtration que les principes de M *de Mirabeau* ne ſont pas fondes Si les impôts ne devoient ſe prelever qu'immédiatement à la ſource de revenus comme le pretend M *de Mirabeau*, et qu'on ne pût jamais exiger qu'une partie du produit territorial, il y a longtems que la Hollande n'exiſteroit plus.

Elle a peu de productions alimentaires, elle eſt preſque entierement privée de terres labourables, de vignes, de bois, quelques près ſont toute ſa reſſource de ce côtè-la. Cependant cette république paie des troupes, a une marine, et a figuré ſouvent en Europe à côtè des grandes puiſſances Les taxes et les impots qu'on y preleve ſont bien plus forts, en tous genres, qu'en France et en Angleterre, et cependant cela n'a pas cauſé la ruine de l'etat il eſt meme encore dans une grande opulence. Si la jalouſie de ſon commerce ne lui avoit pas attiré tant de concurrens, l'etat ne ſe reſſentiroit ſeulement pas des taxes exorbitantes qu'on y paie. Le pain, qui eſt un objet de premiere néceſſité, paie un impot qui en double preſque le prix, tous les objets de conſommation y ſont plus charges qu'en France Les biens fonds, comme maiſons,

actions,

grow very rich, because they would buy their shoes and stockings much cheaper!

Here is the infallible and immediate effect of laying all taxes on land; how is it to be paid? What is to enable the landlords to live after their income is gone in taxes? Explain this. Answer the objection. Your tax on the net product, lay it how you will, and realized to the fair proportion *, will amount to about 15*s.* in the pound absolute payment. What is to be the landlord's return? Will his products rise proportionably in price, so as to enable him to bear it? Impossible. The very terms of the proposed innovation are, that all consumption should at once be so much the cheaper. Will he, in consequence of this change, find that his remaining rental of 5*s.* will go as far as his former one of 20? It does not follow, nay it is by no means clear, that even those commodities which were taxed before would be cheap in proportion to the deduction of such tax, from there not being the same encouragement to produce them—else why do the real

actions, contracts, terres, le sont d'avantage, et malgre cela la Hollande fleurit, et la machine de la finance va son train, par la magie de la circulation et du credit qui opere ces effets salutaires *Traité de la Circulation*, p 134

* The *English* land-tax at 4*s* in the pound nominally, is not so really The true proportion is nearly that mentioned above.

real *consumption* of many articles encreafe in *England* upon being taxed? Render any thing by taxes fomething more of a diftinction than formerly, and you will find that the tax, inftead of checking, will increafe the confumption.—It has been propofed to tax horfes and livery fervants: I have no doubt but both would increafe under a moderate tax *. But a confiderable part of the landlord's expenditure is in articles which never were taxed, the prices of which certainly would not fall; confequently he would have no advantage, though his whole income would fuffer merely with a view to a general fall. Nothing can be clearer than the immenfe balance that would be againft him on that account.

There are no taxes on the moft neceffary parts of provifions, except malt, confequently, you cannot pretend to increafe the confumption by lowering the price (fuppofing the one to follow the other, which is not always the cafe) and if beer was cheaper, yet would it be enormoufly rivalled by all forts of foreign wines and fpirits; men who now are curious in ales, would then have *French* wines.—But not to wafte one's time in proving that there is fome diftinction between black and white, there

* The fame obfervation I find in *Remarks on the Size of Farms and the Price of Provifions.*

there is one general argument which with me is unanſwerable The propoſition is deſigned to eaſe the landed intereſt in conſequence of a general fall in the prices of their conſumption; it is ſaid they now pay not only the nominal amount of the taxes, but as much more in profits on them; if all theſe were ſtruck off, the œconomical writers expreſly ſay the income of land would go as far again, thus their plan of eaſing the land and improving agriculture, is to be by a general *fall of prices* * ! What a monſtrous contradiction! What a contradiction of themſelves! As if any thing could poſſibly be more favourable to agriculture than that general dearneſs which wherever found is the ſtrong ſign of vigour and proſperity.

But let us take a cloſer view of the argument of Meſſrs *Mirabeau* and *Du Pont*.

The former ſays,—" Ce que j'en ai dit eſt ſeulement pour rapeler en un coup d'œil que de quelque maniére que ſe retourne l'impôt, il eſt impoſſible qu'il provienne d'autre

* There is one article, which is of all others the greateſt expence upon huſbandry—*labour*—And this would not fall one penny from the abolition of taxes They have in ſcarce any reſpect raiſed it, and moſt certainly their fall would not ſink it There are alſo many other articles of the conſumption of the landed intereſt, which would not be affected thus their *whole* income would be heavily taxed in order for a deſpicable advantage in the inferior articles of their expence!

d'autre part que du produit, et que s'il n'eſt pris directement ſur le produit net qui conſtitue le revenu, il n'a plus ni baſe, ni bouſſole.—Auſſi eſt ce directement ſur le revenu et ſur le produit net que l'auteur aſſied l'impôt, ainſi que la dîme *." This is M. *de Mirabeau*'s grand idea; firſt, that all taxes fall upon land, which I think I have refuted; and ſecondly, that they ſhould all be raiſed on the neat produce, which he ſtates thus: the total produce he divides into, 1 the farmer's expences; 2. his profit; 3 the remainder ſold at market; out of which third part are to come tythes, the whole revenue of *France*, and the landlord's rent. this ſcale is not drawn with much accuracy, but one word is ſufficient: His third diviſion would not pay one half of what he ſuppoſes; and as taxes and tythe would firſt be paid, the landlord would remain without a penny of rent. He goes on:—" Si l'on veut conſidérer quel eſt le poids des impoſitions arbitraires, ſoit perſonelles, ſoit cenſées territoriales: des taxes ſur toutes les manieres d'agir de contracter, de ſe faire rendre juſtice, &c. des *droits ſur les conſommations*, ſur toutes les tranſi des denres des douanes, &c.—on en conclura que les proprietaires ſeroient fort

* *L'Ami des Hommes*, tom. vii. p. 45.

fort heureux d'obtenir par le payement d'une portion égale à la moitie de leur revenu, l'exemption, de tant et tant de genres de ſpoliation réunis *.——On voit en général que l'impot doit être pris immediatement ſur le produit net des biens-fonds, puiſque de quelque maniére qu'il ſoit impoſé dans un Royaume qui tire ſes richeſſes de ſon territoire, il eſt toujours payé par les biens-fonds †."—This writer thinks the great benefit of his ſcheme is the laying the tax on the *net* not the *groſs* produce of the lands; becauſe he firſt ſecures the farmer's returns and his profit, before any tax is paid, conſequently he eſcapes all taxation. But this idea appears to be falſe and impracticable, for the landlord we muſt ſuppoſe in the firſt place lets his lands at a certain fixed rent, let taxes be paid how and by whom they will, if then the tax is laid on any part of the product, or proportioned in any reſpect to the crop, it will evidently fall on the farmers, lay it on how you will; for though the Marquis may proportion the tax to what he calls *neat* produce, yet a proportion will always hold to the groſs produce. The farmer will pay in proportion to his crop if he gets a good crop he

* *L'*[illegible] *H*[illegible], tom. vii. p 47.
† [illegible] p 171.

he will pay more than if he gets a bad one, and consequently such a tax would in fact be a new tythe, and a most mischievous burthen to agriculture. It is by the direct contrary principle that the land-tax in *England* is harmless, where being laid not on any part of the produce, but rent alone, the farmers and landlord pay just the same, whatever their crops are—whatever improvements are wrought, the profit is all their own, no part going in taxes. It is a strange mistake to suppose that because the tax is laid in proportion to the farmer's surplus, that therefore it should not be burthensome, when the surplus being proportioned to the produce, the farmer must certainly pay in proportion to his crop—which is the very mischief of tythes, nay, and of the taille too whereas the glory of the *English* system is, that NO MORE IS PAID FOR GOOD CROPS THAN FOR BAD ONES.

But M. *de Mirabeau*'s idea further appears to be impracticable; how is a tax to be raised on the farmer's surplus, which he calls *net produce?* how are the tax-gatherers and the farmers to agree in deciding what this surplus is? The latter first takes his expences—then his profit—and the remainder he leaves to the church, king, and landlord: a strange way of stating it, because the landlord should be paid first, and his rent reckoned among the farmer's expences Does the writer mean, that a land tax ſhould be laid proportioned to rent? This has nothing to do with net produce. Does he only in general mean, that the tax ſhould never be ſo high as to touch more than the farmer's ſurplus? This he certainly means in general, but then none of his particulars have any further meaning, and he points at no mode of levying it.

Suppoſe a farm let for one hundred louis d'ors, and to contain two hundred arpents, how would M. *de Mirabeau* lay his tax—by the rent—or by the acre? I ſhould ſuppoſe neither: nor in proportion to the groſs produce. What is his net produce? he muſt divide every crop into three parts in the field, and taking two himſelf, the parſon, the tax-gatherer and the landlord take the third? How can this be practicable! If the farmer carries the whole to his barns, and a compoſition takes place by valuing it—then would frauds multiply, and the whole kingdom be in confuſion.

Let us in the next place examine if M *Du Pont* will caſt further light on this affair, as he has lately entered into a delineation of his ideas on this ſubject in his *Lettre a Meſſieurs de la Société d'Emulation de Londres* *. Which is a performance that ſtruck

* It is an unaccountable affectation in the *French* writers that they will never call *English* things by *English*

ſtruck me a good deal, ſince it is a leſſon to *Britain* to convince us, that our ſyſtem of taxation is abſurd, and that the profeſſors of the œconomical ſcience in *France* could, if we would let them, pull down the fabric of our finances, and build a far better one in its ſtead.

He begins with giving *Mirabeau*'s idea of the *produit net* out of which all taxes ought to be paid, and goes on—"dans ce cas c'eſt une très bonne loi que celle qui etablit l'impôt non pas à une ſomme déterminée, mais dans une proportion connue et ſtable avec le prix du fermage; de ſorte que l'imposition, ſuivant toujours pour régle le prix du loyer des terres, hauſſe et baiſſe avec ce loyer. Par cette loi de nature le gouvernement ne ſaurait accroitre ſes revenus que par l'accroiſſement de ceux du peuple.—"

Here

Engliſh names why is a ſociety for the encouragement of arts to be called a ſociety of emulation? An *Engliſh* writer to talk of the academy of knowledge inſtead of the academy of ſciences at *Paris*, would but talk like a fool and what excuſe ſhould we have for writing *B[illegible]dux* for *Bordeaux*, or *Kain* for *Caen*? yet *Cambridge* in their authors is *Catonbrige*, and M *de Mirabeau* in *L'Ami des Hommes*, talks of *Goodman's chester* The *French* writers that have done me the honour of mentioning the books I have publiſhed, have ſpelt my name ſo that I did not always know myſelf. Even Baron *Haller*, who composes in *Engliſh*, calls me M *Arthard Joung* *Memoires par la Société de Berne*, 1770, p 50

Here M. *du Pont* partly explains M. *du Mirabeau*, that the idea is to rate every farmer with a ſum proportioned to the amount of his neat produce; but, ſays he, it is then right to tax him in proportion to his rent, by which means the ſtate will come in for a ſhare of all the improvements that are made.—The very thing—and I will venture to ſay the thing alone that renders tythes and the taille miſchievous to huſbandry. "La loi, ſays he, qui laiſſe l'impôt invariable d'après un cadaſtre une fois fait, comme celle de votre taxe ſur les terres, *eſt moins bonne* *.——Si la nation proſpére, au bout d'un certain tems elle ſe trouve n'avoir pas une force publique proportionée à ſa puiſſance réelle—elle ſe trouve preſque inevitablement entrainée à des reſources ruinenſes, telles que les emprunts, les *taxes ſur* les conſommations, les droits de douane, &c &c C'eſt ce qui eſt arrivé à votre nation, Meſſieurs."—It is amazing that men of ſagacity and penetration can ſee things in ſuch a light. There is no man

* One would think that theſe writers *would* not ſee the excellence of our ſyſtem, for they blame it for the very reaſon which makes its merit—fondees ſur un cadaſtre ou ſur de pareilles evaluations fixes, une pepiniere d abus generaux et particuliers Certaines terres ne payent pas quinze deniers par livre, et d'autres ſont ſurchargées, vû leur etat actuel *Ephemerides du Citoyen*, 1767, vol iv The ſuppoſition of the tax ever being *ſurchargées* is a very great error

man who has been attentive to the progress of husbandry in this kingdom but what must be sensible, that if our present land tax of a nominal 4*s.* in the pound was a variable one as here recommended, our agriculture would suffer considerably. The grand encouragement it meets with now is the stability of the land tax. If a landlord takes or buys a farm worth only fifty pounds a year, and by improvement makes it worth five hundred pounds a year, he has no increase of tax will any body of common sense affirm that a contrary system, a system which divides his profits with him the moment he makes them, which bears on him in direct proportion to his spirit and his merit—will they assert that such a system is beneficial to husbandry? But to so preposterous a length is this system carried, that these writers want to have it include ALL THE TAXES OF A STATE, so that in *England* the improver would have his improvements immediately taxed at 15*s.* in the pound! And on comparison with such a land tax, excises on the consumption of the luxurious are called *ressources ruineuses*! There is a madness in this hypothetical rage sufficient to confound perspicuity itself.

But M. *du Pont* does not content himself with general reasoning; he gives as an instance of the mischief of customs, those upon *French* wines, (this stroke of patriotism I readily forgive him, yet it is amusing) by assuring us that the forcing our people to pay so exorbitantly for liberty to drink them, is impoverishing them, and by consequence the exchequer itself—*cet impôt est donc payé par les revenus de l'Angleterre.* Who can doubt but that a man is impoverished by drinking claret with a duty of three shillings a bottle on it?—But is he more impoverished by it than M. *du Pont's* landlord with a land tax of fifteen shillings in the pound? But supposing it only fifteen-pence, which is most politick, to make a man pay fifteen-pence because he *possesses* an acre of land, or to make another pay 3*s.* for *consuming* a bottle of claret? A man's having an acre is no proof that he can spare 15*d.* for the state, but his drinking a bottle of claret is a certain proof that he can pay the 3*s.* because it is blended with the first cost, and he pays it before he consumes—and on the other hand, if people will be extravagant and drink what they cannot afford, nothing is wiser than to make the state profit by their folly.

These gentlemen complain much of taxes on consumption raising the prices of every thing, and M. *de Mirabeau* calculates how much farther the *French* landlord's rents would

would go if they were abolished: But this is an effect which sound politicks ought never to wish for: the general dearness of every thing is in all states the greatest sign of prosperity—no instance is to be named of a prosperous and flourishing country being a cheap one: those in which every thing is to be had cheap, are poor and miserable, and exhibit in every respect the reverse of what a statesman would wish to see. I will go farther, and venture to assert, that there is not a class in *France* that would not suffer by a general fall of prices; it is a circumstance that never happens but in consequence of a general decay. And it is surprizing that M. *de Mirabeau* should argue in this manner, who in other parts of his works shews a very proper idea of the importance of a general dearness of commodities, and repeats with approbation from the *Encyclopedie*, ABONDANCE ET CHERTE EST OPULENCE.

At page 21, M. *du Pont* declares generally against all excises and duties, mentions their being falsly supposed to fall equally on the people; and observes, "En vain les faits se sont éléves contre ces préjugés; en vain votre dette national perpétuellement croissante a du vous prouver l'insuffisance & l'illusion d'un impôt ainsi perçu qui porte sur les depenses même de l'etat & qui tarit la ſource des richeſſes renaiſſantes de la nation." This reaſoning is extremely fallacious. Does M. *du Pont* ſuppoſe that our debt is owing to the publick money being raiſed by one mode rather than another? Does he imagine that we ſhould have been free from debts, had all our exciſes been conſolidated into one tax on land? Should we then have been able to have raiſed from 15 to 19 millions within the year? Our debt has been owing to the taxes not producing half what is neceſſary, by no means to the mode of collecting them. At page 27, he aſſerts, that taxes on conſumption, admit not of equality in their diſtribution; which is directly contrary to all experience. He ſays that ſome lands yield a great net produce, ſome a middling one, and ſome little more than the expence of culture; taxes on conſumption, which are eſtabliſhed equally on all three, he ſays, muſt reduce the laſt to waſte. But what can this mean? What have exciſes to do with any land? the exciſe on malt, hops, &c. is not laid *per* acre, but *per* quarter and *per* cwt.; this ſuppoſed inequality therefore is merely ideal.

If he means the taxes on the conſumption *of the products of ſuch lands*, then his obſervation can not be juſt becauſe the tax will be pro-

proportionable to the quantity of product, and consequently cannot be *equally establisshed on all three.*

Nor will M. *du Pont* take the instance of this kingdom, which alone is sufficient to refute him. After stating from *Decker* the mischiefs of our excises, &c. he says, " Et les propiietaires sont obligés en outre de supporter la dégradation de leur patrimoine, laquelle résulte de la *destruction progressive* des richesses d'exploitation, operée par la partie des taxes dont les fermiers des terres ont ressenti le premier coup." This whole kingdom exhibits a fact so decisively contrary to this assertion, that M. *du Pont* must be little acquainted with the effects of our taxes to have let such a passage slip his pen. Instead of a progressive destruction of the wealth of our farmers, owing to excises, we see nothing among them but a progression of wealth and felicity—we have not a farmer who has any conception of an excise—nay, nor of a tax, except on windows, and poor's-rates; these are all the taxes he feels —and if M *du Pont* was to question them on our duties on consumption, nine out of ten would stare, and not know what he meant—so little do they feel the very taxes they pay, from their being blended with the original price of the commodities they consume. This writer proceeding with his argument, tells us, that our exchequer receives but one half of what is raised on the people by our taxes on consumption. I quote this only to set the author right in a fact he much mistakes; even our excises cost only $5\frac{1}{2}$ *per cent.* collecting, every expence included. The following account of the charges of all our taxes, I believe is not far from the truth.

	£.
Land-tax, $\frac{1}{2}$ *per cent.* - - -	10,000
Malt, $5\frac{1}{2}$, - - -	41,250
Excises, $5\frac{1}{2}$, - - -	308,000
Customs, 15, - -	300,000
	659,250

For which expence the exchequer receives neat above ten millions; but if the charges of collection run up to one million, and higher than that no author of credit ever calculated, whence can M. *du Pont* derive his authority for making it ten times as much?

From the terms which this gentleman uses, there is not the least reason to suppose that he means by 10 millions to include the profit made by manufacturers and merchants upon the advance of customs and excises; but as he in other passages complains very much of such taxes raising prices, let us for curiosity suppose

ſuppoſe he had meant to include this, and calculate how near to 10 million ſuch an idea will carry him. We muſt calculate this by allowing the perſon in trade 5 *per cent.* intereſt on his advance; but to obviate objections I ſhall ſuppoſe 7 *per cent.* which gives him 2 *per cent.* profit on the tax.

	£.		£.
Cuſtoms,	2,000,000		
Collecting,	300,000		
	2,300,000	on which 7 *per cent* is -	161,000
Exciſe,	5,600,000		
Collecting,	308,000		
	5,908,000	on which 7 *per cent* is -	343,560
But this includes all inland duties, ſtamps, coaches, &c. on which no advance can be made; however I have reckoned the whole.			
Malt,	613,000		
Collecting,	41,250		
	654,250	on which 7 *per cent.* is -	45,797
			550,357

Here therefore we find that manufacturers and merchants charging 7 *per cent.* on the taxes on conſumption, amounts to but little more than half a million. I do not think we ought to reckon it at more than 7 *per cent.* and for this reaſon, the real expence to them is 5 *per cent.*; and as they can afford to take that, others who charge more might be underſold. However, as we are at preſent endeavouring to elucidate this matter, I ſhall calculate it in another manner; and ſuppoſe that the merchant and manufacturer blends the duty with the prime coſt and all other expences, and then upon the total, charges whatever the neat profit of his trade is. Suppoſe the average profit on trade and manufactures to be 12 *per cent.* then we muſt calculate the advance on the taxes at 12 *per cent.*

	£	£
Cuſtoms and collecting,	2,300,000	
Exciſe, &c - - - -	5,908,000	
Malt, - - - - - -	654,250	
		8,862,250
Of which 12 per cent. is, - -		1,063,470

The whole account of *Britiſh* taxes therefore will, upon this footing, ſtand as follows

Total of all our taxes coming neat in to the exchequer, - - - - - - - -	10,213,000
Expences of collecting, - - - - -	659,250
12 *per cent.* to the merchants and manufacturers on their advance of profit on conſumption, - - - - - - - -	1,063,470
Total, - - - - - - - -	£ 11,935,720

I do not apprehend that any probable account can carry the calculation farther; upon what authority therefore, or on what principles, can M. *du Pont* make the total above 20 millions?

But it well deserves the attention of the œconomical writers, that if their ideas and those of *Locke* and *Decker* be true, M. *du Pont* is much too low in saying, that for 10 millions the exchequer receives, the nation pays 20; for if every man makes such advances on the taxes as they describe —if the farmer sells his ox dearer on account of taxes—if the leatherseller raises his price on account of taxes on candles and soap—if the shoemaker adds to his on account of customs on wine—if the hatter raises his on account of the high price of shoes—if the mercer raises his silks because hats rise—if the merchant importer raises his prices because silks are dearer—and, in a word, if every man in trade adds *all the taxes* he pays to the prices of the commodities he deals in, it is plain, as *Locke* observed, that the whole must fall (not on land) but on the idle consumer; but instead of taxes being thus doubled, they will be multiplied an hundred fold—instead of our paying 20 millions, we should be paying 100 millions, nay, perhaps 1000 millions; the extravagance of which idea shews plainly that the real bearers of the taxes are much more numerous than they suppose —and that in fact people in trade can draw back

back no other taxes on their consumption than such as fall equally and by necessity on every one engaged in the same trade. All the other taxes they really pay, and support the final weight as much as any landlord in the kingdom.

M. *du Pont* is determined to give our society of *Emulation* the meanest opinion possible of the whole system of *British* politicks. Not content with overturning our finances, he attacks the navigation act—" cet acte n'a pas peu contribué à retarder les progrés de votre commerce"—I believe the *Dutch* in the last age would have given a different account; nor can there be any doubt but it was a measure calculated with the utmost wisdom, and the experience of above a century has confirmed the reasoning of the politicians who made it; M. *du Pont* seems not to know that our wisest writers, and those whose works are here in much the highest estimation, concur in this idea, which is so perfectly consonant with the nature of things *.

In

* At page 43, M. *du Pont* falls into a very great error in asserting that the *London* Society expends 40 *mille livres sterling* annually. This is an error of a cypher—let him strike that out, and he will be much nearer the truth.

In another place he ſays, "il a renverſé la conſtitution *Britannique*.—Il a appauvri les maîtres de la maiſon pour enrichir leurs valets de leurs dépouilles. Il a principalement contribué à former ces fortunes pécuniaires qui ont jetté la *Grande Brétagne* dans le delire funeſte des emprunts publics †." What is this to the purpoſe? he might as well have ſaid in general that TRADE had done all this; which has nothing to do with the enquiry. Has it been an encouragement to trade? This he acknowledges in theſe words. And as to its being a monopoly, which is *Decker*'s objection, experience tells us the contrary, and that from the competition between our own ports and our own merchants, freights are as cheap, and commodities as readily tranſported as if all *Europe* had been our carriers. As to navigation, ſhipping, and ſeamen, all theſe *phyſiocratical* writers laugh at ſuch matters, but they forget that an extenſive navigation, much ſhipping, and many ſeamen, are the farmers beſt markets —they are themſelves markets—they by wealth create markets—not to ſpeak of that maritime power which M. *du Pont* miſtakenly ſays in the ſame piece, is to be bought.

† *Ephemerides du Citoyen*, 1769, vol. vi.

bought.—Ships and cannon may be bought, but money will not buy ſeamen.

He would do well to inſtance any export of our commodities in which the navigation act ever proved a monopoly. Let him enquire the freight of the immenſe quantities of corn *Britiſh* ſhipping landed in *France* in 1748, 49, and 50; and yet the export of our corn is a monopoly to ſhips navigated by *Britiſh* ſeamen.

The author in various parts of his letter ſpeaks of our taxes on conſumption as impoveriſhing the people to the leſſening of conſumption: but herein he is again utterly miſinformed, ſince the conſumption of every article that has been exciſed, has increaſed under the accumulated weight. No article has been heavier taxed than malt and beer—and none conſumed by people leſs able to bear it, yet has the quantity almoſt regularly advanced under all the growing weight of ſuch heavy duties.

Upon the whole, this gentleman and the Marquis *de Mirabeau*, with many other *French* writers, ſeem to have recommended the abolition of all taxes on conſumption in favour of a ſimple land-tax, rather for the ſake of getting rid of farmers of the revenue, and other great abuſes, than from any poſitive conviction of the excellence of the plan: and in the purſuit of the notion they

they have run into the two common errors, a diſpoſition to condemn every thing they find at home; and on the contrary, in their recommendation to launch into an hypotheſis, to which every circumſtance, every fact, and every thought muſt be ſquared. I know nothing more likely to lead to erroneous concluſions. It was a ſtrange blunder to carry the ſame idea to *Britain*.

Theſe gentlemen do not ſeem in any of their works to make a proper diſtinction between different countries. For inſtance, between thoſe where the income ariſes only from the ſoil—thoſe where the ſoil yields much the greateſt income—and others where trade and manufactures are the moſt conſiderable. Had they made this diſtinction, they could not have allowed themſelves the licence of ſuch *general* expreſſions, as if their noſtrum was equally adapted to every poſſible conſtitution. What do they ſay to *Holland*?—Would they abſorb all the *Dutch* exciſes into a tax upon land, which one might almoſt ſay hardly exiſts? Would they, like our Sir *Matthew Decker*, lay it upon houſes, and thereby let the trader, who ſpends five thouſand a year, be taxed no higher than the fiſherman who ſpends only fifty pounds? neither of whom poſſeſs one acre of land—And will they venture to aſſert affert the inconfiderable body of *Dutch* landlords would be eafed by paying all the enormous amount of *Dutch* excifes directly in a tax on the produce of their lands, rather than have, as at prefent, the accumulations of thofe who advance the taxes? Would thefe gentlemen accept a *Dutch* eftate in fo bleffed a predicament? This is an inftance, perhaps the ftrongeft, of a country, for which their fyftem appears at firft fight to be ridicule itfelf.

On the other hand, let us fuppofe a country where there is neither trade nor manufactures, and confequently where the national income arifes only from land rents. If the publick revenue in fuch an one is raifed by excifes, the landlords, who from the fuppofition are the only confumers, pay not only the tax, but the profit made on advancing it. Here therefore their fyftem is fo far rational; but even in this cafe there follows the quere, Whether they would not lofe more than to the amount of this advantage, by the new tax on their *produit net*, which would be a tax on their improvements, in direct proportion to the amount of fuch improvements. Hence, therefore, I fhould even in this cafe be againft their fcheme, and had rather that the general body of indolent landlords fhould ſhould pay accumulated exciſe, than have induſtrious improving ones taxed in proportion to their induſtry.

Theſe are two inſtances, the one in which their ſyſtem would be prepoſterous; the other, in which it would be attended with the feweſt inconveniences. The example of *England* lies between both.

The income of our ſoil is very conſiderable, but does not make much above half the total income of the ſtate. The profits and labour in commerce, manufactures and arts, are of a vaſt amount; conſequently to exempt them all from taxation, and throw the whole burthen on land, would be unequal and oppreſſive in the higheſt degree.

In *France* the income of the ſoil bears a much greater proportion to the total income than in *England*, and conſequently their ſyſtem would do leſs miſchief there than here. But it is by a ſtrange mode of reaſoning that they ſhould recommend a plan to us, becauſe in *France* it is to a certain point more expedient than in ſome other countries.

In anſwer to all this, I know they would advance as before, that their propoſition is by no means to burthen the land more, becauſe the land already pays all taxes, and in no ſyſtem can it pay more than all: but on their plan it would pay the *all* with moſt eaſe.

By what other logical ledgerdemain than what *Locke* and *Decker* uſed, they make out this poſition, I know not; that it is falſe, will admit of no doubt—that every thing *Locke* and *Decker* advanced on this point, has been refuted by experience, as well as writings, there is as little doubt.

Suppoſe a merchant of *Marſeilles* trades to the *Levant*, and that his commerce conſiſts of exporting *French* cloths in return for cotton, ſilk, fruit, drugs, coffee, and ſilver; and upon this trade makes a profit of forty thouſand livres a year. Now the queſtion is, who pays the exciſes that in any way affect the manufacture of the cloth exported, or the cotton and ſilk imported; the cuſtoms on the drugs, coffee, &c; and laſtly, the manufacturers and merchants profits not only on the direct line of trade, but on the advance of the exciſes and cuſtoms?—*Anſwer*, The conſumers of thoſe commodities. *No*, ſay theſe gentlemen, *it is les proprietaires des biens-fonds*, the landlords alone.

Suppoſe the coffee, for inſtance, landed at *Marſeilles*, and a cuſtom paid on it, ſuppoſe

pose it next to pay (as not coming from their own islands) an excise; and further, suppose it to pay at the gates of a city the entrée: it is consumed, part by the merchant who imports it, part by the manufacturer of the silk and cotton, and part by a *French* landlord. These three purchasers of the coffee certainly pay all the duties, and all the profits made by advancing them —what I would urge is, that the merchant who drinks his part, pays in the last resort, his share of the taxes as much as the landlord. And I desire to know in what manner the tax on that drank by the merchant and the manufacturer can possibly come to the landlord? *Locke* and *Decker* in answer will say, that these men will charge the expence on the consumers of the other commodities they deal in: they might as well say they would do the same by the money they lost at the gaming tables; and because they lost a thousand livres at hazard sell their silk and cotton so much the dearer.

Let us attend to the manner in which a merchant sits down to calculate the prime cost to him of the commodity he deals in. Suppose it wine; and let us state ideal sums, their exactness is not of consequence, suppose 36 pipes.

	£.	s.	d.	£.	s.	d.
Invoice of 36 pipes, - -				409	10	0
Duty with fees, -	347	15	4			
Port entry with ditto,	79	3	4			
				426	18	8
Freight, &c. - -	63	18	0			
Priſage, - - -	9	0	0			
				72	18	0
Inſurance with convoy on 400 *l.* at 5 *per cent.* - - - -				20	0	0
Landing, at 3*s.* 4*d.* *per* ton,				3	0	0
Porterage, - - - - - - -				3	12	0
Cooperage, at 1*s.* 4*d.* *per* ton,				1	4	0
Leakage, 5*s.* a pipe, - - -				9	0	0
				946	2	8
Which is *per* pipe, - -				26	3	4
Suppoſe the merchant's profit 23 *per cent.* - - - -				5	16	8
Coſt to the conſumer, excluſive of expences in moving from the merchant's vaults,				32	0	0

Now if the *French* writers ideas be juſt, the merchant, beſides the above charges, ſhould add ſuch as theſe.

	£.	s.	d.
	32	0	0
Expences in coffee, tea, ſugar, &c. beyond what the above 23 *per cent.* will allow,	1	10	0
Point lace, and diamonds for my wife, - -	3	0	0
N. B. Merchants wives in *England* wear theſe commodities.			
Further, as I am perfectly well inclined to drink as well as to ſell wine, and my 23 *per cent.* not being ſufficient, *inde*, - - -	1	8	0
Price which I muſt charge the conſumer, - -	*37	18	0

The

* Sir *M Decker*'s idea that every man advances the price of the commodities he deals in, proportioned to the increaſe in *all* the articles of his expence, of which he gives an inſtance in ſhoes, is contrary to common ſenſe and all experience. Thus he ſays, the grazier adds the advance in ſhoes to the price of his beaſt. Impoſſible, the price of it in the market will not be regulated even by the expence of its food, much leſs of its maſter's ſhoes. He farther makes the tanner's journeymen raiſe their wages on account of the advance in ſhoes, another inſtance which ſhews how little he underſtood the nature of taxes. In what manufactory of the kingdom did he find 100 or 50 *per cent.* advance in labour ſince the exciſe duties? And he

The merchant may charge what he pleaſes, but where is the conſumer who will pay 37 for what he can get at next door for 32?

I ſuppoſe 23 *per cent.* or whatever is named on the above expenditure; but if the merchant charges more than reaſonable, he will be as much underſold by his neighbour as if he charged his wife's gilt chariot, or her loſſes at quadrille.

Thus there are certain expences, under which a commodity cannot be procured; there muſt alſo be a reaſonable profit for the merchant; and if there were no conſumers but landlords, certainly the land would pay the whole; but as the commodity is conſumed by all ranks—all ranks pay their ſhare.

It is the cuſtom of ſome gentlemen in *England* to import their own wine; they then ſave a part of the 5*l.* 16*s.* 8*d.* *per* pipe

---

he makes every man who deals in leather or ſhoes, raiſe his price proportioned to the taxes on ſoap and candles, in a word, he ſuppoſes every man to make an advance in his commodity, proportioned to the general dearneſs of living—and becauſe ſuch a proportion appears reaſonable, he took it for granted, whereas nothing is farther from fact. See *Eſſay on the cauſes of the decline of foreign Trade* which decline never exiſted, ſo far from it, that our exports, and particularly of woollen goods, were then greater than ever known before, as is abundantly proved by Mr. *Smith*, in his *Memoirs of Wool.* Yet Sir *M* complains moſt of the decline in the woollen fabricks.

pipe (not the whole of it)—then, ſay the *French* writers, ſurely the gentleman if he buys of the merchant, pays not only the duty, but 23 *per cent.* more—Certainly, I reply, for all he conſumes—*On no more,* ſays a dealer in dowlas, who ſtands by, *for I buy part of the merchant's wines, and of courſe pay my ſhare of the taxes.* But who buys your dowlas? *The Dutch and Americans*—and conſequently pay the duties. *I alſo,* ſays a tobacco merchant, *buy wine of this man:*—Who conſumes this tobacco? *Germany and the North*—they therefore pay their ſhare.

But there is a farther circumſtance which muſt not be forgotten, and which may be ſaid to eaſe the landlord even of the ſhare which belongs to him, which is his own conſumption:—This is the great national wealth which accompanies taxes, or at leaſt is always found, where they and trade abound together, as in *Holland, England,* and *France,* raiſing the prices of the landlord's products, ſo as to indemnify him for his taxes, which, though not a regular drawing back in the way a trader does, yet has the ſame effect: he is enabled from this national wealth, to raiſe his rents, and the price of the farmer's products riſing with all other commodities; this burthen, like all the reſt, falls equally on the whole body of consumers. I do not say that the supposition I have now been making is always the case—but if the landlord paid an excise which he could regularly draw back, then the effect would be just so, and the circle complete: That is, every man advancing his share of excises, but paying no more than in proportion to his consumption.

In the next place, let us take the case of a stockholder, a man with a thousand a year in the public funds The excellency of our excises is, that they bring every article of this man's consumption to contribute to the public revenue: Excises and customs are alone what he can feel. he cannot drink a bottle of wine, buy a yard of lace, or an article in furniture, &c. without paying a tax this idle consumer therefore, is made to contribute—Is this no advantage to land?—He sells nothing which the landlords buy, and consequently cannot accumulate duties on them.

Out of the supposed 23 *per cent.* I stated above, there is to be deducted the interest of the merchant's capital, or 5 *per cent.*; also, all his expences of trade, or charges of merchandize, such as clerks, writers, vaults, coopers, paper, books, postage, long credit, bad debts, &c. which perhaps will reduce the 23 to 12 or 15; and there

are

are many trades and manufactures not ſo good as a wine merchant: ſuppoſe we ſay 12 *per cent.* as a medium neat profit.—Now can there poſſibly be common ſenſe in the landed intereſt ſubmitting to the total of taxation, in order to eſcape 12 *per cent.* addition on the part of their conſumption?

Suppoſe M. *du Pont*'s propoſition executed, and all our taxes laid on land: what would be the conſequence, granting it poſſible for the land to bear them? Would not trade, manufactures and arts eſcape taxation, that is, the poſſeſſors of half the national income? And is this a way to render taxes an equal burthen? But in what manner is the landlord made amends? This immenſe tax on the farmer's neat produce is to be no exciſe which he can draw back and throw upon the conſumers of corn, conſequently he can afford to pay no more rent than before to the landlord; but much leſs; nor is there one attendant circumſtance that can raiſe the price of his products, and thereby recompence him: What advantage is to ariſe to him farther than the 12 *per cent.* the mercantile advance on the landlord's conſumption—No probable one; for, as to the benefits of a free port trade when cuſtoms are at an end, the probable conſequences are much againſt the nation; one circumſtance of which would be a free import of corn, not very favourable to the farming race—but which, in ſome years, would be heavy enough upon them.—It may be ſaid, the duties on malt would ceaſe, and the conſumption of barley be greater. I much queſtion it; at beſt it is but a conjecture; whereas we certainly know that with an increaſe of tax there has been an increaſe of conſumption *.

Thus,

---

* A modern writer, whoſe information is undoubted, and whoſe abilities are confeſſed, ſtates the duties on conſumption at two periods thus:

	£.
—"Average of net exciſe ſince the new duties, three years, ending 1767,	4,590,734
Ditto before the new duties, three years, ending 1759, - -	3,261,694
Average increaſe, - -	1,329,040

Here is no diminution Here is, on the contrary, an immenſe increaſe. This is owing, I ſhall be told, to the new duties, which may increaſe the total bulk, but at the ſame time may make ſome diminution of the produce of the old.—Let us take, as the beſt inſtance for the purpoſe, the produce of the old hereditary and temporary exciſe, granted in the reign of Charles II whoſe object is that of moſt of the new impoſitions from two averages, each of eight years.

Average

Thus, with a view to very doubtful advantages, they are, in order to eaſe themſelves of 12 *per cent.* advance on taxes on con-

	£.
Average firſt period, eight years, ending 1754, - - -	525,317
Ditto ſecond period, eight years, ending 1767, - - -	538,542
Encreaſe, - -	13,225

Such is the ſtate of the oldeſt branch of the revenue from conſumption Beſides the acquiſition of ſo much new, this article, to ſpeak of no other, has rather encreaſed under the preſſure of all thoſe additional taxes to which the author † is pleaſed to attribute its deſtruction. But as the author has made his grand effort againſt thoſe moderate, judicious and neceſſary levies, which ſupport all the dignity, the credit and the power of his country, the reader will excuſe a little farther detail on this ſubject. That we may ſee how little oppreſſive thoſe taxes are on the ſhoulders of the publick, with which he labours ſo earneſtly to load its imagination. For this purpoſe we take the ſtate of that ſpecific article upon which the two capital burthens of the war leaned the moſt immediately, by the additional duties upon malt and upon beer:

	Barrels.
Average of ſtrong beer brewed in eight years before the additional malt and beer duties, - -	3,895,059
Average of the eight years ſince the duties, - -	4,060,726
Encreaſe in laſt period, -	165,667

† *State of the Nation.*

Here

consumption, to accept the whole amount, and instead of 4*s.* pay 15*s.* in the pound, while all the other idle consumers in the nation are to drink their claret at 1*s.* 6*d* a bottle, and wear foreign manufactures duty free—in a word, their whole consumption to

---

Here is the effect of two such daring taxes as 3*d* by the bushel additional on malt, and 3*s* by the barrel additional on beer. Two impositions laid without remission one upon the neck of the other; and laid upon an object which before had been immensely loaded They did not in the least impair the consumption it has grown under them It appears, that upon the whole the people did not feel so much inconvenience from the new duties, as to oblige them to take refuge in the private brewery. Quite the contrary happened in both these respects in the reign of King William, and it happened from much slighter impositions No people can long consume a commodity for which they are not well able to pay. An enlightened reader laughs at the inconsistent chimera of our author, of a people universally luxurious, and at the same time oppressed with taxes and declining in trade For my part, I cannot look on these duties as the author does He sees nothing but the burthen. I can perceive the burthen as well as he, but I cannot avoid contemplating also the strength that supports it. From thence I draw the most comfortable assurance of the future vigour, and the ample resources, of this great misrepresented country, and can never prevail on myself to make complaints which have no cause, in order to raise hopes which have no foundation" The *French* writers, who often quote *the State of the Nation*, should read this admirable answer to it it would enlarge their conceptions not a little. *Observations on a late State of the Nation*, 3d edit. 1767. p 44.

to be exempted from all taxation—and all this mighty operation is to be founded ſolely on the chimera that the land pays all taxes.—That Mr. *A.* the landlord pays the cuſtoms on Lord *B.* the ſtockholder's claret. That Mr. *C.* another landlord, is burthened with the duties on tobacco ſmoaked in *Germany*. And Mr. *D.* a third, has the exciſes on tea drank at *New York* to pay. If theſe ideas are juſt, there is a contradiction in mine not far ſhort of frenzy.

Suppoſe all cuſtoms and exciſes aboliſhed, let me aſk this ſimple queſtion; How would the merchant or manufacturer contribute to the publick revenues? At preſent he pays taxes in the whole expenditure of his *profit*. The moment he is a mere conſumer inſtead of a trader, he ranks with landlords, and pays at the laſt hand duties on all the commodities he buys.—Further; how would the ſtockholder, or him whoſe income was from mortgages, contribute to the public? Not a penny would be paid by them; if they pleaſed they might expend their whole income in encouraging the induſtry of *Frenchmen* and *Italians*, by conſuming their manufactures, without contributing a farthing to the ſtate. To what purpoſe, conſiſtent with common ſenſe, could ſuch an exemption be given them? Such would live duty free, while land paid 15 *s.* in the pound!

pound! The first, greatest, and most essential principle of taxation is *equality* The wit of [illegible] could never de[illegible] system so com[illegible] on consumption, [illegible] converse of their merit be found so perf[illegible] in the union of taxes on the neat produce of the land?

A *German* prince, the Margrave of *Baden Dourlach*, pleased with the writings on what our authors pompously call *La Nouvelle Science*, the œconomical science, and I suppose meaning perfectly well, has made the experiment, as we are told [*], in the considerable village of *Dietlingen*, in 1770. He there abolished every excise, and duty whatsoever except the tythe, and in return accepted the 4th of the neat produce of gardens, grass and arable lands; and the 6th of vines; that is to say,

	liv.	*s.*	*den.*
From an arpent of arable land, of the first quality	6	10	11
Ditto the medium quality	2	10	11
Ditto bad quality -	1	14	11
Ditto good grass -	8	14	6
Ditto bad grass - -	6	0	0
Ditto the best gardens -	11	12	8
Ditto the next -	8	14	8
Ditto vines - -	8	14	6

And M. *du Pont*, in a note on this observes,

[*] *Ephemerides du Citoyen*, 1771, vol. vii. p. 209.

ſerves, that it muſt be changed every ten years, becauſe an acre in the loweſt claſs may be advanced by improvement to the firſt. Thus we ſee that in every inſtance theſe friends of the farmer are for taxing his improvements: they muſt have a portion of the produce varying with improvements: we know what this is in our tythe; a tax would be univerſal, which the tythe is not. —What a curſe upon the agriculture of a country would ſuch a ſyſtem be! Nay; as if they would not ſee the effects of their own taille, he obſerves, that the means to judge of improvements are the cattle the farmer keeps—"La quantité des beſtiaux peut donner une idée aſſez juſte de la ſomme des avances, dont ils forment toujours la meilleure partie.—Quand le nombre des beſtiaux eſt *tel* ſur *telle* étendue de terrein, les *avances de culture* et les *repriſes du cultivateur* doivent être de *tant*.—Quand les avances de la culture et les repriſes du cultivateur ſont de *tant* le *produit net* ſur une récolte de *telle* quantité, à *tel prix*, eſt de *tant*."—But in this whole paper there is no ſatisfaction given us how exciſes are aboliſhed in one part of a prince's territory and not in all—This is a difficulty to which I cannot readily imagine a ſolution without a much greater expence than the experiment was worth.

M. *Quesnay* gives in the *Encyclopedie* a ſet of maxims upon which his diſciples have founded much of their new ſcience; there is in theſe maxims a great mixture of penetration and prejudice. Here they are:

I. *Les travaux d'induſtrie ne multiplient pas les richeſſes.*

This is the idea upon which they partly found the neceſſity of making the ſoil pay all taxes; but what a ſtrange aſſertion! In what manner will M. *Queſnay* get rid of the exception, *Holland*? Does not induſtry in that country multiply riches? Is it not attended with the ſame effect in *England* and *France*? To aſſert that the ſoil is the original of all wealth, would be juſt; but to ſay that manufactures and commerce add not to national wealth, is beyond conception. Let us ſtate a ſuppoſition. A country produces beſides its own conſumption, 100,000 quarters of wheat; 500,000 pounds of wool; 50,000 hides; 5000 tons of hemp, and 10,000 tons of iron; which ſurplus of its product is exported in 300 ſail of foreign ſhipping, navigated by 5000 ſailors. We will ſuppoſe theſe commodities ſell for 500,000*l.* which is of courſe annually received part in caſh and part in foreign produce. Suppoſe the legiſlature of this country, in order to enrich the people, introduces or enlarges manufactures

factures sufficiently to work the wool and hemp into cloth; the hides into fabrics of leather, and the iron into hard wares; and instead of exporting the wheat, feeds these new manufacturers with it. Let us, to make the idea stronger, suppose the statesman to erect these fabrics within an enclosure quite cut off from the common intercourse with the rest of the people. What is his process? In order for his designed works he wants a portion of the people; a demand that will in all countries be easily supplied. As he encreases the numbers of workmen in his enclosure, the export of those raw commodities lessens, till it ends upon his having hands sufficient for working the whole. Here then is a change wrought, but not to the old inhabitants; before, they sold their surplus products to the foreign shipping; now they sell it at the gates of the statesman's enclosure—it is the same to them; their interest is neither promoted nor injured. Now let us attend to the progress of the new manufactures; the raw materials being worked into the fabrics abovementioned, amount to the value of £ 2,000,000—these the statesman puts on board ships he has built, and having by degrees trained up seamen, he sends these fabrics to a foreign market, where he disposes of them, and taking in exchange

 such

ſuch commodities as are wanted in his own country, receives the balance in bullion. Here then we may ſtate ſome effects of the new policy.

The number of ſubjects is encreaſed by all that are employed in the manufacture and tranſport of thoſe commodities, which formerly were exported raw. This increaſe ariſes from the increaſe of demand for labour, the conſequence I explained on another occaſion. The people in his incloſure are juſt the ſame to him as an increaſe of territory; they have a regular, permanent income *created* by themſelves of 1,500,000 *l.* which is the value their labour adds to the rough materials purchaſed without the walls of the incloſure. This income ſupports them, and is open to levies for the public ſervice as much as the products of the lands. How can M. *Queſnay* poſſibly aſſert that the labour of this induſtry does not multiply the wealth of the whole nation? The incloſure is peopled without leſſening the population of the country; 1,500,000*l.* is gained more than before, which is to ſupport the manufacturers; they in the common courſe of multiplication will yield a ſurplus of people for ſoldiers, ſailors, &c. and in the expenditure of their income will add to the national revenue ſo much by taxes on conſumption, that it may be poſſible for the ſtateſman to eaſe the landlords thereby of a

part

part of thoſe on the products of the land. I aſſert that the labour of theſe people is to all intents and purpoſes as really and effectually *wealth* as the income of the lands. Nor has M. *Queſnay* in any of his works given one reaſon to prove the contrary. Inſtead of an encloſure for manufacturers, ſuppoſe a ſmall iſland full of them near a large one, a territory under the ſame government; will not the income gained by the inhabitants of the little iſland be as much the income of the ſtateſman's ſubjects as that of the great one? Will he not have taxes and men from them? will not his people be increaſed? will not their navigation give him ſeamen? To what other purpoſe, intent or idea can the income from the lands in one iſland be called wealth, and that from manufactures in the other not allowed the ſame definition? I have kept the manufacturers, merchants and ſeamen diſtinct from the people, to throw the idea into the ſtrongeſt light, but the effect is the ſame if they are ſcattered through the whole territory.

II. *Les hommes ſe multiplient à proportion des revenus des biens-fonds.*

Very true in ſome caſes, very falſe in others. In a ſtate where the only income is land it may, under ſome circumſtances, be true; but not in others. Suppoſe the multiplication from the land ſtopped (as it always is) for want of a greater demand of the ſurplus of its population, it then ſtops becauſe the people, if it bred more, would not be able to get an income, but if manufactures, arts or commerce are introduced or increaſed, to demand more hands from the population of the ſoil, *then* that population will multiply, though the revenue of the land remains the ſame. It is therefore a great error to ſuppoſe that the income of the ſoil alone regulates the population of it.

III. *Les travaux d'induſtrie qui occupent des hommes* au prejudice de la culture *des biens-fonds, nuiſent à la population, et à l'accroiſſement des richeſſes.*

An ideal caſe, which is impoſſible to happen. A demand for hands in every thing creates hands; agriculture is always firſt eſtabliſhed in a country; when manufactures come they demand hands of agriculture, which will have plenty to ſupply them if this goes on ſo far that agriculture wants hands, ſhe will demand them of the towns, and the towns will ſupply her. Both theſe caſes are very common, and no inconveniences follow; if labour and prices in general riſe, agriculture does not ſuffer by it.

IV. *Les richeſſes des cultivateurs ſont naître les richeſſes de la culture.*

It is impoſſible to ſtate a truer maxim.

V. *L'agriculture produit deux ſortes de richeſſes. ſavoir le produit annuel des revenus des*

des propriétaires, & la restitution des frais de la culture.

You may make this distinction if you please, but with equal justice you might say, it produced several other species of income. In *England* I should say, first, the soil yields a gross product, which forms the following divisions of income:

1.	The landlord in rent,	5
2.	The clergy in tythe,	$1\frac{3}{4}$
3.	The state in the land-tax,	$0\frac{1}{2}$
4.	The industrious poor in labour,	$3\frac{1}{2}$
5.	The non-industrious poor in rates,	$\frac{1}{5}$
6.	The artizans in wear and tear,	$1\frac{1}{3}$
7.	The farmer in his profit.	$4\frac{1}{2}$*

And for the information of my foreign readers I have set down against each article, the proportion it bears to the rest. That is, if 20 is the gross product of *England*, the rest will be as above.

VI. *Les richesses employées aux frais de la culture doivent êtres reservées aux cultivateurs & être exemptes de toutes impositions.*

Most certainly; and this tythe and rates excepted is clearly and decisively the case in *England*; yet would these writers persuade us that our system of finance is a bad one.

VII. *Lorsque le commerce des denrées du cru est facile & libre les travaux de main-d'œuvre sont toujours assurés infailliblement par le revenu des biens-fonds.*

* These make $17\frac{1}{4}$, the other $2\frac{3}{4}$ are seed and teams.

A very juſt idea.

VIII. *Une nation qui a peu de commerce de denrée de ſon cru, & qui eſt réduite pour ſubſiſter à un commerce d'induſtrie, eſt dans un état précaire & incertain.*

Holland is an inſtance that this truth (for there certainly is truth in this maxim) muſt have ſtrong exceptions *Holland* is in a precarious ſtate, not from ſubſiſting by commerce inſtead of agriculture, but from the ſmallneſs of her territory. Greater neighbours, if permitted by others, might ſwallow up *Holland*, ſo they might *Switzerland*; ſo they always have done *Milan:* this cauſe of weakneſs has nothing to do with the employment of the people: but will any perſon pretend to aſſert, that *Holland* would be more powerful if ſhe ſubſiſted by the huſbandry of a ſoil, the rental of which, would not keep out the ſea! Commerce has made the *Dutch* more powerful than many ſtates, far richer in territory. This maxim therefore is only ſaying, that ſmall ſtates (for ſuch only can come within the deſcription) are not ſo powerful as great ones!

IX. *Une nation qui a un grand territoire & qui fait baiſſer le prix des denrées de ſon cru pour favoriſer la fabrication des ouvrages de main-d'œuvre, ſe détruit de toutes parts.*

Uncontrovertible.

X. *La non-valeur avec abondance n'eſt point richeſſe. La cherté avec diſette eſt miſère.*

misére. L'abondance avec cherté (permanente) est opulence.

An incomparable idea, which deserves to be written in letters of gold.

XI. *Les avantages du commerce extérieur ne consistent pas dans l'accroissement des richesses pecuniaires.*

In what then do they consist?

XII. *On ne peut connoître par l'état de la balance du commerce entre diverses nations, l'avantage du commerce, & l'etât des richesses de chaque nation.*

This opinion certainly is not just. Where there are no mines, the balance of national payments (which, with a few exceptions, is the balance of commerce) is the means of wealth—and it is wealth that encourages every branch of industry, agriculture as well as manufactures. A great domestic circulation—a flourishing husbandry—and abundance of national wealth, without a favourable balance of trade, is a chimerical idea—of which an instance cannot be produced in the whole globe.

XIII. *Une nation ne pourroit entreprendre contre le commerce de ses voisins, sans déranger son état & sans se nuire à elle même, surtout dans la commerce reciproque qu'elle auroit directement ou indirectement établi eux.*

Nothing can be more mistaken than such ideas; of which truth innumerable instances may be given. See the commerce of *India*, which has been successively enjoyed by the *Genoese*, *Portuguese*, *Dutch*, *French*, and *English*; and by none of them without the destruction of their neighbours. What is the monopoly of spices? What is the monopoly of the commerce of colonies, which all nations upon such good grounds keep to themselves? What is the navigation-act of *England*, that epoch of the maritime commerce and power of this country? What are the duties laid by northern nations on the commodities of their southern neighbours? When a country is situated like *France*, *Spain* and *Italy*, and at the same time enjoying colonies in the *West Indies*, what comparison can there be between the demand of such a country for the commodities of *Poland* or *Denmark*, with the demand in these for the commodities of the south? Would not an equal commerce without duties impoverish the north? And would not the diminution of its wealth ruin the industry and even agriculture of their own subjects? This is a distinction between nations formed by nature herself; and if industry is equal between them, that superiority must be beneficial to one, and injurious to the other. A general free trade, as there has been no example of it in history, so is it contrary to reason. But why will not those writers look around them? Where does commerce flourish

flourish most? Upon what principles does it flourish? It flourishes most in *England* and *Holland*, upon principles, and owing to a policy diametrically contrary to what these writers would inculcate. Let them produce their instances. Why will they eternally wrap themselves up in hypothetical visionary propositions, of which no experience was ever gained, and in which nothing but conjecture can guide them? Yet upon such foundations do they arraign the policy that carried the COMMERCE of *Holland* to the highest pitch of grandeur *; and the principles which have rendered the AGRICULTURE of *England* flourishing, and her people happy!

One word more to my countrymen, in general reply to these theorists. Our agriculture has long flourished—and is now flourishing and improving—our landlords and farmers wealthy and happy—our taxes heavy. but so equal and well administered that nobody feels the weight but the idle and extravagant consumer.—while our landlords raise their rents, and the farmers are happy in paying them; while all classes of the people expend more than ever they did in former times; while all parts of the island are improved by publick works; and ornamented by pri-

* See the India Commerce, &c. &c.

vate ones; in a word, while the great characteristic of a flourishing state in every thing appears, ABONDANCE ET CHERTE EST OPULENCE, while the nation is happy in such a variety of circumstances flowing from her present policy, would it not be madness to adopt or even to commend a system which tends so powerfully to eradicate every blessing we enjoy?

But impartiality demands of me a due tribute to the genius of these writers in other circumstances than such as I have quoted. Mess. *Quesnay* and *du Pont* in many of their works, display great sagacity, much knowledge, and every where a very sincere desire of being serviceable to the public: In a word, they shew themselves to be writers that no man would wish to oppose, nor should I have been induced to assert opinions contrary to theirs, had not the same duty to my country which they owe to theirs, called on me to differ from ideas, which I should have trembled to see realized. M. *de Mirabeau* in his *Tableau Oeconomique* has some admirable observations on the advantages of great farms; on the export of corn, on the superiority of national wealth to population †, and on some

† It is very extraordinary that this writer, after discovering this most useful maxim, should recall his opinion,

ſome other points. In theſe he ſhews the clearneſs of his underſtanding, and his freedom from popular prejudices—in theſe I readily allow him diſtinguiſhed merit, and am ſorry that on any occaſion I ſhould feel a neceſſity of differing in opinion with a man whoſe humanity I love, and whoſe abilities I revere.

If in return for M. *du Pont's* letter to the *London* Society, in which he gives ſo much advice to this country, I ſhould venture to offer advice to the government of his, I ſhould do it in few words. Relative to the material object, taxation, I ſhould ſay—Your agriculture is deſtroyed by your land-tax being proportional to the products of the ſoil—and you are cramped by the exemption of the nobles: Eaſe your huſbandry by aboliſhing the taille, and throw the burthen into additional taxes on conſumption, you will thereby tax the farmers only when they are luxurious conſumers, and you remedy the nobles exemption, by making every rank and claſs pay in proportion to their expences. In caſe the amount of the preſent taille could not be added to the preſent taxes on conſumption, then let the deficiency be laid on in the form of the *Eng-*

opinion, and declare that wealth was an inferior object to population, and that numbers of people were alone the cauſe of riches, yet this is his poſition in the letters annexed to *La Socrate Ruſtique*, 12mo

English land-tax on rents, and like that, be at an invariable rate. But if the represen-tations of your writers are near the truth, there are ſuch enormous expences in the receipt of your taxes, that a better conduct in that reſpect, would almoſt make up for the deficiency of the taille. If this is the caſe, certainly the intereſts of your country demand a reform.——

Thus have I gone through this long examination of the ſentiments of theſe authors; I thought it a work neceſſary to my deſign, which is to point out how agri-culture may beſt be encouraged. As I explained the ſyſtem of *England*, and recom-mended the imitation of it to foreigners, and endeavoured to ſhew the great obſtacles to huſbandry in moſt countries; it was na-tural to throw in the caution againſt adopt-ing, in the career of improvement, propo-ſitions, which, though made by able wri-ters, appeared to me to have a very fatal tendency: this it is that induced me to examine with ſo much attention, the hypo-theſis which the modern *French* writers have built in what they call the oeconomical ſcience.

SECT. II.

POPULATION A SECONDARY OBJECT.

IN the confideration of methods for advancing the interefts of agriculture, a legiflature may be in danger of following bad advice not only in matters of taxation, but in feveral other points: Among thefe the attention that is proper to be given to population, deferves particular notice. Since in feveral inftances recommendations may be offered, which at firft fight may feem difadvantageous to population, and on that account rejected; it will therefore be proper to explain in a curfory manner upon what principles it is that agriculture fhould never be in any inftance difcouraged, with a view to render a nation more populous, fuppofing fuch difcouragement could be attended with that effect.

What I would here inculcate, is the idea (in cafe of a fuppofed competition) of keeping population ever fubordinate to agriculture. If a meafure is beneficial to the latter, give no attention to thofe who talk of injuring population.—If you act primarily from an idea of encouraging populoufnefs, you may injure hufbandry; but if your firft idea is the encouragement of the latter, you cannot hurt population.

If

If this idea was acknowledged to be juſt, there would be no neceſſity for a diſcuſſion of it—but as many are of a very different opinion, it is neceſſary to urge a right conduct, though upon motives apparently deceitful.

I have before mentioned that application of the ſoil to be moſt beneficial, which yields the greateſt neat profit in the market —*Aye*, ſays another, *provided it be food for man, thereby promoting population.* But I admit no ſuch proviſion; and I am clear that the population of a country will be moſt advanced by the farmer's growing rich, whether by hops, madder, or woad, as well as corn: but granting the truth, ſtill let the farmer act as he finds beſt, becauſe he had better increaſe his wealth than the nation's people.

The farmers are deſirous in ſuch and ſuch diſtricts to convert their arable lands to graſs—*No*; they are told, *that will injure population.* This reaſoning is all on falſe principles. Do not the huſbandmen beſt know what their lands are proper for? If they deſire a change, is it not plain they do it for their own intereſt? Will they not grow more wealthy from hence? Will they not proportionably encourage and conſequently increaſe all the claſſes that depend on, or are connected with them? And how can a conduct in ſuch a train, be in the end an injury to population?

M. *de*

M. *de Mirabeau* has obſerved in *France*, and I have repeatedly made the ſame obſervation in *England*, that great farms are of far more advantage to huſbandry than ſmall ones: the ſame gentlemen tell us, *no matter*; *ſmall farms are the moſt beneficial to population*.—I have proved this to be falſe from the regiſter of all the farms on more than 70,000 acres of land in various parts of the kingdom; but granting they are right, yet the advantages of agriculture are never to be oppoſed on that pretence; for a good, ſpirited and accurate cultivation carried on by wealthy farmers, is of more conſequence to the nation than population.

This whole matter is reduced ſimply to this; National wealth raiſed by induſtry, is more advantageous to a nation than an increaſe of people. Why are you ſtrenuous for population? It can only be with views of national defence. But the number of people in a modern ſtate, is by no means the meaſure of ſtrength* this is wealth alone. Men were never wanting where money, flowing from induſtry, was plentiful, but if money is wanting, your population is of no conſequence. All modern experience is but a collective proof of this.

My principles are theſe: I mean to befriend population, and I think the only way to

* See this further treated in *Propoſals to the Legiſlature for numbering the People*, 1772.

to do it is to promote every branch of national induſtry, and never throw out any reſtrictions, laws, or rules with a view to population—ever let it be a ſecondary object flowing from wealth, if you would in fact have it the firſt. Farmers, manufacturers, merchants, &c. conducting their buſineſs after their own ideas, and from the increaſe of their private wealth, enabled to be more active in their reſpective provinces, and increaſing the general conſumption of all commodities, muſt in the very nature of things promote population infinitely more than it is poſſible for you to do by your cautions, your reſtrictions, and your regulations.

Thoſe who are ſo eager in favour of population ſhould reflect, that a very numerous people raiſed by any means but the gradual progreſs of wealth and induſtry, would, in moſt caſes, be burthenſome. Suppoſe the farms ſo ſmall as to be juſt able to feed a family, and that the farmers were (as they muſt be in ſuch a caſe) their own landlords—ſuppoſing by ſuch a minute diviſion of the territory the people ſhould increaſe, but to what purpoſe? Merely to ſtarve one another; they can ſell nothing, wanting the whole produce for their own ſupport—land-taxes on them would reduce them to beggary, and they can conſume no exciſable commodities, for how are they to buy them? Thus ſuch a ſyſtem gives you no public revenue—nor yields any products for exportation, scarce any even for sale—Of what good therefore is this part of your territory? Why it breeds people. True; but does it maintain them? No? Here therefore would be a surplus of population; but you want no such surplus—your army is full, your navy is full, and your manufacturers have far more hands than they can employ—Why then increase your people?—They can be nothing but a public burthen, if they do not leave a country which cannot support them.

This country, and I have reason to believe it is the same in *France*, and most certainly so in *Germany*, has men enough to spare from industry for any wars that we may find it necessary to wage. Whoever will take the trouble to consult the political tracts and the debates in parliament towards the close of the war in the year 1748, will find re-iterated complaints of the want of men, and bold assertions that none could be found to continue the war; yet in ten years we were in the midst of another that employed more than double the men of the former; and when it was ending again, heard the old complaints of a want of men. and the reason was the high premiums given to those that enlisted in the army. But this did not prove that you had fought off the surplus of your population,

every

every man's experience, I might ſay in almoſt every village, certainly in every town of the kingdom, would tell him the contrary of that; it only proves that, as the ſurplus decreaſed, the price aroſe.—It is the ſame in the purchaſe of all other commodities; no buyer but what knows that he muſt pay according to the quantity in the market—and he feels prices riſe, without dreaming that he is to go home without his commodity. That the want of ſoldiers never went beyond this ſcarcity, which would appear in the moſt populous countries that ever exiſted, we have the greateſt reaſon to believe, from the quick and mighty execution of all publick and private works at the ſame time. It was preciſely during the laſt years of the war that our maſter manufacturers employed more than ever they did in any former period, our merchants employed more ſeamen; if you examine the ſtatutes of that time, you will ſee more turnpike, drainage and navigation bills; and in no former period did you ever know ſo large ſums expended by private people in buildings, lawns, plantations and lakes: all theſe were ſo many bidders at the auction of men againſt the government: the conſequence was, prices aroſe; but are we therefore to ſay the ſcarcity was real? Are we to ſay that there were few goods at a ſale, becauſe from many bidders they went high?

SECT. III.

FREEDOM OF CULTURE.

ANOTHER notion of much the ſame kind with this falſe one of population, and connected with it, is the government of a country iſſuing edicts againſt the culture of certain crops—ſuch as vines in *France*, *Spain* and *Portugal*. Thoſe countries have ſuffered ſo much for want of corn, that they think endeavours ſhould be uſed to feed themſelves: this is certainly very right; but the means they take is to drive the huſbandmen from one branch into another; knowing wine can be better ſpared than bread, they want to convert the vineyards into wheat fields; this is falſe politicks. It is evident, that the farmers find the vineyard culture the moſt profitable, or they would not be deſirous of getting into it, which is alone ſufficient proof that they do right in purſuing it.—Probably the money they make by their wine will much more than pay for the corn that could have been raiſed on the ſame ground.—But ſuppoſing the government deſirous of cutting off any ſuch importation, yet the evil is one whoſe direct tendency is to remedy itſelf; for if the vineyards multiply ſo as much to leſſen the culture of corn, the price of it will riſe, and every day bring the profit nearer to that of vines, and conſequently the culture would ſpeedily increaſe. But if the government of a country is deſirous of increaſing any product of its lands, the direct and proper way is to encourage the culture of it without depreſſing that of any other. If your territory does not yield corn enough, give the farmers a better and more ſteady price for it, by encouraging exportation; eaſe the huſbandman of thoſe taxes which diſable him from purſuing his buſineſs with ſpirit; in a word, make the culture of corn profitable to him, and fear not but he will raiſe enough of it. I have been ſurprized to read in the works of the *French* writers, inſtances of edicts not only to prevent an increaſe of vineyards, but even to grub up ſuch as have been planted ſince certain periods. This is a ſyſtem of abſurdity which appears to me aſtoniſhing. It has alſo very lately been the caſe in *Portugal*. I have reflected on this policy with as much attention as I am able, and I cannot conceive upon what principles it can be embraced.

SECT. IV.

RISE OF RENTS.

ANOTHER erroneous idea may easily take place in relation to rents. In my journies through this kingdom I have often taken notice, of how much consequence it is to the welfare of agriculture here, to improve the rental of estates; as I have remarked that those parts of the country which are much under let, are generally cultivated in a very incomplete and slovenly manner.

This remark I know to be just in *England*; but that it is so in other countries is by no means clear. Here our farmers enjoy every advantage that can result from liberty, law, taxation, and other circumstances; if therefore they do not make use of such advantages, it must be owing to their being contented with merely living, by means of low rents, instead of aiming by industry at wealth: But in other countries where liberty is precarious—law the will of the prince, and consequently of the great—taxes excessively burthensome—markets low—and few circumstances very favourable——in such the farmers must necessarily have spurs enough to be industrious, there must be more danger of activity being extinguished by oppression, than damped by any favour in rent; consequently it would be very dangerous to recommend this conduct to such a country, though found so beneficial in *England*.

SECT. V.

FREE CORN TRADE.

ANOTHER instance wherein it may be imprudent in one country to copy the sensible regulations of another, is seen in the case of the absolutely free corn-trade of *Holland*. I have, in various passages of this essay, spoken much in favour of a free export of corn—but in some cases, I think a free import would be disadvantageous.

That it is a most wise measure in *Holland* cannot be doubted, and for these reasons: In relation to corn, the *Dutch* have but two interests, those of commerce, and consumption. For the former, corn, like other commodities, cannot be too cheap, because the cheaper it is with them, the greater the trade must be with all their neighbours; and as to the consumers, the cheaper the better for them. If the States think bread too cheap, they can raise the price by excises, which

which accordingly is their practice; and thus the cheapness of corn is beneficial to the state.

But carrying these circumstances in our eye, they offer a strong instance of the caution with which we should recommend the practice of one country to another. Several writers, and especially one for whose abilities I have no slight esteem *, have warmly expressed their opinion in favour of *Britain*'s adopting this system, which is so advantageous to *Holland*: But herein I think there are reasons against them, which at least deserve attention.

I have just shewn that there are only two interests in *Holland*, that of trade, and that of consumption. But in *Britain* the case is extremely different; for besides these interests, we have another which deserves to the full as much attention as either of the former—that of agriculture—an interest totally out of the question in *Holland*. Here, therefore, is a palpable difference between the circumstances of the two countries, entirely overlooked by the authors I have just mentioned. To the two interests in *Holland*, corn cannot be too cheap; but to the third interest in *England*,

 it

* *Inquiry into the Connection between the Size of Farms, and the present Price of Provisions* 1773

it cannot be too dear—how, therefore, can the ſame policy be proper for both countries? The aim of our police is to keep corn at a moderate price for the conſumer, without ſuffering it to fall too low, on account of the grower.

The argument which I ſhould ſuppoſe would be uſed in anſwer to this, is the denial of a free import of corn having a tendency to ſink the price, becauſe where huſbandry is ſo good, it can be raiſed as cheap as any where elſe. But the truth of this I can by no means admit Corn is a commodity which varies very much in price, merely from the difference of crops, and they do not fail in all countries alike—it has been no unuſual thing to have a good crop in *Poland* and a bad * one in *England*, a good one in *England* and a bad one in *France*, a good one in *America*, and a bad one in *England*; caſes which, as they have happened and have in future nothing impoſſible in them, we may ſurely reaſon from.

The equality of the price of corn ought not to be regulated by the import, but by the product. if the crop is extremely plentiful,

* Whenever I mention bad crops, do not let it be ſuppoſed I have the common idea of ſcarcity, I mean no more than thoſe variations which will ever be found, and which affect prices beyond the proportion of the plenty or deficiency.

tiful, the price ought certainly, and will be very low. on the contrary, if it is very deficient, it ought to be high, but when there is a ſcarce crop, what would the farmers do if a free importation poured in corn from a country where the crop was plentiful? The author of the *Enquiry* gives a table to ſhew at what price the *Engliſh* farmer can afford to ſell according to his products; and it is from that table extremely evident, that the import in ſcarce years would do him infinite miſchief, if not abſolutely ruin him; and the only reaſon why he has not felt this of late years is, that other countries have had corn as dear as our own, and conſequently a free import, when there is none to come, muſt be perfectly innocent.

We ſhould remember that a good crop in *France*, *Sicily* and *Barbary*, at any time anſwers the demand of *Spain*, *Portugal*, and part of *Italy*; and then the ſurplus of *America*, in caſe of a free import, might all be poured into the markets of *Britain*, with how much danger to our huſbandry may be ſeen from the table given by the author of the Enquiry, where he ſhews that a quarter of wheat is landed at *London* from *America* for the expence of 14*s*.— and when their export to the Streights fails, corn with them is 20*s*. a quarter only. but ſuppoſe it 35*s.* it makes 49*s.* in *England*; whereas by his other table he proves that when the *Engliſh* farmer's crop is 2½ quarters, no bad one on an average, he cannot ſell under 56*s.* *

Thoſe who think there would not be any danger of an import from *America* at too low prices, ſhould conſider the charges of ſhipping flour from thence. The following is an account of the prices at which flour was actually brought from *Philadelphia* to *London*, before the late high prices in *America*.

	£.	*s.*	*d.*
A barrel of 2 cwt. at from 8*s.* to 8*s.* 6*d.* *per* cwt. -	0	16	6
Barrel - - - -	0	1	0
Fee for branding - -	0	0	1
Freight - - -	0	4	6
Commiſſion and inſurance -	0	1	1
Port charges in *London* -	0	1	4
	1	4	6

Another

* Our knowledge of the agriculture of the colonies is too imperfect to allow us to reaſon in a poſitive manner, but from all the information I have been able to get, and alſo from the prices in *America*, I am confident they can afford wheat much better at 20*s.* a quarter than we can at 40*s.* The advantages enjoyed

Another account makes this as under:

		Penſylv. Money.	
One barrel of flour, weight neat 225 lb. at 13 *s.* *per* hundred, and to which add, caſk, branding, nails, &c.	1	8	0
Inſurance to *England* at 2½ *per cent.* and part policy -	0	0	9
£.	1	8	9

Charges.

		Sterl.	
Freight to *England* *per* barrel -	0	5	0
Cartage, ware-houſe, &c.	0	1	6
	0	6	6

Exchange, at 165 - -	0	10	9
	1	19	6

---

joyed by agriculture in that country much exceed thoſe of any other under heaven; let but the following circumſtances be conſidered, and this cannot but appear, *viz* Land to be had in property at a very ſmall price—and what exceeds every other circumſtance, ADDITIONS AT WILL—No tythe—Taxes very light—No poor rates—Materials for building extremely cheap—Great eaſe of ſupporting cattle.—And in oppoſition to theſe powerful circumſtances, there is no counter article, for I do not think the price of labour to be ſuch, as it does not exceed that of *England*.

225 lb. neat flour, costing 1*l.* 19*s.* 6*d.* gives 19*s* 7¼*d.* for 112 lb. which sterling is 11*s.* 10½*d.*

2 cwt therefore (equal to 6 bushels of wheat) come to 1*l.* 3*s.* 9*d.* landed in *England*

From *New York* the account is:

	£.	s.	d.
2 cwt. flour - - - -	0	18	0
Charges as above - -	0	8	0
	* 1	6	0

These 2 cwt. of flour are equal to six bushels of wheat; so that the *Americans* sold that grain in *London* at 4*s* a bushel from *Pensylvania*, and at 4*s.* 4*d.* from *New York*, which is *per* quarter 32*s.* and 34*s.* 8*d.* Will any person assert that our *English* farmers can rival such prices?

Since that period, prices at *New York* and *Philadelphia* have risen, owing, as I am informed, almost singly to the increased export to *Europe*, a circumstance depending on the fluctuation of the *European* markets. But in the more southern colonies, the prices are yet very low. I have lately received the following account from *South Carolina*:

Price

* See Appendix, No. VIII for prices of flour in *America*

	£.	s.	d.
Price of wheat *per* bushel -	0	2	10½
3 bushels make a barrel of fine flour - - -	0	8	7½
Barrel - - - - -	0	1	0
Freight to *Charles Town* -	0	2	0
Ditto to *London*, 10 barrels a ton at 40*s*. - -	0	4	0
Landing, wharfage, &c. -	0	0	6
	0	16	1½

The barrel weighs 2½ cwt consequently the hundred weight comes to 6*s*. 5*d*. ½. a degree of cheapness never yet rivalled in *England*.

But without entering into any such enquiries, we may in general venture to assert that the great object of a free import is to lower the price of corn; to reduce high prices owing to poor crops to the same standard as the rate of good crops in other countries. if it means not this, it can mean nothing; and how well adapted such a system is to encourage husbandry in the importing country, must surely be obvious without much explanation.

Following the example of the *Dutch*, is to us highly inconsistent on a second account, which is the difference of government. That of the States is one of the

most

moſt ſtern and ſevere in *Europe.* Any meaſure adopted by the legiſlature, is carried punctually and rigorouſly into execution—the opinion of the lower claſſes is overlooked—obedience is demanded and enforced. The author of the enquiry gives a ſingular inſtance of this, that while the people were almoſt ſtarving—much nearer to it than any thing we have an idea of, yet would they not prohibit for a moment the exportation of corn, although they would not allow a potatoe to be ſent away: Now let me aſk theſe ſtrenuous admirers of *Dutch* policy, if any thing of this ſort is to be expected from a miniſtry in *Britain?* They want what they are pleaſed to call a perfect freedom in the corn trade: let them explain what they mean by that freedom: I know not what they mean; but I can tell them what it would be—We ſhould have a regular freedom of import—whatever our farmers might ſuffer, this would certainly be ſecured: but whenever the price became diſagreeable to the mob, then our *freedom* of export would be at an end. this would be the event of that *perfect* freedom in favour of which our bounty on export at low prices is to be ſacrificed, a meaſure which has brought ſo many millions into this country.——I cannot forget hearing the miniſter minifter in the Houfe of Commons declare, that *a liberty of export muft not be given, for the difcontents of the people were great, and fuch a meafure would make them yet greater:* a declaration following an examination which proved the average price to be only 4*s.* 6*d.* a bufhel. Now, I beg leave to urge, that while the people (*i. e.* thofe who certainly wifh to eat as cheap as poffible) are in matters of export to be directors—furely a perfect freedom in the corn trade is a mere chimera, applicable enough to fome governments, but by no means to ours.

Is it not therefore a conduct that may be pernicious to the interefts of agriculture, to recommend in a country governed as ours is, fuch fchemes, which every one muft know to be impoffible to be fairly executed —the above meafure is likely fome time or other to be adopted; but as to a free export when corn is very high at home (a cafe fo poffible, that it would actually have often happened of late years) thefe gentlemen muft be certain it would never be allowed: So we fhould have the mifchief of their free import, without the good of their export.

Some of thefe writers, who are fo earneft for a free trade in corn, alfo plead for a general free port trade, which is very confiftent with their former propofition,

 being

being a ſtroke aimed in favour of manufactures and commerce at the direct expence of agriculture. It is nothing more than ſaying to the landed intereſt, *Gentlemen, we will do you and your huſbandry the favour of laying 8 s in the pound on you, inſtead of four; and in return for this you ſhall have the liberty of eating, drinking and wearing foreign luxuries cheaper than ever*—very much to be ſure to the national benefit *.

---

* The very ingenious and obſerving Mr *Smith*, in reply to ſome wild performances, remarks, "These gentlemen, it is to be obſerved, are great admirers of the policies of the *Dutch*, whom they eſteem the greateſt maſters in the art of trade, and who poſſibly are ſo, for their own ſituation and circumſtances. But it does not therefore follow that they are a perfect pattern for all the world beſides, though *London* and *Amſterdam* reſemble each other, yet *Great Britain* and *Holland* are very unlike The chief ſtock of the latter, comparatively is money. It has not natural product ſufficient for its own conſumption, nor manufacture enough for its domeſtic uſe and foreign trade The former hath *a large eſtate in land* producing ſtores of many kinds in great plenty, and abundance of manufactures far beyond what it can uſe or readily vend So that *Great Britain* differs from *Holland* much as a *country farmer* does from a *London* ſhopkeeper"—Upon theſe conſiderations, I am humbly of opinion that all the fine notions which ſome have entertained for making *England* what is called a FREE PORT, are quite chimerical, could the great obſtacle in their way, the duties and cuſtoms, be transferred elſewhere." *Memoirs of Wool*, vol ii. p 523.

SECT. VI.

SIZE OF FARMS.

A STATESMAN, in his ideas of improving the agriculture of his country, ought to give a perfect freedom to landlords and tenants, the one in letting their estates in whatever sized farms they please, and the other in hiring them But there are writers that will give very different advice, who will assert, that instead of giving such entire liberty, both landlords and tenants ought to be restrained in the circumstance of rendering farms great—since it is supposed that great farms are pernicious to population, and raise the prices of provisions too high. Now as listening to such ideas would in any legislature be a most mischievous circumstance, it is necessary to offer a few general reasons to shew the necessity of giving perfect liberty in this respect This will be done in few words, as I have in another place from facts shewn the fallacy of the remark *.

A con-

* *Six Months Tour through the North of England*, vol iv. p 192 251. 253 267

A confiderable farmer, with a greater proportioned wealth than the fmaller occupier, is able to work greater improvements in his bufinefs, and experience tells us, that this is conftantly the cafe; he can build, hedge, ditch, plant, plough, harrow, drain, manure, hoe, weed, and, in a word, execute every operation of his bufinefs, better and more effectually than a little farmer: In the fame manner as a wealthy manufacturer always works greater improvements in a fabric than a poor one. He alfo employs better cattle, and ufes better implements; he purchafes more manures, and adopts more improvements; all very important objects in making the foil yield its utmoft produce. The raifing greater crops of every fort, fo far increafes the folid publick wealth of the kingdom; himfelf, his landlord, and the nation are the richer for the fize of his farm; his wealth is raifed by thofe improvements which are moft of them wrought by an increafe of labour; he employs more hands in proportion than the little tenant, confequently he promotes population more powerfully; for in every branch of induftry *employment is the foul of population.* Thus he employs more people and he creates more wealth, which again fets more hands to work, and in the whole of his courſe does more effectual ſervice to his country *. The gentlemen who maintain a contrary opinion muſt virtually aſſert that good huſbandry is pernicious, bad huſbandry beneficial; a poſition which I leave them to meditate on.

Dr. *Price* has the following obſervation: —" Let a tract of ground be ſuppoſed in the hands of a multitude of little proprietors and tenants who maintain themſelves and families by the produce of the ground they occupy, by ſheep kept on a common, by poultry, hogs, &c. and who therefore have little occaſion to purchaſe any of the means of ſubſiſtence. If this land gets into the hands of a few great farmers, the conſequence muſt be, that the little farmers will be converted into a body of men who earn their ſubſiſtence by working for others, and who will be under a neceſſity of going to market for all they want: And ſubſiſtence in this way being difficult, families of children will become burthens, marriage will

U be

* The proper and only right encouragement for agriculture is a moderate and gradual increaſe of demand for the productions of the earth: this works a natural and beneficial increaſe of inhabitants; and this demand muſt come from cities. *An Inquiry into the Principles of Political Oeconomy.* By Sir *James Stewart*, vol 1. p. 54.

be avoided, and population will decline*. —At the ſame time perhaps there will be more labour becauſe there will be more compulſion to it. More bread will be conſumed, and therefore more corn grown; becauſe there will be leſs ability of going to the price of other food. Pariſhes likewiſe will be more loaded, becauſe the number of poor will be greater. And towns and manufactures will increaſe, becauſe more will be driven to them in queſt of places and employments.—This is the way in which the engroſſing of farms naturally operates. And this is the way in which for many years it has been actually operating in this kingdom."

It is a very barren diſquiſition to enquire into the different means of promoting population, without we previouſly ſhew that the increaſe of people will be of any uſe comparable to the evils that will attend it. The Doctor ſets out with the idea that the minute ſub-diviſion of landed property is favourable to population: It may be ſo. But

* A writer who had very good information concerning *England*, and knew *France* perfectly, ſays, ſpeaking of the former Le payſan & le laboureur ſont dans l'aiſance, & n'étant point vexes, ils multiplient, & fourniſſent à l'etat des cultivateurs, des marins, des artiſans & des manœuvriers. *Traite de la Circulation*, p 71.

But what would a nation of cottagers do for their defence? They would become the prey of the firſt invader: they are to have neither manufactures nor commerce; for, ſays he, a flouriſhing commerce whilſt it flatters may be deſtroying *. What does this mean but proſcribing it? For we muſt take mens ſentiments in their tendency, and not admit the ideal meaſure and degree of trade and luxury which they will allow, as if it was in human power to ſay to wealth, So far ſhalt thou go, and no farther. This nation of cottagers therefore muſt pay all taxes, which we may ſuppoſe ſufficiently productive to ſupport the magnificence of a ſhepherd king—no army—no fleet—no

wars

* I cannot paſs this opportunity of remarking, that the complaints of commerce, luxury, and an unequal diviſion of the lands being prejudicial to population, have been very often repeated—If the reader would ſee the ſubject treated in a much more maſterly manner than any late writer has handled it, let him conſult Mr WALACE's *Diſſertation on the Numbers of Mankind*, 1753; where every thing is ſaid againſt them that can be ſaid, yet is the author candid enough to allow much to commerce and the arts, and ſpeaks of them as occaſions of depopulation, not ſo much in the country where they are practiſed as in the world at large, ſee p. 22 Yet do I not think his ſyſtem is well founded The circumſtance that *the countries wherein the neceſſaries of life are the cheapeſt, are the worſt peopled*, is an anſwer to three-fourths of his arguments.

wars—What has ſuch a ſituation to do with the ſtate of the modern world! If the author ſays it is extravagant to carry his idea ſo far, I reply, ſuch a ſuppoſition ſhews the neceſſity of limits—ſhews that we muſt have ſomething elſe in a modern ſtate than the cultivators of ſeven jugera. —If this is admitted, how far is the exception to go? Who is to lay down the line of diviſion, and ſay, Here propriety ends—there exceſs begins? In a word, the great fact proved by this argument is, that you muſt give up a degree of population in favour of more important objects—that is, you muſt admit commerce and wealth —This muſt be admitted—I deſire no other conceſſion: your whole ſyſtem at once tumbles about your ears.—My politicks of claſſing national wealth before population, needs no exception—it ſets population at defiance—Yours of giving populouſneſs the firſt rank, neceſſitates you to call in a ſuperior to your aſſiſtance—and like all ſuperior powers called to the ſupport of the weaker, it deſtroys their independance.

But to proceed: the Doctor ſays, when the land is got into few hands, the little farmers muſt become labourers: Certainly; and in that ſtate are juſt as uſeful to the nation as in their former. But, ſays he, ſubſiſtence then being difficult, they will not marry. So marriage, in a given ſtate, thrives in proportion to the ability of maintaining families. In the back country of *America*, where every child is 50 acres to the father, and the wife 100—where there is no ſociety beyond the cottage, and where a woman is neceſſary almoſt to the exiſtence of a man—I admit this.—In a modern *European* ſtate, I deny it: I appeal to every man's obſervation for telling him that celibacy is more common among the wealthy than the poor—and that the claſſes leaſt able to ſupport a family, marry more readily than the rich.—At the ſame time, ſays the Doctor, there will be more labour: then I reply, there is every thing we want, for labour is the valuable effect of population. In a great farm there is but one idle perſon, in a ſmall one there is the ſame*. Sure, therefore, the ſupernumerary farmers are a mere burthen to the ſtate; an idea applicable to every one who ſtands in the place of a labourer without performing his office, but conſumes thoſe products that ought to go to market.

There is one argument I have heard in converſation againſt large farms, which

 appears

* One can ſcarce ever be accurate in uſing ſuch terms as *large* and *ſmall*, by ſmall I do not mean only farms of 20 or 30 acres, but others upon which mere idle occupiers are found.

appears more specious than any to be found against them in Dr. *Price* It is said, that large farms are in fact machines in agriculture, which enable the cultivators of the soil to do that with few hands which before they did with many, resembling a stocking-loom, for instance, which enables the master manufacturer to turn off half his hands, and yet make more stockings than ever. A lively argument, but false in almost every particular; indeed the resemblance holds no farther than the capacity of performing in some operations much more with ten men in one farm, than with the same number divided among five farms; of which there can be no doubt But I appeal to all persons conversant in husbandry, if this holds true through one-tenth of the labour of a farm; witness ploughing, harrowing, sowing, digging, mowing, reaping, threshing, hedging, ditching, and an hundred other articles, in which one man, separately taken, performs the full tenth of ten men collected. The saving of labour is but in few articles, such as carting hay or corn; carting dung or marle; keeping sheep, &c.

But take the comparison in another light. Who dungs most? Who brings most manure from towns? Who digs most chalk, clay or marle? Who cultivates most turneps? Which hoes them best? Which plants most pease,

peaſe, beans, potatoes, &c. in rows for hand-hoeing? Who digs moſt drains? Who digs the largeſt and deepeſt ditches? Which gives the ſoil the moſt numerous, deep and effective ploughings? Which brought into culture the moſt waſte land? Who in all this, and many things more, expends moſt labour in proportion to their acres, the great or the little farmers? That any man who pretends to know wheat from barley ſhould aſſert ſo prepoſterous an idea as the *poorer* occupier to be the *beſt* cultivator, is not a little aſtoniſhing. Nothing appears to me ſo reaſonable as the contrary; and when I compared the population of 250 different-ſized farms, the fact turned out as every one might ſuppoſe *.

As to the change of the conſumption from meat to bread, it is perfectly harmleſs —for I know no good in one being conſumed more than in another, as long as meat is dear enough to induce the farmers to keep proper ſtocks of cattle for manure. But it is a little extraordinary if the conſumption of meat declines ſo much, that the price ſhould continue ſo high.—Farther, towns and manufactures will increaſe—

* The ſingle circumſtance of much of the labour of ſmall farms being ſervants unmarried, and nine-tenths of that of great ones labourers married, makes a greater difference.

This is a great misfortune in the Doctor's political creed—but I would recommend him, if he will hold national wealth in contempt, to consider manufactures in that most beautiful idea of Mr. *Hume*'s—*a store-house of labour for the public* · those hands which are employed in these fabrics yield a surplus always at the service of government —but what navies, what armies are recruited from farmers? The people employed in raising food must be tied to the soil, and so we every where see them. The fewer employed (consistently with good husbandry) the better; for then the less product is intercepted before it reaches the markets, and you may have so many the more for manufacturers, sailors and soldiers.

This is a mode of reasoning, which I think is perfectly fair. I do not expect any reasoning should convince those who will not be convinced by facts; for I may say with a *French* author, La dépopulation étoit devenue à la mode*; who also observes very justly: Je suis très porté à croire que les *Anglois* ont aussi LA MANIE de dénigrer leur population.

* *De la Felicité Publique*, tom. ii. p. 133.

SECT. VII.

MANUFACTURES AND COMMERCE.

IN too many of the writings on the œconomical ſcience which have within theſe twenty years appeared in *France*; writings which I mention rather than the publications in *England*, becauſe they have been greatly ſuperior, the advocates for huſbandry have ſeemed too much to arrange themſelves rather *againſt* commerce and manufactures, than *with* agriculture: M. *de Boulainvilliers* in his well known work * enters into very long details of the miſchiefs ariſing from commerce, colonies and manufactures, and he has been followed by ſeveral other writers. But I think ſuch ideas are extremely miſchievous: on the contrary, I eſteem them as of infinite conſequence to the well-being of agriculture, whenever the latter is not ſacrificed to the former by prohibitions and reſtrictions on the export of corn laid with a view to feed manufacturers cheaper; views never anſwered by ſuch a policy. If the conduct of a ſtateſ-

* *Les Interets de la France mal entendus*, 3 tome. 1755.

a ſtateſman ſhews ability, I had rather he would neglect agriculture than manufactures and commerce, and for this reaſon, agriculture requires only a negative encouragement—let it alone, and it will thrive; you cannot hurt it unleſs you are *active* againſt it, in taxation, corn laws, &c. But, on the contrary, trade and manufactures are children of more ſickly and difficult growth; if you do not give them active encouragement, they preſently die; witneſs nine-tenths of our foreign treaties—witneſs our public companies, *ſuppoſed* to be neceſſary—witneſs our eternal wars made for the defence or acquiſition of trade—witneſs half the acts of the legiſlature: every thing in this country ſhews the attention that is neceſſary, or at leaſt that is given to commercial intereſts If I am aſked, of what good all this is to agriculture, I reply, it makes us a wealthy people—it makes every thing dear —and I have already ſhewn, that great national wealth is one of the moſt effectual points in the encouragement of agriculture. I do not think it is neceſſary to add, that ſuch a conduct may be carried to exceſs—Views of trade may ſo exhauſt a country's revenues as to bring on a burthen of public debts, more miſchievous than all the evils that can reſult

from

from a want of trade* I am not reaſoning on the abuſe of a right maxim; nor do I aſſert

---

* As I have in various paſſages found myſelf under a neceſſity of differing in opinion concerning proviſion, population, &c from the very ingenious author of the *Obſervations on Reverſionary Payments*, I ought not to let ſlip any opportunity of paying my tribute to his abilities in other parts of his work. I think his propoſition for paying or leſſening the national debt by the uninterrupted operation of a ſum ſacred to compound intereſt, is ſet forth, explained, and all objections anſwered in the moſt clear and ſatisfactory manner, inſomuch that the author well deſerves the thanks of the community for that part of his performance. Perhaps the idea of ruin from our debts is carried too far, but be that as it may, the having an opportunity of placing any ſums at compound intereſt by way of freeing a portion of taxes as a treaſure in reſerve, and not doing it, is certainly infatuation nor can I conceive a reaſon againſt it, unleſs it be the propoſition whenever made ſuppoſing a reduction of our taxes Such a ſuppoſition is extremely impolitick; it is ſo contrary to the particular intereſt of the crown, that there is an abſurdity in ſuppoſing it will ever be thought of, conſequently to connect the circumſtance of *payment of debt*, with *reduction of taxes*, is to raiſe a prejudice againſt the whole Indeed the two circumſtances are abundantly different, payment of debt ſtrikes one as highly neceſſary, but as to a neceſſity of lowering the taxes, I ſee none, nor do I think any good would flow from it, except in a very few inſtances, which might eaſily be changed without any reduction. The object of freeing a part of the national income from incumbrances, in order for other applications, is a much more neceſſary and obvious work than the reduction of taxes —See Appendix.

assert that this has yet happened in this country.

Certain it is that manufactures and commerce provide an excellent market for the farmer, at the same time that they give that wealth to the public, without which agriculture cannot thrive And this beneficial effect, in every country except *England*, is unattended with any great burthen of unprovided poor in case of a failure or decline of a manufacture; because, although the community in general has a load upon their charity, yet is not the evil tied to the farmer. In this circumstance, from the absurdity of the poor laws, which threaten more than any other circumstance the agriculture of the kingdom, and I might in fact say every branch of industry in it; operates very differently from what one could wish, and occasions, wherever manufactures are established, a most heavy burthen of poors rates, partly borne by the tenant in the customary form, and partly by the landlord, who is obliged to let his farms so much the cheaper.

Yet as this disadvantage belongs more to the false policy of our poors laws than to any circumstance necessarily flowing from manufactures, it would not be right generally to find fault with them on that account. other nations who make them a great

great object of their endeavours, ſhould take warning by our example, and if they find any ſupport of their poor further than charity affords neceſſary, that they may take care the burthen ariſing from manufactures may fall on manufactures, and by no means on agriculture.

Hence therefore we may venture to aſſert, that the encouragement of manufactures and commerce, and in general of all branches of induſtry, is a ſure way to encourage agriculture, provided the legiſlature attends to a few circumſtances which ſhould not be forgotten. *Firſt*—Not to burthen agriculture with taxes proportioned to its products, in order to leſſen thoſe on conſumption. *Secondly*—Not to prohibit, or in any way reſtrain the export of the earth's productions, on ſuppoſition of feeding manufacturers the cheaper. *Thirdly*—To make manufacturers ſupport their own poor. Theſe conditions are ſo ſimple, and at the ſame time ſo juſt, that a compliance with them can never be reckoned a reſtraint on any branch of national induſtry.

APPEN-

APPENDIX.

NUMBER I.

Memoir drawn up, and laid before the Lords Commissioners of the Treasury, containing An Historical Review of the statutes that have been made relative to the Corn Trade, and Proposals for ascertaining the prices of Middling British Corn for the purpose of exportation.

Now first published.

BY GOVERNOR POWNALL.

VARIOUS laws from time to time have been
made and enacted, directing when *H* 6 *an* 15 c 2.
corn might be exported and when im- 20. c 6.
ported, marking the prices at which 23. c 5 *P & M* 1 & 2.
such respective grains shall be sold the c 5
rule whereby the ports are to be opened *El* 1 c 11 § 20.
and shut to the exportation and impor- 13 c. 13 35 c 7 § 25.
tation of corn And also directing what *Ja* 1 c 25 § 26
duties should be paid inwards and out- 21 c 28 § 3.
wards, according to such prices. Yet *Car* 1 c 4. § 24. *Car* 2 12 c 4
“ no provision was made by the said § 11
Acts for ascertaining and determining 15 c 7
the said prices *.” 22 c 13.

Therefore for the first time, an act passed in the first year of *James* the Second, entituled, *An additional Act for the Improvement of Tillage*, directs, That the justices of the maritime counties have power by the 1685 1 *Ja* 2 c. 19. § 3

* Words of the Statute of 1 *Ja* 2 c 19

the oath of two men, being neither merchants nor factors for the importing of corn, nor anyways concerned or interested, and having a freehold of 20*l.* *per ann.* or a leasehold of 50*l* *per ann.* to determine the common market prices of middling *English* corn, &c. and then to certify the same to the chief officer or collector of the customs

All foreign corn imported is to pay duty according
§ 4 to those certified prices

This enquiry, determination and certificate are to be made by the justices at their quarter sessions
§ 3 at *Michaelmas* and *Easter* yearly, for the kingdom at large—and for the city of *London* in the
§ 5 months of *October* and *April*

N. B Those prices thus determined and certified are to continue six months.

Several bounties were granted on the exportation of corn, when the prices of the respec-
1688
1 *W.* & *M* c 12 tive grains therein mentioned did not exceed the prices in that statute respectively mentioned.

Remark The law of *James* II had it been actually carried into execution (which it was not) respected only the rates to be paid by *foreign corn imported.*

There was not at the time of passing this bounty law any rule for ascertaining and determining the prices up to which the several bounties on the several grains were respectively payable.

The law itself contains no such rule or regulation, nor has any been made since to this day, except in
2 *Ge.* II c 18 the case of bere *alias* bigg, oatmeal,
§ 5 and malt made of wheat, as shall be hereafter explained.

We will therefore pursue the various alterations and amendments which have been successively made in the mode prescribed for ascertaining and determining *the prices* which were to regulate *the importation of foreign corn*—and *the duties payable thereon.*

In

In the 2d year of *Geo* II a law was made, called "An Act to ascertain the custom payable for corn and grain imported, for better ascertaining the *price* and *quantity* of corn and grain for which a bounty is payable on exportation" The first clause recites the whole act of *James* II and then recites as the ground of this new law, "That the justices of the "peace for some of the counties of this kingdom "have, notwithstanding the last mentioned act, "omitted or neglected to settle the price of corn at "their quarter sessions, and to return certificates "thereof—whereby great loss has arisen to the revenue, and detriment to the farmer and fair trader." 1729 2 *Geo* II c 18. § 1, 2, 3, 4, 5

Therefore the act directs, that the justices who have omitted to settle the prices of corn at the quarter sessions after *Michaelmas* last, are to settle it at the next quarter sessions by examining and determining *what the prices were* at or about *Michaelmas* last—and all persons concerned are to govern themselves by the *prices thus set*, as though according to the old law they had been actually set at the quarter sessions after *Michaelmas* last § 1.

Corn imported since the 1st day of *Michaelmas* quarter sessions, and duty not paid, forfeited. § 2.

If justices in time to come shall omit or neglect to examine, determine and certify the prices as by law directed, the chief officer or collector of the customs, "*where foreign corn or grain shall be imported,*" empowered to receive the several duties of *the corn so imported*, according to the lowest price of the several sorts of corn or grain, as *per* 22 *Car* II.

Officers to *measure* corn *exported* The bounty to be paid according to the *quantity* thereby computed. § 4.

The act uniting the two kingdoms of *England* and *Scotland* passed since the *English* act, granting a bounty on the exportation of certain grains. § 5.

An article of the union gave a bounty on the exportation from *Scotland* of here or bigg, and of oatmeal.

X By

By an act in the 5th year of the reign of *Anne*, 5 Ann c 29 § 10 this bounty was extended to bere *alias* bigg, *exported from England*, and by the same act it was determined and enacted, that a bounty on malt made of wheat, exported, should be payable. This act therefore of the 2d of *Geo.* II supposing that the regulations for ascertaining the prices according to which the duties on *foreign corn imported* should be paid, were general rules and regulations that extended to ascertain the prices of *British corn exported*—which it is seen herein above they did not—does under this mistake enact, that the like powers, certificates and regulations, and other matters and things abovementioned, shall extend to the ascertaining the *prices* and quantity of bere *alia* bigg, oatmeal, and malt made of wheat *intended for exportation.*

N B The case then after this law had passed, stood thus —There was a method (such as it was, *an ineffectual one*) for ascertaining the prices according to which the duties on *foreign corn imported* should be paid, and according to which the bounty on bere *alias* bigg and oat meal, and malt made of wheat should be paid But yet the rules by which the prices at which the several sorts of corn and grain specified in the bounty act might be exported, and to which price the several respective bounties were payable, still remained undetermined and unauthorized

Let us then see what the next law respecting the matter did.

In the 5th year of *Geo* II an act passed "for "amending and making more effectual 5 Geo II c 12 "an act made in the first year of "King *James* II intituled, *An additional Act for* "*the Improvement of Tillage.*"

This recites, that in the act of *James*, *provision was made for examining and determining the common market prices of middling English corn and grain*, which was however INEFFECTUAL. Then directs, that for the better *ascertaining the common market prices of middling English corn and grain*, and for *preventing the fraudulent* IMPORTATION of foreign corn and grain,

grain, the justices of the peace in such counties of *England, wherein foreign corn or grain* shall or may be hereafter *imported*, at every of their quarter sessions shall give in charge to the grand jury to make enquiry and presentment upon their oaths of the common market prices, of the respective sorts and quantities of corn and grain mentioned in the 22 of *Car* II.

N. B. Although this law was made since the bounty, yet this ascertaining of the prices is expressly only to prevent the *fraudulent importation* of foreign corn—Is to be executed in such counties wherein foreign corn *shall or may be imported*, and refers, not to several sorts of corn and grain, which by the bounty act and the 5th of *Anne* are to receive a bounty *on exportation*, but only to the 22 of *Car*. II. respective to the duties payable on *importation*.

This presentment to be made in open court, to be certified to the custom-house where such corn and grain shall be imported, to be hung up there—And all duties on importation appointed to be paid by 22 *Car*. II. are to be paid according to these prices so certified. § 2. § 3

N B Here the mode of ascertaining the common market prices is altered, and the prices certified are by this law to continue only *three months*, which before continued *six months*.

The mode of proceeding in *London* to continue as before under the act of *James*. § 4

Bounty on *corn ground* to be regulated by weight. 24 *Geo*. II c. 56.

By the 31st of *Geo* II. (an act for the due making of Bread, and regulating the assize and price thereof, &c.) another mode is directed for the returns of the prices of grain. But this is done only for the purpose of setting the assize of bread; and the custom-house cannot regulate itself by it. 31 *Geo*. II c 29.

By an act of the 6th year of the reign of his present Majesty, the Mayor and Aldermen of the city of *London* may determine the prices of corn in the months of *January* and *July*, as well as in *April* and *October* yearly 6 *Geo* III c 17.

By

By an act passed in the 10th year of the reign of his present Majesty, weekly returns of the prices of grain are to be made, and published in the Gazette.

10 G. III. c. 39.

But this has no reference to importation or exportation, nor can the custom-house regulate themselves thereby.

The case then standing thus, that the law of King *James* II. is ineffectual—that the law of King *George* II. is not always executed, and that neither of these laws have any reference to, or can regulate the prices as to exportation, the custom-house, having *no legal rule* to regulate themselves by, have adopted without law (if not contrary to law) a mode of their own. They oblige the exporter in the body of the *entry outwards* to swear that the prices of the corn or grain so entered for exportation, did not exceed the bounty price *the last market day*.

For the doing this, they have *no authority* by law: And when done, this does not authorize to give a debenture for the bounty, or even to suffer the exportation.

Vide *Crouch's* Compleat Guide to the officers of his Majesty's Customs, p. 42.
N. B. This is what the Custom-House go by.

They are therefore, as a succedaneum, directed and intrusted by their superiors in these words: "If the "officers *are satisfied* that the respec- "tive prices of corn do not exceed "the limitations for the bounty (which they are care- "fully to inform themselves of from market day to "market day, remembering that they must be ac- "counted as at the time of shipping and not of "entry) and the exporter has given the collector a "certificate under his hand, containing the quantities "and qualities of the corn so shipped, &c."

Vide ibid., p. 43.

Now this is not only, as I said above, without the authority of law, but contrary to law—as the oath to be taken respecting the prices of corn, by which the [illegible]-house is to regulate itself as to the duties on [illegible] it could have reference to the

bounty

bounty act and to exportation) muſt be taken by *two* perſons—and neither of theſe merchants or factors for the importing of corn, nor any way concerned or intereſted, and muſt have an eſtate of 20*l.* *per ann.* freehold, or 50*l* *per ann* leaſehold.

The concluſion of the matter is:

I. That the laws for aſcertaining the prices of corn which are to regulate the importation and duties thereon, are ineffectual and not carried into practice.

II That except for the article of bere *alias* bigg, oatmeal, and malt made of wheat, there is no law for aſcertaining the prices which are to regulate the exportation and bounty paid thereon.

III That the mode purſued and practiſed is unfounded—is open to frauds—and has given occaſion to many impoſitions

The remedy propoſed is to repeal theſe ſeveral vague and ineffectual laws, which neither are executed at all, nor can to the purpoſes intended—To reduce all the *proviſions* † contained in them into one bill, to render them practicable, and to point their effect to the real end intended, by

1ſt, Reciting the preſent ſtate and inefficiency of them.

2dly, Repealing them.

3dly, Enacting the purview of them by proviſion, which may reach the end, taking care to inſert all and every regulation *ſo pointed* as the legiſlature have already enacted, and all ſuch others as may be farther neceſſary

The general ſcope and purview of ſuch bill will be,

I. That the juſtices ‡ at their general quarter ſeſſions do, by all ſuch methods, and from all ways of information as the laws direct, or as by this propoſed law ſhall be directed, *enquire* what have been the

 common

† The Regiſter of weekly prices anſwers (in the publication) ſo many good purpoſes, beſides the matter of export, I ſhould apprehend that it might very properly be a part of the proviſions Mr *Pownall* mentions remaining As it ought to be rendered perpetual, it might very properly be done in a general act Y

‡ Of the maritime counties only are neceſſary

common market prices of corn and grain for three months past

II That having special regard to the case, whether the markets have been falling, or rising, they do *determine* what shall for the next three months which are to come, be deemed the prices of such respective corn or grain that is to say, what shall be deemed the port price —According to which, importation or exportation shall take place, and according to which, the duties and bounties shall be paid

III. That they do certify this to the respective custom-houses within the county —And that this, and this only, be the rule to be observed at such ports

How to oblige justices to do it

IV. This bill to contain a proviso to guard against the only thing which can happen to the hurt of the landed interest, viz That if, upon the ports being opened (according to the prices certified as above) for importation, any such large quantity should be imported so as to load the markets in a way that may prove a discouragement of tillage—the facts of which will appear by the falling of the market prices,—that is to say, that if the *port price* shall have been fixed above 48 *s* *per* quarter, and by an overflow of importation the actual market price should, within the next three months to come, sink suddenly or rapidly below 44 *s* *per* quarter, that then the said justices, at any adjourned or special sessions, may, for the remaining part of the three months, alter the certificate to such price as the *immediate state of the market* shall justify

These certificates and determinations to be hung up openly at the several custom houses.

All the provisions respecting the measurement of quantity, the mode of ascertaining the quality to be re-enacted If it were not thought better, as it most certainly would be, to determine the quantity which was to pay duty, or to receive bounty, *by the* WEIGHT, both as to corn unground, as well as (which the law now directs) to corn ground.

Such

Such a simple regulation would have an immediate tendency to encourage good husbandry † in the tillage of, and to avoid a thousand frauds in the commerce of grain.

It would prevent many frauds as to the bounty,—many in contracts—and would have an effect to give our British corn a preference in the foreign market—and would, at the same time, lead to the importation of such as would never interfere with our own corn, in our own markets, even upon the most ample importation of foreign corn.

Although there might arise a thousand perplexities and difficulties, and hence some danger, in any law directing corn to be *sold by weight*, yet the thus directing the duties and bounties to be so paid, could have none I can venture to say that this matter has been fully considered.

I take the liberty of laying this state and proposal before the Lords Commissioners of the Treasury. I wish it to be referred to the Commissioners of the Customs—and I will be ready to communicate or give explanations in detail upon every point which may arise.

Richmond, Surry, July 15, 1773.

† An observation which carries conviction with it Y.

NUMBER II

Rise of Prices—page 3?

IT has been, by some writers, supposed that the high prices of corn since the year 1756, have been confined to *England*, an idea which was favourable to the causes they attributed the evil to, a worse police respecting markets, engrossers, forestallers, &c. To say, that prices have of late very generally risen in other parts of *Europe*, will be a reply to much of this nonsense, and it will also account, in the most satisfactory manner, for the rise in our *American* colonies I transcribe the following tables from M. *Engell's Essai sur la maniere la plus sure d'etablir un systeme de police des grains*. Berne, 1772.

I.

The sack of wheat, weighing 212 pounds, was sold in the divers markets of the *Palatinate* from 1751 to 1769 inclusively, at 4 *florins* and a half to 6*fl.* 5*s.* and in 1770, at 13*fl.*

II.

Price of spelt at *Berne*.

	Batz.		*Batz.*		*Batz.*
1751 —	70	1758 —	92	1765 —	75
1752 —	70	1759 —	75	1766 —	85
1753 —	80	1760 —	60	1767 —	80
1754 —	65	1761 —	60	1768 —	78
1755 —	60	1762 —	60	1769 —	90
1756 —	65	1763 —	56	1770 —	130
1757 —	85	1764 —	64		

The sack of wheat, or spelt, weighs 190 to 200 pounds

III.

Price of wheat at *Dijon*.

1753 — *sols*	62 to 70		1757 — *sols*	55 to 65
1754 ———	50 — 65		1758 ———	65 — 76
1755 ———	48 — 55		1759 ———	70 — 75
1756 ———	50 — 59		1760 ———	55 — 65

1761 — *sols*	48	to	58	1767 — *sols*	85	to	88
1762 ——	38	—	45	1768 ——	84	—	200
1763 ——	45	—	50	1769 ——	85	—	92
1764 ——	60	—	65	1770 ——	85	—	107
1766 ——	72	—	80	1771 ——	140	—	160

The measure of *Dijon* weighs 46 to 47 pounds.

IV.

Price of corn in the *Canton* of *Bale*.

	Liv	*s*	*d*		*Liv*	*s.*	*d.*
1754 ——	8	2	6	1763 ——	7	16	8
1755 ——	7	12	6	1764 ——	7	6	8
1756 ——	9	5	0	1765 ——	8	15	0
1757 ——	11	7	6	1766 ——	10	10	0
1758 ——	10	17	6	1767 ——	10	6	8
1759 ——	10	12	6	1768 ——	10	15	10
1760 ——	9	2	6	1769 ——	11	19	6
1761 ——	7	15	0	1770 ——	25	0	0
1762 ——	8	15	0				

V.

Price of corn at *Geneva*.

	Florins.		*Florins.*		*Florins.*
1700 —	30	1720 —	21	1740 —	33
1701 —	33	1721 —	21	1741 —	26
1702 —	32	1722 —	21	1742 —	28
1703 —	34	1723 —	16	1743 —	25
1704 —	32	1724 —	16	1744 —	25
1705 —	21	1725 —	21	1745 —	28
1706 —	18	1726 —	21	1746 —	31
1707 —	21	1727 —	24	1747 —	40
1708 —	45	1728 —	21	1748 —	50
1709 —	95	1729 —	21	1749 —	50
1710 —	36	1730 —	21	1750 —	25
1711 —	36	1731 —	21	1751 —	30
1712 —	36	1732 —	22	1752 —	30
1713 —	40	1733 —	20	1753 —	30
1714 —	40	1734 —	21	1754 —	23
1715 —	36	1735 —	23	1755 —	22
1716 —	24	1736 —	19	1756 —	24
1717 —	21	1737 —	19	1757 —	36
1718 —	20	1738 —	18	1758 —	35
1719 —	25	1739 —	25	1759 —	34

	Florins		Florins		Florins
1760 —	24	1764 —	22	1768 —	29
1761 —	24	1765 —	36	1769 —	34
1762 —	23	1766 —	36	1770 —	63
1763 —	22	1767 —	32		

The meaſure is the *coupe*, weighs from 108 to 112 pounds, of 18 ounces.

NUMBER III.

Decline of Manufactures—Page 87.

IT is very difficult to know what is the real ſtate of any manufacture; ſo difficult, that I believe it is ſcarcely ever attained, except when a committee of the Houſe of Commons is appointed for the purpoſe, with power to ſend for perſons, papers, and records. The late appointment of ſuch a committee to enquire into the ſtate of the linen manufacture in *Great Britain* and *Ireland*, has brought to light ſome very important facts relative to that manufacture. The point of ſuppoſed declenſion, mentioned in the text, after the concluſion of the laſt war, appears to be no ſuch point in reality. this is an extraordinary circumſtance, for in the journies I have made through this kingdom, I found accounts very general of the decline that followed the peace, I am therefore ſurprized to find that this was not the caſe with the linen manufacture, as appears by the following table of export of *Britiſh* and *Iriſh* linen from *England*.

Years		*Britiſh* Linens Yards		*Iriſh* Linens. Yards.
1743	—	52,779	—	40,907
1744	—	49,521	—	28,255
1745	—	56 240	—	101,928
1746	—	175,328	—	695,002
1747	—	238 014	—	595,277
1748	—	330,747	—	723,663

Years.		*British* Linens Yards		*Irish* Linens. Yards
1749	—	414,834	—	965,897
1750	—	588,874	—	742,032
1751	—	527,976	—	854,490
1752	—	437,277	—	968,319
1753	—	641,510	—	1,039,967
1754	—	1,382,796	—	843,973
1755	—	41,367	—	51,040
Average of ſeven years peace,		576,373	—	772,245
1756	—	394,746	—	719,135
1757	—	1,016,754	—	2,005,575
1758	—	1,942,667	—	2,117,109
1759	—	1,693,087	—	1,956,572
1760	—	1,413,602	—	2,352,583
1761	—	1,272,985	—	1,819,329
1762	—	1,762,643	—	2,930,476
Average of ſeven years war,		1,355,226	—	1,985,825
1763	—	2,308,310	—	2,588,564
1764	—	2,134,733	—	1,858,780
1765	—	2,095,933	—	1,663,670
1766	—	2,236,086	—	1,770,634
1767	—	2,444,181	—	2,227,142
1768	—	2,687,457	—	2,270,160
1769	—	3,056,950	—	1,855,159
Average of ſeven years peace,		2,423,664	—	2,033,444
1770	—	3,210,506	—	2,707,482
1771	—	4,411,040	—	3,450,224

Since 1771, the manufacturers have complained much, and their complaints were the occaſion of this committee But upon this I muſt make two obſervations which appear to me eſſential. Firſt, the year 1771 is greater than 1770, by

		British		*Irish*
Yards	—	1,200,534	—	742,742

Which

Which in the *British* is a greater rise by a million of yards than that from 1769 to 1770, this great superiority of 1771 was owing to the flow of trade that followed the dissolution of combinations in *America*, consequently is an improper year to take singly for comparison. The only fair method of comparing different periods is to average several: thus, if 1771, 1772, and 1773 equal on an average those of 1770, 1769, and 1768, no person can, upon any principles, deduce a decline. The stagnation of credit following the bankruptcies in *May* 1772, was a wound to every fabric in the kingdom; but as in its nature it was temporary, there can be little doubt of a revival: and accordingly trade of every sort is now fast reviving.

The linen manufacturers, it is true, came to parliament for relief, supposing the stagnation they experienced not owing to that of credit, but an increased import of foreign linens. The following table is transcribed from the report of the committee,

Years		Total import Yards		Re-exported Yards
1752	—	27,856,122	—	7,187,110
1753	—	35,372,977	—	7,448,672
1754	—	30,871,973	—	6,981,528
1755	—	31,947,447	—	7,542,694
1756	—	31 759 234	—	8,461,726
1757	—	28,429 072	—	8,461,031
1758	—	29,770,104	—	7,969,160
1759	—	25 059 533	—	10,482,730
1760	—	27,988,972	—	10,079,851
1761	—	30,428,[illegible]24	—	6,740,960
1762	—	18,827,853	—	5,990,706
1763	—	26,634,851	—	8,046,355
1764	—	28,092,215	—	7,889,265
1765	—	25 497,795	—	6,394,147
1766	—	25,624,107	—	7,171,891
1767	—	21,054,411	—	7,147,784
1768	—	23,112,349	—	8,046,960
1769	—	25,431,102	—	7,102 527
1770	—	27,101,313	—	8,461,546
1771	—	28,213,121	—	10,4[illegible]0,129

Now

Now from this table it appears equally clear, that the import is not increased to 1771, it is on the contrary lessened, nor is the re-export lessened If when the accounts come to be made up for 1772, and 1773, a great increased import is seen, than these gentlemen may have reason to complain

The tables here transcribed being quoted for the purpose of shewing that this manufacture went on regularly increasing after the peace, it is not a part of my business to touch upon what has happened since 1771—they have proved what I produced them for clearly—as to the rest, I was induced to hint what I did, because I am always, from principle, suspicious of commercial complaints The lengths to which the woollen manufacturers carried such complaints near forty years ago—the asseverations they made—the proofs they brought—the arguments they used--the attention given them by parliament—all tending to evince and *prove incontestibly*, that the woollen manufacture was *going to the dogs*, at the very time when it was flourishing in an higher degree than was ever before experienced—this is with me a circumstance that gives suspicion at manufacturing complaints—and will never allow me to believe facts that do not clearly appear in such tables of exportation as those I have now quoted. If, on the average of several years, a decline is *proved*, measures of encouragement ought certainly to be taken, but as to temporary stagnations, arising from evidently temporary causes, they do not appear to call for permanent alterations, if any thing is hazarded by such alterations the alarm of ruin that is gone forth among all our other manufacturers at *the idea* of measures, carries an appearance of impropriety, for such alarms are generally groundless. The committee appointed to enquire into the whole affair, will fairly and candidly examine all parties—they will discover, first, whether there is any great decline, next, they will enquire if a corresponding decline has appeared in other manufactures—then the causes of such partial or general declension will be examined—

and

and if it appears that causes, which bear particularly against the linen trade, have produced such effects, they will very wisely recommend to the house such measures as may remove those causes. On the contrary, if they find that the effect is not singular but general, and flowing from causes which will gradually remove themselves, they will then, doubtless, determine that new and restrictive measures are unnecessary.

One circumstance has fallen within my own knowledge relative to the present state of *Ireland*, which gives me reason to think the evil complained of is not owing to any cause particularly bearing against the linen fabric. The number of farms at present upon the landlords hands in that kingdom is very great, and tenants every day throwing up others, or breaking upon them I have been applied to by several very considerable landlords for my advice on this their situation, and upon making enquiries into the causes of this effect, asking if the products of the land sell at lower prices than they used to do—or if the farmers expences have arisen considerably—I have been answered, that products of all sorts sell better than ever they did—and that expences have not risen — Nor was it till I had repeated my enquiries of different persons, that I found the whole of their evils owing to the stagnation of credit—yet was it proved to me incontestibly Very many farmers hired their lands on credit—conducted their business on credit, and settled their children in other farms on credit, and this whole system receiving a fatal blow in the bankruptcies of *May*, &c 1772, such a distress followed among these sons of credit, that infinite numbers were ruined Now if agriculture could be so affected by the failure of credit, is it to be wondered at that manufactures suffered in a greater proportion, being more dependant on commercial credit and is not this a very strong collateral proof that the declension of the linen trade is owing principally to this cause?

Before

Before I finiſh theſe obſervations, I ſhall expreſs a wiſh that the committee may publiſh, in their farther report, a table of the annual export of all woollen fabrics.—It is a common opinion that that manufacture is declining—I much ſuſpect the truth of it, but to prove the real fact, cannot but have its uſes—it will probably ſtop many groundleſs complaints.

EMIGRATIONS.

IN the courſe of the examinations which the linen committee has taken, the emigrations from *Ireland* were an object much enquired into—they ſeemed to many gentlemen an object of alarm.—What I have obſerved in the preceeding papers was deſigned by way of reply to the falſe ideas too current in books, pamphlets, and news-papers.—I did not imagine that ſo wiſe an aſſembly as a *Britiſh* houſe of Commons would ever deſcend to opinions ſo much below their level. Why are you uneaſy at theſe people leaving *Ireland?* To what purpoſe would you have them ſtay at home? their going is proof enough that they ought to go—or in other words, there were more than you could employ. *Oh, but that is owing to the decline of the linen trade, and if that riſes again, the hands will not be found.* Do not indulge ſuch idle fears: raiſe the manufacture as quick as you pleaſe, it will, in its moſt rapid progreſs, create hands by every motion: the abſence of thoſe that are gone will be a premium to the induſtry of thoſe that remain, by filling their hands with conſtant work, and prove ſuch an encouragement to population that nothing will be able to oppoſe its progreſs. It would be a moſt beneficial thing to this country, if the unemployed people at *Norwich*, *Colcheſter*, *Sudbury*, *Bocking*, &c. were ſeized with the *Iriſh* ſpirit of emigration, we ſhould, twenty years hence, be the more populous on that account. In a word, this is a link of that chain of reaſoning which I traced before. Look firſt to employment, as the principal object, and trouble not your head about population, if you cannot keep up your

quan-

quantity of employment, your people will decrease in spite of fate, and they will decrease more from the unemployed hands remaining a burthen on the industrious, and starving them by competition, than if they should emigrate as fast as their employment declined. Would but gentlemen reflect on the whole train of this reasoning, they would not think any part of it paradoxical It has been with surprize that I have heard gentlemen of acknowledged abilities, saying, *If some measure is not taken to keep these emigrants at home, the country will be ruined* Whereas, the surest method of doing mischief would be to stop them. Increase your employment and you will retain hands enough to answer that employment—let the rest take their way to that happy clime where *hands create employment* Which is not the case in *Europe* †. But if you would retain them without doing mischief, offer them some of your waste land in property, and you will soon find that they will then stay in *Ireland*, having found that at home for which they wanted to go abroad—*employment*

The emigration of the husbandmen from the North and West of *Scotland*, has occasioned as much conversation in that kingdom, as the emigrating manufacturers in *Ireland* There is a considerable difference between them, for farmers and husbandmen emigrating are an extreme clear proof, that they are very unpolitically treated at home in some point of rent, houses, leases, or personal service For I shall venture to assert, that if a landlord conducts his estate on good principles, even with his own profit the first object, that his tenants and labourers will never emigrate Raising rents with judgment is an excellent operation for all parties, but some contrive to make it the very engine of loss and folly. I find, however, from some very sensible observations in the *Edinburgh Magazine*,

---

† I have [illegible] some persons express themselves as if they wished a [illegible] laid [illegible] the exportation of men Such an idea I have [illegible] found recommended in *France*, in a book which, from beginning [illegible] vulgar error *De Corps de la D[illegible]* [illegible], page 20.

gazine, that the emigrations from that country are not considerable the authors, also, observe, that the war carried off between 50 and 60,000 of the ablest bodied men in the north and west of *Scotland*, which, for a time, distressed every branch of demand, yet in a very few years numbers were greater than ever, and hands for every demand so plentiful, that many wanted work an instance which is a very strong illustration of the reasoning I have offered, and proves that the absence of those men operated as a premium to the increase and industry of those who remained.

Now I am upon the subject of emigrations from *Scotland* and *Ireland*, I must add a remark or two on the methods followed in raising rents. People of large fortune will look only to saving trouble, and they send an agent to raise their estates, as if it was a work as easy as raising a barn. In *Ireland* the buildings on many estates consist of labourers cabins only, who may so far be called farmers, as they have each their little field or two. These labourers depend on and are under-tenants to farmers who live in towns at some distance, the landlord deals only with these farmers, and the cabbins are left at their mercy The most pernicious system that ever was invented Was I entrusted with the management of a great *Irish* estate, I should set all these labourers free from the farmers, and make them tenants to the principal, and so far from raising their little farms, I should sink the rent where it was screwed very high, their cabbins I would put into repair, give them as much more land at a reasonable rate as they desired—and assist the most industrious, in proportion to their industry. In a word, my first operation should make all the mob in the country my friends upon principles of justice, and then I would go to work with the farmers, and make them pay what their lands were really worth. In this part of the business however there ought to be many considerations, particularly under the circumstances of 1. Buildings, 2. inclosures, and 3 leases. The two first articles must either be at the direct or the indirect expence of the landlord—the latter is in all cafes the heavieft upon him. If he throws an expence upon his tenant, which he ought to bear himfelf, he muft grant ample deductions on that account—and he muft not only do this, but muft farther fee his tenant fpending that money on buildings and fences, which ought to be expended in the culture of the land—This is as heavy upon him as the former—he bears both thefe weights—and he precludes improvements upon the *Englifh* fyftem. Let any man who underftands hufbandry and figures, calculate thefe circumftances, and fee what profit the *Irifh* landlord makes by neither building houfes nor digging ditches. As to leafes, they fhould be for 21 years, never for lives.

NUMBER IV.

Reply to Dr. Price —Page 91.

To the Printer *of the* ST JAMES'S CHRONICLE.

SIR,

THE Rev Dr. *Price*, in his very ingenious *Obfervations on reverfionary payments*, has drawn fuch a picture of the declining population of this kingdom, as muft alarm and terrify all well-wifhers to their country, and much exhilerate the fpirits of our neighbours This *opinion*, for I can call it nothing elfe, is publifhed in a work, the principal part of which confifts of a chain of demonftrative proofs, the author being remarkably attentive not to advance any affertions in his calculations of the value of reverfions, &c without giving the pofitive facts on which he builds, and at the fame time, being a gentleman of confiderable literary reputation, whatever is found in his book muft carry a much greater weight than the fame fentiments would have if found in inferior company. The confequence is, that the idea of our depopulation will become more general,

clamours

clamours about engrossing farms, and the high prices of provisions, will be more riotous; and the old worn-out declamations against luxury be again common in the mouths of our politicians It is not only an author's readers that converse about his sentiments, the discourse is retailed among numbers. *The kingdom is depopulated!* Who says it is depopulated? *Why Dr. Price, who has written so excellently on reversions.* Immediately the assertion spreads, and connected with the idea of being as clearly proved as any other assertion in his book. *Engrossing farms depopulates the kingdom.* This is supposed to be proved as satisfactorily as the *value of joint lives for a given number of years.*

But here, Sir, I beg leave to observe, by way of consolation to my countrymen, that a very great distinction is to be made in the doctor's book. The positive assertions he has ventured on the number of the people, engrossing farms, &c. are by no means attended with any but conjectural proofs; no positive ones, that is, he offers us such and such *opinions*, supported by *arguments*; which, if you approve, you may accept, and if not, reject. But this is not the case with the other parts of his work, he there commands your assent by facts; not solicits it by arguments founded on suppositions.

The following are the propositions which Dr. *Price* labours to establish

I. That the number of the people is fallen a million and a half since 1685.

II. That the present number is four millions and a half.

III. That the depopulation is partly owing to the engrossing of farms.

From an attentive perusal of the work, I can find no other data from whence these conclusions can be drawn than the following

1. The number of houses calculated from the hearth books by *Davenant*, were, at the restoration, - - - 1,230,000

In

In 1685, ditto - -	1,300,000
In 1690, ditto - -	1,319,215
2. The number in 1759 (*from Considerations on Trade and Finances*) -	986,482
In 1766, ditto - - -	980,692
3 Individuals per house at *Norwich*, found to be in 1752 - - -	5
Ditto in *Oxford* (exclusive of the colleges) and at *Wolverhampton* - -	4 4/5
Ditto in *Birmingham* and *Coventry* -	5 1/4
Ditto in *Shrewsbury* - -	4 1/3
Ditto in *Holy-Cross* - -	4 1/3
Ditto in *Northampton*, *Manchester* and *Liverpool* - - -	4 1/4
Ditto in *Ackworth*, *Newbury* and *Speen* -	4
Ditto in *Calne* - -	4 1/2
Ditto in *Altringham* - -	4 1/7
Ditto in *St. Michael's*, *Chester* - -	4 5/6
Ditto in *Leeds* (partly conjectured) -	5
4 Individuals *per* Family in 14 Market-Towns (*from Dr Short*) Little more than - - -	4 1/4
Ditto in 65 country parishes, not quite -	4 1/2
Ditto in *Leeds* - - -	4 1/5

Upon these authorities I shall observe, that the number of houses given by *Davenant* is not from an actual enumeration, (for none was ever yet made) but *calculated* from the hearth tax. This may be just; but reasons are not wanting to think the contrary.

Here it is to be observed, that Dr. *Halley* calculated them (see *Houghton's Husbandry*) from the same authority, in 1691, at 1,175,951, which agrees so badly with that of 1690, as to make a prodigious error in one account, and shews how extremely fallible the authority is.

Dr *Brakenridge* gives the number, in 1710, to be 911,310, which is less than at present It is to be noted, that Dr. *Price* takes no notice of these accounts. It may be said, that Dr *Brakenridge* does not mention the office whence he got the list, but his character

is

is too well eſtabliſhed to ſuppoſe him utterly miſtaken.

If the liſts from which the Doctor calculates be true, the number of houſes in 1766 were leſs by 249,308 than in 1660.

The liſt of 1691 gives 56,826 more houſes in *Yorkſhire*, *Middleſex*, *London*, *Kent*, *Eſſex*, *Surry*, and *Suſſex*, for that year, than for 1758, which is ſimply impoſſible (*See Three Tracts on Corn Trade.*) From hence is to be ſeen what credit is to be given to the calculations of the laſt century.

Let us compare the two periods	£.
Cuſtoms at the Revolution, produced	*1,015,000
At preſent, above - -	2,000,000
The exciſe at the Revolution -	† 666,383
At preſent - - -	4,600,000
Total of imports and exports in 1668	‡ 10,000,000
In 1763 - - -	26,651,854
Rental of the kingdom in Sir *William Petty*'s time, after the Reſtoration - - -	**9,000,000
At preſent - - -	20,000,000
Years purchaſe of land then ‡‡	17½
At preſent - - -	33½
Intereſt of money from 1660 to 1690,	£ 7 6 6
From 1730 to 1760 - -	3 13 6

Agriculture needs no compariſon

In the name of common ſenſe, if the kingdom contained in the former period a million and a half of ſouls more than in the latter, about what were they employed?

Does the Doctor imagine, that the ſuperiority of all theſe circumſtances can indicate a *leſs* numerous people, by a *quarter*, than in the former period? If Dr *Price* can conceive theſe circumſtances to exiſt, and at the ſame time mark a population inferior to that of 1660, I muſt ſay, by the ſame rule, that the

 moſt

* *Davenant's Eſſay on Ways and Means*, 1695, p 36. † Ib p 36
‡ *Davenant's Works*, Vol II p 15
** *Petty's Political Arithmetic*, p 151. ‡‡ Ibid.

moſt populous age of *Britain* muſt have been the reign of the Conqueror.

In the next place, reſpecting the preſent liſt, it is ſuppoſed (and I apprehend juſtly) that theſe are much the moſt accurate ever taken, but I muſt remark, that a gentleman (equally eminent for his abilities, his eloquence, and his accurate inveſtigation of theſe affairs) has informed me, that by taking particular accounts of ſeveral pariſhes, the inhabitants, houſes, births, &c he finds the number of houſes falſely reported to government in 1759, &c being in *every inſtance* FEWER than the real number This is extremely probable to be univerſal, and of which the Doctor might have taken a hint, from the great difference between the number of houſes in *London*, as appears in the pariſh books, and from *Maitland*'s accurate and laborious examination. This circumſtance is *eſſential*. It deſtroys the foundation of all the arguments to prove our depopulation, at one ſtroke

Laſtly, as to the number per houſe.—Suppoſe the houſes 980,692, and the average

5	to a Houſe, as at *Norwich*,	the total is	4,903,460
5	——— as at *Leeds*,	———	4,903,460
$4\frac{4}{5}$	——— as at *Oxford*,	———	4,717,320
$4\frac{4}{5}$	——— as at *Wolverhampton*,	———	4,717,320
$5\frac{3}{4}$	——— as at *Birmingham*,	———	5,638,979
$5\frac{3}{4}$	——— as at *Coventry*,	———	5,638,979
$4\frac{1}{3}$	——— as at *Shrewſbury*,	———	4,249,665
$4\frac{1}{3}$	——— as at *Holy Croſs*,	———	4,249,665
$4\frac{3}{4}$	——— as at *Northampton*,	———	4,658,287
$4\frac{3}{4}$	——— as at *Mancheſter*,	———	4,658,287
$4\frac{3}{4}$	——— as at *Liverpool*,	———	4,658,287
4	——— as at *Ackworth*,	———	3,922,768
4	——— as at *Newbury*,	———	3,922,768
4	——— as at *Speen*,	———	3,922,768
$4\frac{1}{2}$	——— as at *Calne*,	———	4,413,114
$4\frac{1}{7}$	——— as at *Altringham*,	———	4,062,867
$4\frac{5}{6}$	——— as at *St. M Cheſter*,	———	4,740,008
Average,	-	-	4,587,000

At *Oxford*, the Colleges are rejected—at *Ackworth*, the Hospital—and at *Calne*, the Poor-house: These omissions are named, nor have we any information that similar deductions are not elsewhere used. But upon what principles can such a calculation be made? As the application of the facts is to know the general average not *per* family, but *per* house, the largest seminaries of people ought to be included, or the result cannot come near the truth. This is so apparent, that it must strike every one at first sight. Yet does Dr. *Price determine* the general number by the average of the particulars, after all such buildings are rejected. So that a house with a family of ten, two of whom are at college, is called eight, yet the college no where included—And the same with hospitals, poor-houses, &c. This is such a method of calculating as I cannot comprehend—for in it 2 and 2 do not make 4

No parish at *London* is included, where the numbers *per* house must certainly be more considerable, though perhaps more than a tenth of the total are there*. No place in which any great nobleman or rich commoner resides—What allowance is made for all the body of seamen? the army, which in 1759 was above 100,000, also the men fought off by the war, but which peace soon recruits? The number taken *per* house of only one family, we find 4,587,000. To these are to be added the superiority of *London* and

 its

* It deserves notice, that Dr *Price* procured an account of part of *Pancras* parish, wherein the numbers are above seven to a house, which is explained away by saying many were lodgers

Within the Bills there were in 1737, 95,968 houses, *Pancras* and *Marybone* not included, call it only 100,000, and if they are classed in whatever probable manner you may fix on, the number will turn out greater than the Doctor's idea

20,000	at	12	———	240,000
20,000	at	10	———	200,000
20,000	at	8	———	160,000
20,000	at	6	———	120,000
20,000	at	5	———	100,000
				820,000

its environs to $4\frac{1}{2}$ *per* house, the inhabitants of all colleges, schools, hospitals, poor-houses, and prisons; all soldiers and seamen, all persons without settled habitations, &c. You are farther to add the deficiences in the list of houses, which *cannot* exceed, and which *may* fall short, as we know it does, and reckon for these the *real* average *per* house. And when all these circumstances are considered, the reader, it is apprehended, will not approve of the positive expression used by our author "Four millions and a half are *probably* too large an allowance, five millions *certainly* so" (Page 60 of *Supplement.*) To what purpose such an assertion can be ventured, unsupported by facts, unless to convince the world that *the nation is ruined*, I know not.

As to the number of individuals *per family*, it is in this enquiry useless, unless it was proved that every house contains but one, which is impossible to prove. But I should be glad to know, whether an hospital, a prison, a college, a school, &c. were reckoned as families? The author takes no notice (except in the case of *Leeds)* of the difference between *house* and *family*, so that we have no certain satisfaction on this head.

Lastly, Sir, I come to the cause of this imaginary depopulation, which the Doctor attributes chiefly to *engrossing farms* I will offer no *reasons* in support of that which I have already *proved.* From a comparison of the population of 250 farms, containing more than seventy thousand acres, I have shewn that farms of above 500 acres are in population superior to smaller ones, as $8\frac{1}{4}$ to $6\frac{1}{2}$ (*Six Months Tour*, vol iv. p 192, 251, 253, 267) I will change my opinion when a longer list, taken with more care and impartiality, is produced, that proves a contrary fact And I have there given the reasons why it is impossible the fact should be otherwise.

Attributing the high price of provisions (*Supplement*, p 19) to any causes that can be remedied by government, must have an extreme bad effect on the

minds

minds of the people, it is like all we hear about jobbers, badgers, foreſtallers, &c. It is a miſtake to ſuppoſe, that large farms can have any ſuch effects, unleſs the ſoil, when well cultivated, yields leſs food than when full of beggary and weeds.

The Doctor from M. *Muret* ſpeaks alſo of laying arable lands to graſs, as a cauſe of depopulation. This has nothing to do with the ſize of farms. This *Swiſs* writer ſpeaks alſo of engroſſing farms; but the author ſhould recollect an eſſential difference between *England* and *Switzerland* in this reſpect. In the latter, the ſmall farms M *Muret* ſpeaks of, are generally ſmall eſtates, that is, the property of the farmer I find this in almoſt every page of the *Berne Memoires*, but this is a direct exception to ſmall farms. It is poſſible (but this again is a point which wants proof) that ſmall farms *in property*, may be favourable to population, for the farmer may afford a much better culture than that miſerable one univerſally ſeen on them when rent is paid.

No part of this ſubject will admit of general, random aſſertions, exceptions muſt be made, or a writer can only miſlead.

If the prices of proviſions be high, it muſt be owing to the cheapneſs of money, or a natural ſcarcity, but the people never recur to natural cauſes, they always dreſs up a phantom among their neighbours, and call it jobber, badger, butcher, or what not, to whom they attribute every evil under the ſun. But who will be ſo hardy as to aſſert that proviſions are dear? What do you mean by dearneſs? Would you have wheat at the ſame price when a kingdom has thirty millions of ſpecie as when it had but twenty, or when it has twenty, the ſame as when it had ten? Before you talk of the comparative dearneſs of two periods, prove to me, that the quantity of ſpecie in both is equal. For want of attending to this circumſtance, the people are blown up into diſcontent, by writings which cannot poſſibly have any good effect. If my commodity is wheat, and I pay for moſt of my conſumption double the price of 80 years ago (and juſtly too, owing to the different value of money) ought I not to receive double the price for my wheat?

But the truth is, the prices of commodities muſt always vary according to the variations of *demand* for them, and the *quantity* that is brought to market to anſwer that demand. If the people either increaſe in number, or conſume more, or a better ſort of food than formerly, in either caſe the demand increaſes and prices muſt riſe. If on the contrary, the demand continues the ſame, but the quantity is leſs, the ſame effect muſt follow. If the people decreaſe, or eat leſs, or a worſe ſort of food than formerly, and the ſame quantity is brought to market, then prices muſt certainly fall. In all which caſes, whatever is found to be the price of a commodity, OUGHT TO BE the price of that commodity, ſince it is evidently regulated by the variations in the demand, and the quantity which ſupplies it. Nothing, therefore, can be more pernicious, and at the ſame time futile, than to attempt to regulate that by laws, rules, ſtatutes, and proclamations, which regulates itſelf by the vibrations in the market. And I do not comprehend, how a country can greatly increaſe in wealth, through induſtry, without the *quantity of wealth* having a conſiderable effect in theſe vibrations. (*But for a contrary opinion, ſee Sir James Steuart*, vol. 1. p. 394).

To return to population—I have lately taken great pains in procuring liſts for ſatisfying me on this head. —I ſhall continue to collect them, and doubt not being able to convince the publick, as far as any authority, except directly numbering the people, will allow, that the numbers, ſo far from declining, advance conſiderably; which may be ſeen by the great increaſe of births in very many places ſince the Reſtauration. The gentleman I mentioned above has made ſimilar reſearches, and the event is with him univerſally the ſame. Dr. *Price*, though he has been ſo converſant in ſuch regiſters, takes not the leaſt notice of this, from which I conjecture, that he alſo might find it thus.

But whether the people are increaſing or not, it is certainly of high importance to know the real and the whole truth, this can only be gained by numbering them I publiſhed laſt year, *Propoſals to the Legiſlature*, for that purpoſe, and ſince opinions ſtill continue ſo contrary, the neceſſity of that meaſure is greater than ever

It is my being an enemy to all writings that can increaſe the groundleſs diſcontents of the people concerning the rates of proviſions, &c. or convert into the melancholy proſpect of a ruined nation the unparalleled proſperity of this great and populous kingdom, that has urged me, Sir, to trouble you with this letter, and by no means a fondneſs for contradiction: I honour the abilities of the author from whoſe opinion in one point I differ, and my aim, believe me, is nothing but the acquiſition of real facts.

I am, Sir, your's, &c

ARTHUR YOUNG.

North Mims, March 28, 1772.

NUMBER V.

Law of Settlements.—Page 95.

SINCE the above paſſage was written, a bill has been brought into parliament, and is now under conſideration, to prevent unneceſſary and vexatious removals of the poor I have read this bill, and been preſent at the debates that happened on its progreſs, and I am induced to add a remark or two on the propoſition, becauſe, to find fault with our laws as I have done in the above paſſage, and to take no notice of a propoſed amendment, might be thought an inattention.

The

The argument ſhould, I think, go principally to this point To remove the POLITICAL evil, incurring as ſmall a PRIVATE inconvenience as poſſible. So great an object cannot be acquired without hazarding ſome inconveniences, but in queſtions of this ſort, it ought to be an eternal rule, at the ſame time that you look at the inconvenience, to view alſo the benefit. Compare them, and then draw your concluſion. That it is an object of vaſt importance, no body can doubt, the preſent laws are cruel, injudicious, unpolitical, and pernicious To tie a man down to a ſpot where his legal ſettlement may be, and cut off that natural liberty of mankind of moving where he pleaſes, is certainly a cruel law, and in its nature, a direct effort of tyranny, for the effect is ſlavery —To ſuppoſe that the expenditure of the poor rates, is the price at which this right to tyrannize is purchaſed, appears very erroneous, for the evil falls where the benefit never comes—nor is the latter, individually taken, the conſequence of the former. Yet if the one was to be ſuppoſed the price of the other, both will be acknowledged the effects of mere power—you chuſe to inflict an unnatural reſtriction, you chuſe to give a benefit—but both are the efforts of your power It is therefore impoſſible to ſay, with any propriety, that the maintenance of the poor in their age ſhould be conſidered as a ſufficient compenſation for the ſlavery of their youth.

But the ſtriking light in which the buſineſs ſhould be viewed, is that of a POLITICAL evil. In this reſpect the obſervations I made at the paſſage referred from, are ſuch as I ſee no reaſon to change; the cauſes of population in this country are ſo powerful, that we do not feel the effects of contrary cauſes, but that they exiſt, no one can doubt, in the laws of ſettlements And if population was out of the queſtion, the effect on the general aggregate of induſtry, ought alone to evince their abſurdity. The preventing a man from living in the place where he thinks he can beſt maintain himſelf and family, and forcing him

him to ſtay where he finds that he cannot, is ſuch an abominable ſyſtem, that to attempt to eſtabliſh its abſurdity is almoſt an affront to common ſenſe. In ſhort, the firſt principles of the propoſition are ſound, and founded upon the moſt immutable laws of nature and policy.

The only queſtion is, how will you get rid of the evil? Will you make the poor the judges of the propriety of their own removals—or will you lodge that truſt in juſtices of the peace, by giving them a power of refuſing certificates? The latter propoſition appears to be one of thoſe palliatives, which plaiſters over an evil, but can never effect a radical cure. Such a truſt ought to be lodged in no man—much leſs in a juſtice, who living, perhaps, in the neighbourhood of the man who aſks a certificate, and who wants, poſſibly, to remove into a pariſh where the juſtice has an eſtate, is refuſed, leſt that burthen ſhould be the conſequence which, at preſent, people have ſuch an idea of. Gentlemen of fortune who perhaps ſit in parliament, and know the liberal principles which actuate their brother members, may be too apt to ſuppoſe that juſtices in general act upon ſuch principles—but he muſt be a poor obſerver that is not ſenſible, very many of the tribe deſerve no ſuch idea—merit no ſuch truſt—and ought not to be confided in for acting contrary to what they think their intereſt.

A propoſition was made, that the perſon wanting to remove ſhould bring proof before the juſtice, that he cannot get employment—but this would be open to ſuch horrid abuſes and impoſition as would totally defeat the ends of the bill, ſince nothing would be eaſier than to prove, that the man might have employment at home, and by that means kept from moving, though his ſtay at home be under the moſt oppreſſive circumſtances

The great objection made to the bill, was the idea that it would encourage vagrancy and frivolous removals, increaſe litigations, and raiſe poor rates. I ſhould not have any great ſcruples at recommending

mending the meaſure, even if all theſe evils were proved deciſively to flow from it Becauſe it is much better to incur ſuch inconveniencies, than to continue in a ſyſtem ſubverſive of the firſt principles of policy. But this conception is out of the queſtion for—*firſt*, the bill abſolutely excepts vagrants and other delinquents. *Secondly*, removals being frivolous, that is, the reaſon for them not ſufficient, is a contingency that muſt depend on individuals exerting their natural right in any point of conduct whatever. The poor muſt remove at their peril, if they find themſelves miſtaken in their expectations, and cannot find the employment they looked for at one place, they will ſeek it at another, but to ſuppoſe they will take up their reſidence where work is not to be had, is an idle idea, and when they become chargeable, then the old law comes again into play, and they are removed It is impoſſible to attain the good looked for from this bill, without the attendant evil of many removals being injudicious—but it would be a moſt tyrannical ſyſtem to reject the exertion of this natural and political liberty, becauſe that liberty, like all good things, *may* be abuſed.

Reſpecting the increaſe of litigation, it is very difficult to gather this conſequence from the meaſure:—at preſent every man may be removed that ſettles where he has not a legal ſettlement or a certificate, and removals are common every where, and every day: how diſputes can increaſe from cutting away five ſixths of the opportunities of removing, does not appear to me. Whether a man is chargeable or not, litigations from removals now are common—But if this bill paſſes, the removals can only take place after being chargeable, thus the removal orders are leſſened, ſurely, therefore, the litigations muſt leſſen with them

As to poor rates increaſing from this meaſure, it is the ſtrangeſt aſſertion that any man could well make. Enabling the induſtrious poor to ſettle where their induſtry can be exerted to the beſt effect, is

indiſ-

indisputably a premium upon that industry, and how an encouragement of that sort should impoverish them to such a degree as to raise the poor rates for their support, is a contradiction in terms. Nor can I see how the granting this liberty to the industrious can fail of proving beneficial to their industry, how many are the instances wherein men are tied down to the profit of their own labour, without being able to make any advantage of that of numerous families, from the want of power to move where a more general demand exists! How many others wherein a man is forced by those cruel laws to support his family upon eight or nine shillings a week, when by a removal, he might with equal ease earn near twice the money in a different calling! How many instances of ploughmen being sent, from mere suspicion of becoming chargeable, to places where weavers only are wanted—weavers being packed away to coal-pits, and colliers sent to fishing towns. Is this rational? And will any man give the idleness of his imagination so much play as to indulge such inconsistencies as asserting, that such a conduct is judicious, and a means of enabling the poor so to support themselves, as to prevent rates from increasing!

One word more as to population—Is it a rational system to keep industrious workmen from filling empty houses? To keep industrious men and women from marrying, and becoming the parents of an industrious progeny? Does not such a conduct effectually operate against the population, the wealth and the happiness of the kingdom? But do your work effectually, and repeal that ill judged law which prevents any cottage being built without four acres of land annexed to it.

NUMBER VI

Observations on the Register Act —*Note, page* 144.

To the Printer *of the* ST. JAMES's CHRONICLE.

SIR,

HAVING just received intelligence that a motion was very soon to be made in the House of Commons, for the repeal of the act for registering the price of corn, I think there will be no impropriety in examining the principles upon which such a proposition can be made, that if those principles are cogent enough to satisfy the people of the expediency of the measure, we may applaud the idea, and, on the contrary, condemn it in case they are found nugatory and insufficient

It is near two years since the average prices of corn have been laid before the public by authority of parliament. This has been a period sufficient for the consideration of all objections to such a publication, and it has also been sufficient for the friends of it to reflect on the advantages which they suppose may flow from it. I shall begin with the former, and enquire into the force and validity of those objections which have come to my knowledge.

It is in the first place asserted, that publishing the price of corn has this ill effect It dissatishes the farmers in the eastern counties, upon their finding that corn is so much cheaper there than in the west of *England*, the consequence of which is, inducing them to raise the price.

Those who found their objections upon this plea, must be very ignorant of the nature of the corn trade, and also of the common effect of such knowledge. That the farmers in one part of the kingdom would wish to have their corn as dear as in any other part, I readily allow, but I utterly deny that they can possibly realize their wishes, and because they want it dearer,

dearer, make it ſo. Who can be ſo weak as to imagine, that the low price in the eaſt is owing to the moderation of the farmers, or the high rate of the weſt to their avarice? Corn is cheap in the eaſtern counties becauſe ſo much is raiſed; they are, properly ſpeaking, corn counties, the *demand* likewiſe is leſs, for want of manufactures, *Norwich* being the only capital manufacturing place in all the eaſtern part of the kingdom. It is dear in the weſt, becauſe their lands are more generally graſs, and becauſe their demand is greater; owing to the immenſe manufactures there carried on.

Theſe are the reaſons for the difference, Sir, and by no means the wiſhes and avarice of farmers, or their poſſeſſing a knowledge of the prices in the different parts of the kingdom. If this cauſe of high prices, (*viz.* the proportion between the price and the quantity raiſed) was better conſidered, we ſhould not ſee the Houſe of Commons buſying themſelves ſo long in counteracting or remedying the decrees of providence

But the idea of keeping the kingdom ignorant of the truth, is founded on the ſame principles as the old injunction in *France* of tranſporting corn from one province to another They would not ſuffer it to be ſent from *Normandy* to *Brittany*, leſt the former ſhould want it and pay too dear at home, and we have ſome politicians who are not for letting the farmers in *Norfolk* and *Suffolk* know how dear corn is in *Warwick* and *Staffordſhire*, leſt they ſhould ſtop the ſale and make it ſtill dearer. This is all abſurdity On the contrary, take every meaſure to let them know this fact let the farmers, factors, and dealers, know how dear it is in certain counties; they will only be ſo much the quicker in ſending corn to ſo good a market, the conſequence of which is to ſink it, and reduce the price the nearer to that general level at which it ought to be throughout the kingdom. Were it poſſible to keep one part quite ignorant of the price in the other, can there be any doubt but the diſproportion would be vaſtly greater?

How is a demand to be supplied, if the existence of it is not known?

But, Sir, we may grant the truth of this preposterous position, and yet these gentlemen will be never the nearer their mark, for granting that the eastern counties knowing corn to be so much dearer in the western ones, should enable them to raise the price, I reply, that upon the same principles this knowledge among the western *consumers* would be equally powerful in making it cheaper. The same register which tells the east that corn is dearer in the west, likewise tells the west that it is *cheaper* in the east, and why should not such knowledge as well enable them to lower their own prices, as to allow the other part of the kingdom to raise theirs? A *Norfolk* farmer says to a consumer, *I will not sell my wheat at 5 s. You see it is 7 s in* Warwickshire. *Why are we to sell cheaper?* This is the argument. Surely the consumer at *Warwick* may as well say to the farmer, *I will not give you 7 s for your wheat, you see it is only 5 s in* Norfolk, and he may add, *if you will not take the same, I will go to the importer* This, I think, is sufficient to shew the fallacy of such an argument.

In the second place, the enemies of the registry bill assert, that it does not give the prices of corn, on the contrary, that it gives false prices, and therefore had better give none

This is an objection I have often heard in conversation, and as often answered, by observing that *the price of corn at market*, spoken in a general way, is not the price of some fine sample which Mr. *this* or Mr. *that* sells at, but the average of the market, that is to say, if all the wheat sold at market was thrown into one heap, the price of a sample taken from that heap would be the average price of the market Nor is the price that of the customary bushel, which varies greatly, but of the Winchester measure

Whenever these circumstances are duly attended to, the prices published by Mr *Cook* will be found the true

true average prices of the market. I have examined them ſince the firſt publication, and I find ſuch a conſiſtency throughout them, that it is impoſſible there ſhould be any material errors in the account

Theſe are the only objections I have heard which ſeem to carry any weight; others there are, but too trivial to deſerve an anſwer. As ſuch objections have been thought ſufficiently ſtrong to found on them a motion for a repeal, I ſhall take the liberty to examine the contrary ſide of the queſtion, and ſee if no good reſults from the publication.

It has at one ſtroke overturned the lying reports which uſed to be circulated of the high price of corn. When the world was ignorant of the truth, every man quoted that price which was convenient to his argument, and 8, 9, and 10 *s.* a buſhel were not unfrequently heard of, when no ſuch price fairly exiſted.

When a man had a mind to harangue on the price of wheat, he told us that ſuch a neighbour of his ſold at ſo and ſo, not adding that his corn was the fineſt ſample in the market, and another juſt arrived from a diſtance, lifting up his hands and eyes at the miſery of the poor, uſed to tell us, that wheat at ſuch a place was 9 *s* a buſhel, forgetting at the ſame time to inform us, that the meaſure was 11 or 12 gallons and yet, on ſuch vague intelligence were the ideas of people on this important point founded! Before this act paſſed, parliament and the miniſtry were buſied in remedying evils that never exiſted; and all the information they could gain of prices was from factors and dealers, who could never be unintereſted in their opinion Now the caſe is changed, and they have every day much better authority before their eyes than that of all the dealers in *Britain*, authority particularly valuable, becauſe it is *diſintereſted.*

It is almoſt incredible that there ſhould be any men ſo totally blind as to delight in darkneſs, and becauſe they cannot or will not ſee themſelves, urge the propriety of hoodwinking all the rest of the nation Till this act passed, we never fairly knew what was the price of corn, and every measure of the corn trade was transacted in the dark. Our knowledge of this branch of national œconomy would now be wonderfully different from what it is, if we had similar registers from *James* the first's reign, such would be abundantly more satisfactory than the *Windsor* prices of the *best* wheat, and in only *one* market of the kingdom This part of our domestic policy would then have been long ago understood, and instead of volumes of conjectures, we should have had tables of facts.

The regular publication of the price of corn tends more strongly than any other measure to prevent its being extravagantly dear in certain counties, because the knowledge of such an evil is the immediate occasion of a remedy It enables the nation to judge rationally of exportation and the common means of collecting the prices will, by degrees, familiarize the officers through whose hands the business goes, to be accurate and careful in the business, to a degree of which we do not at present think, a circumstance which may in future prove of no slight consequence to quite different views

If any person proved to me (which, by the way, is impossible) that the prices published were not absolutely accurate, I should still be of the same opinion: If the authority is not good, give me better Who will assert, that a more exact knowledge of the price of corn may not be gained from the tables than from the random impertinence of conversation, from the assertions of dealers and factors, from the reports of travellers, and from the lying tales of boasting gentlemen farmers, who, to give you an opinion of their husbandry, talk of prices which have as much to do with the national concern, as prices at *Jericho*? If the register bill gives us not this, I will agree in its condemnation

It is for these and other reasons, Sir, that I cannot but esteem this act as the most valuable in corn affairs (next to the general prohibitions of the import of foreign corn, and the bounty act) that ever paſſed the legiſlature of this kingdom, and, as ſuch, moſt heartily wiſh, that inſtead of its repeal, I may ſee its perpetuity

The Houſe of Commons, I ſee, is much employed in endeavouring to lower the price of proviſions. As far as gaining intelligence goes, they will do good; for the knowledge of facts can never have any other tendency. But by facts I do not mean ſuch random aſſertions, calculations, and opinions, as I have ſeen in the papers among the evidences they have received, ſome of which, whether true or falſe, are little to the purpoſe in point, they may receive much more ſuch, and at laſt find that parliament is unable to cope with nature; and that the effect of much money or bad crops is not to be remedied Opening the ports is a meaſure that pleaſes the people, but *England* will not be fed by imports from countries where wheat is much dearer than with her. Our poor rioted laſt year becauſe they paid ſeven farthings a pound for bread, while their brethren in *Holland* eat it at four-pence and four-pence farthing In ſome parts of *France* it was five-pence, in *Switzerland* ſix-pence, and in *Germany*, barley, beans, horſe-dung, and the bark of trees, formed the bread eaten by the poor, through a conſiderable part of laſt ſummer A fact I have from good authority Had it not been for the encouragement agriculture has received in this kingdom, our poor might have been in the ſame predicament, and if parliament is zealous in lowering prices, it muſt be done by the ſame means. Let them take means to bring into culture ten millions of our waſte acres a ſingle vote to raiſe fifty thouſand pounds to begin ſuch a work, would at one ſtroke do more than all the nonſenſe that will be talked, or all the acts that will be paſſed, for two months to come.

There never was a ſcarcity of corn in any country that was remedied by meaſures taken after ſuch ſcarcity was felt, an hundred proofs of this will occur at once to thoſe who are in the leaſt converſant in the corn history of *Europe*; even attempts to effect it have proved mischievous, in alarming the people; for they are apt to thing a scarcity much greater than it is when they see government employed in reducing it, and an alarm of this nature never spreads without prices rising much beyond the proportion of the real defect in the crop. Nothing can be more pernicious than addressing parliament to do impossibilities, unless it be parliment's undertaking them, and, for the sake of quieting the minds of the foolish part of the people, acting as if it thought the evil to be remedied; the consequence of which is, leaving the mischief much greater than it was found. While the house is busied upon provisions, the poor will be quiet, but when they find nothing done, they will not be persuaded that nothing could be done, and then they will riot, and pull down graineries, and burn barns full of corn, in order to make wheat cheap.

The measures to be taken to remedy the scarcity, are such as are applicable to any period first, gain a knowledge of useful facts, in which the publication of the prices of corn stands foremost; and, secondly, sink the future prices by increasing the quantity raised, which can only be effected by bringing our immense wastes into culture

Excuse, Sir, the incorrectness of this letter, which is written immediately on receiving intelligence of the motion for repealing an act, the good effects of which are every day felt I am called away to the care of a few fields, in which I endeavour to produce more corn than they produced before; and this, I think, is the way to make wheat cheap.

I am, Sir, your's, &c

ARTHUR YOUNG.

North-Mims, Dec 14, 1772.

P. S. Corn Dealers, I can easily believe, may be against the act in question, for such an open and numerous publication can little suit the purposes of private interests, which are peculiarly answered by the [illegible] in general being ignorant, and the dealers [illegible] the [illegible] knowledge to be found.

NUMBER VII.

Smallneſs of Sums voted for National Improvements.—Page 171.

THE following paper of the expences of government from the revolution to the ſeventh year of his preſent majeſty, I drew up ſome years ago with a different view, but I inſert it at preſent to ſhew in compariſon the attention that has been given by our legiſlature to the demands of war, and the arts of peace

		£.
Expences of the revolution, -		1,020,000
Navy, - - -	140,743,623	
Army, - -	166,551,041	
Sundries, - -	23,273,795	
Subſidies, - -	13,404,204	
Eaſt *India* company, for military force,	120,000	
Enemies' depredations	285,075	
Total war and its conſequences, -		344,377,738
Foundling hoſpital, -	418,527	
Public buildings, -	691,200	
Britiſh muſeum, -	36,000	
Streets and roads, -	66,500	
Rye harbour, - -	23,363	
Longitude, - -	5,000	
Land carriage fiſh ſcheme,	* 2,500	
Priſons, - - - -	20,800	
Total public works and uſeful eſtabliſhments,	- -	1,266,890

 Colo-

* This article was meant well, and therefore I have inſerted it, but certainly it was a moſt futile trifling affair. A premium to ſupply the tables of people of fortune had it been deſigned for the poor, it would have been confined to ſprats and herring.

Colonies, - -	908,615	
Survey of *America*, -	5,203	
Manufactures, - -	14,000	
Pot-aſh, - - -	3,000	
African ſettlements and trade,	546,715	
Total colonies, trade, and manufactures,	- -	1,477,533
Sufferers by the earthquake at *Liſbon*, -	100,000	
Ditto, by fire at *Charles Town*,	20,000	
French proteſtants, -	13,000	
Mrs *Stephens*'s medicines,	5,000	
Total charities and gratuities,	- -	138,000
Capt *Cornwall*'s monument,	3,000	
To Sir *Wm. Johnſon*, -	5,000	
Total rewards for bravery exerted in the ſervice of the public,	-	8,000
Coinage,	887,655	
Burning infected ſhips,	23,935	
Caſh ſtole, - -	4,191	
Loſt by an agent, -	8,715	
Maſters in Chancery,	11,485	
Mr *Lowndes*'s mortgage,	1,280	
Jekil's legatees, -	13 582	
Rebels and forfeited eſtates,	158,753	
Heretable juriſdiction,	152,037	
Union tolls, - -	7,641	
Journals - -	7,278	
Expences of law, -	372,050	
Sundry articles, - -		1,648,602
Expences of the court, - - -		56,936,733
Intereſt of debts, - - -		170,298,551
General total, being the amount of all the money raiſed on the ſubject for the public ſervice during 79 years,		577,172,047
General medium *per annum*,	7 305,988	

In

In the following ſpecification the intereſt of the debt is divided among the above articles, in the exact proportion between them and the whole amount.

Revolution, - - -		£. 1,438,581
War.		
Navy, - -	202,813,683	
Army, - -	233,969,431	
Sundries, - -	32,500,602	
Subſidies, - -	18,604,604	
Eaſt *India* company, and depredations,	540,204	
		488,428,524
Public works, - - -		1,790,760
Colonies, trade, &c. - - -		2,105,433
Charities and gratuities, - - -		195,200
Rewards of bravery, - - -		11,300
Sundry articles, - - - - -		2,336,602
The court, - - - - -		80,865,647
		£. 577,172,047

If we ſuppoſe the total 20, the parts will then be,

Revolution, - - - - -		$0\frac{1}{21}$
War.		
Navy, - - - - -	$7\frac{13}{38}$	
Army, - - - - -	8	
Sundries, - - -	$1\frac{68}{387}$	
Sudſidies, - - -	$0\frac{1}{2}$	
Eaſt *India* co. &c. - -	$0\frac{1}{32}$	
		$17\frac{695}{587172}$
Public works, - - - - -		$0\frac{1}{17}$
Colonies, &c. - - - - -		$0\frac{1}{15}$
Charities, &c - - - - -		$0\frac{1}{160}$
Rewards, - - - - - -		$0\frac{1}{2700}$
Sundries, - - - - -		$0\frac{1}{13}$
The court, - - - - -		$2\frac{430}{587}$

This ſtate of the expenditure of the public money ought to ſilence the anſwers which are uſually given to propoſitions for ſmall ſums being voted as an encouragement to that part of agriculture which evidently

dently wants it, from the lands remaining in the same state of waste and desolation that has disgraced the kingdom for a thousand years While the national wealth is dissipated by millions in military projects, why refuse a few thousands for the solid advantages of cultivation to the wastes—industry to the people—popularity to the minister—and fame to the monarch?

I have classed the Foundling Hospital rather as it was intended, than from its effect. If the principles of population explained in the preceeding pages be well considered, I apprehend it will be thought that the policy of establishing hospitals for foundlings is contrary to those principles It is encouraging that vicious population which cannot support itself You save many lives, it is said, but the very saving these lives must have the effect of starving other people. The thing wanted is not people, but employment; if you increase employment with the foundlings, you do good, but the increase of employment alone would have the same effect in a much better way. You assert, that you bring up many people, who would otherwise have died in the cottages, and encourage the increase of children by rendering them no burthen to their parents But why are they a burthen? Why do they not increase? Because there is no demand for them. They would increase fast enough if you employed them and your taking these children, bringing them up, and fixing them elsewhere, is (like naturalizing foreigners) only starving those with whose labour they come into competition, and consequently destroying with one hand as many as you rear with another This ought to convince us that all measures, taken professedly with a view to encourage population, are nugatory and idle, and that the only possible means of doing it is by increasing regular employment

But there is another circumstance which has rendered our foundling hospital pernicious This is the irregularity of its support, the progressive grants of parliament gave a great encouragement to that ſort of increaſe I mentioned above, and then comes a ſudden ſtop. What could be the conſequence of this, but great diſtreſs among thoſe people who had entered into procreation of ſome ſort or other under the idea of their ſurplus being taken off by the hoſpital? the ſudden ſtagnation of this demand muſt have juſt ſuch effects as the ſudden decline of a manufacture—doing more miſchief to population than it could before have done good

This four hundred thouſand pounds I conſider, therefore, as thrown away but ſuppoſing it had been laid out progreſſively in bringing into cultivation our moors,—this would have anſwered the deſign moſt effectually, for the increaſe of employment would have increaſed the people, without taking the bread from any one, or throwing the leaſt difficulty on the increaſe of other places. at the ſame time that this was effected, the whole progreſs of the expenditure would have added to the national income and wealth, and thereby have become a new cauſe of farther populouſneſs. WHEN WILL THERE ARISE A MINISTER WITH SPIRIT AND PATRIOTISM SUFFICIENT TO INDUCE HIM TO LET ONE POOR TWENTY THOUSAND POUNDS FOR WASTE LANDS APPEAR, IN THE LONG GRANT OF SO MANY HUNDRED MILLIONS!

NUMBER VIII.

Price of Flour in America.—*Page* 282.

IT will appear from the following table of the prices of flour in *America*, that the idea of the colonists not being able to rival the farmers of this country in their own markets, is a very false notion.

New York.

Flour	£	s	d
March, 1760, at 17*s*. 6*d* *per* Cwt		17	6
Cask, contain 2 Cwt		1	0
Insurance, weighing and carting, at 4*d* *per* cask,		0	2
Currency, -		18	8
Exchange at 165, is sterling, -		11	$3\frac{3}{4}$
Commission, -		0	$6\frac{3}{4}$
		11	$10\frac{1}{2}$
1760, *April*, —		18	0
May, —		18	0
June, —		18	0
July, —		17	9
Sept. —		18	0
Oct —		18	3
Dec. —		18	0
1761, *May*, —		18	0
Aug —		16	0
Nov. —		17	0
1762, *Feb* —		18	0
March, —		18	0
May, —		18	6
Sept.	1	2	0
Oct -	1	3	3
1763, *Jan* -	1	4	0
Feb -	1	2	0
March,	1	1	0

Philadelphia.

Flour.	s.	d.
March, 1760, at 15*s* 6*d* *per* Cwt	15	6
Cask, containing 2 Cwt 2*s* 4*d* $\frac{1}{2}$,	1	$2\frac{1}{4}$
Commission on 16*s* 8*d*. $\frac{1}{4}$, at 5 *per cent.*	0	10
Currency, -	17	$6\frac{1}{4}$
Exchange at 154, is sterling, -	11	$4\frac{1}{2}$
1760, *April*, —	16	8
May, —	15	9
June, —	15	3
July, —	15	3
Sept —	15	0
Oct —	15	3
Nov. —	15	9
1761, *March*, —	15	0
April, —	14	6
June, —	14	10
Aug —	15	0
Sept. —	15	3
Oct —	16	6
1762, *Jan* —	15	9
Feb —	16	0
March, —	16	0
April, —	16	0
Oct. —	17	9

New-York		s	d
	April, —	17	0
	May, —	18	6
	June, —	18	9
	July, —	17	6
	Aug —	17	9
	Sept. —	17	0
	Oct. —	16	0
	Nov. —	15	3
1764,	*May,* —	14	6
	June, —	12	6
	July, —	13	0
	Aug —	13	9
	Sept. —	14	0
1765,	*Feb.* —	13	3
	March, —	12	6
	April, —	13	3
	May, —	14	0
	June, —	15	0
	Aug —	16	0
	Nov. —	15	6
	Dec —	14	6
1766,	*Jan* —	15	6
	June, —	16	0
	July, —	16	0
	Sept —	16	0
1767,	*Feb* —	19	0
	April, —	19	0
	May, —	18	0
	June, —	18	0
	July, —	19	6
	Aug £. 1	0	6
	Sept. — 1	0	6
	Dec —	19	6
1768,	*March,* —	19	6
	May, —	19	0

Philadelphia		s.	d.
1763,	*May,* —	16	0
	June, —	15	8
1764,	*June,* —	12	0
	Sept. —	13	0
	Oct —	12	10
	Nov. —	15	3
1765,	*April,* —	12	9
	May, —	12	6
	June, —	13	8
1767,	*July,* —	19	0
1768,	*May,* —	17	4

From this table it appears, that fine flour sold there sometimes at from 12*s* to 16*s* *per* cwt. and generally at 15*s*. to 18*s*. currency, which is from 7*s*. 6*d*. to 10*s* and from 9*s*. to 11*s* sterling *per* cwt Say on a general average 9*s*. for that which is equal to three bushels good wheat.

NUMBER IX.

Effect of Compound Interest in payment of the National Debt.—Page 299.

THE effect of compound interest as given by Dr *Price* suggests, I must own, to me a different idea from that of easing the nation of taxes which are no burthen to it I should rather apply it to establishing a fund for increasing the revenues of the nation in future, in order to enable the government to expend considerable sums in the encouragement of agriculture, manufactures and commerce.

It is evident from the Doctor's tables, that a moderate annual appropriation to sinking debts might be made the means in future of commanding the greatest sums of money.

Let us suppose the scheme adopted in 1774, and six hundred thousand pounds a year applied inviolably to the extinction of debt, which we will suppose to bear 5 *per cent.* interest, and let us call our present debt 130,000,000*l* and suppose it increased in future as below.

Years		*Debt*	*Debt paid*	*Debt reduced to.*
1774,	——	£ 130,000,000	——	——
1784,	——	130 000,000	7,546,734	122,453,266
1789,	——	130,000,000		
	Suppose a war to have added	100,000,000		
		230,000,000	12,947,136	217,052,864
1804,	——	230,000 000	39,863,307	190,135,693
1824,	——	230,000,000	125,608,800	104,391,200
1844,	Twenty years encouragement of agriculture, manufactures, commerce and colonies, at 8 mill a year,	160,000,000		
		390,000,000	353,117,106	36,882,894
1861,	Seventeen years ditto, at 10 mill a year,	170,000,000		
	A war, &c.	264,855,094		
		824,855,094	824,855,094	——

Without attending to the minute accuracy of ſuch a calculation (ſomething of which ſort I wiſh the Doctor had given, to ſhew what might yet be done with the debt of this country) it appears from it that by means of applying only 600,000 *l* a year, which is not one-third of the ſinking fund, we might ſafely continue to run in debt for ever, but ſuppoſe for 87 years longer, during which period we might expend in war above 364 millions; and in cultivating the arts of peace 310 millions, by means of which every uncultivated acre in the three kingdoms might be made equal to the moſt fertile ſoils, great bounties might be given on the export of manufactures, new colonies eſtabliſhed, and commerce extended, and at the end of the period, the nation might find itſelf without a penny of debt, and in poſſeſſion of an immenſe clear revenue. By this means, thoſe exertions in the arts of peace ſo neceſſary and important, and which are ſo much neglected in this country, might with eaſe be executed. To borrow at ſimple intereſt for theſe objects, while a fund for payment rolls on at compound intereſt, is making the higheſt advantage poſſible of the funding ſyſtem. inſtead of expending the eight and ten millions *per ann* in peace at the periods minuted, if a ſmaller ſum was begun with in 1774, and continued regularly through the 87 years (for inſtance near four millions) it would be the ſame thing in the payment, and every branch of the national induſtry ſo greatly encouraged, that all taxes would be abundantly more productive than at preſent, and render the intereſt of 217 millions, a weight not much heavier than 130,000,000 *l*. at preſent I have been induced to run into this perhaps wild note, to ſhew what may yet be done by a ſmall beginning. Dr. *Price* laments the paſt much more than he propoſes for the future if ſuch a plan was now begun, we ſhould have no reaſon to lament its not having been executed, and when once it is begun and really deſtined to its end, the more you borrow the

the better, for, it will discharge more than you can know what to do with, and after it has been operating some years, you may safely borrow any sums, as it will be difficult to run in debt so fast as your fund will pay.

NUMBER X.

Corn Laws.—Page 40.

THE corn laws of *Britain* being entirely changed by the late permanent act, which was brought in by Governor *Pownall*, it is necessary, for the information of foreigners, to give an abstract of that act, by which they will see what our present system is.

I. The act took place the first day of *January*, 1774.

II. When Wheat is above 48 *s. per* quarter,
Rye — above 32
Barley — above 34
Oats — above 18
all duties on importation to cease.

III. Instead of former duties, new ones laid of
6 *d per* quarter on wheat,
2 *per* cwt. on wheat flour,
3 *per* quarter on rye,
2 *per* quarter on barley,
2 *per* quarter on oats.
These duties designed to ascertain the quantities imported.

IV. When prices are such, that importation by this act is not allowed, wheat or wheat flour, rye, barley, or oats may be imported duty free, if immediately deposited in warehouses in the presence of the proper custom-house officer, and under the joint locks of the king and the importer The corn not to be taken out for home consumption till the duties are paid as if commonly imported. But for re-exportation,

tation, it may at any time be taken, a bond being given as security, that it shall not be landed in any part of *Britain*.

The design of this clause is, to enable merchants to carry on a trade in corn at a time when the prices here will not allow importation for home consumption.

V. When wheat is at or above 44 *s. per* quarter,

Rye	———	28,
Barley	———	22,
Oats	———	16,

exportation to cease; except

2500 qrs. to *Gibraltar*,
3500 qrs. to *Minorca*,
500 qrs. to *St Helena*,
5000 qrs. to *Guernsey* and *Jersey*,
2500 qrs. to *Isle of Man*.

VI. When the price of wheat is under 44 *s. per* qr.

Rye	———	28,
Barley	———	22,
Oats	———	16,

the following bounties shall be paid on exportation:

	s.	*d.*
For wheat - - -	5	0 *per* quarter,
For malt made of ditto	5	0,
For rye - -	3	0,
For barley - -	2	6,
For malt made of ditto	2	6,
For bear or bigg -	2	6,
For oats - -	2	0,
For oat-meal - -	2	6.

VII. Merchants re-exporting corn, which on importation paid duties, to have such duties repaid them.

NUMBER XI

Proportion between the price of meat and wheat. —Page 137.

FLEETWOOD quotes from *Stowe* another ſet of prices for the year 1533. A fat ox, 1*l.* 6*s* 8*d.* A fat wether, 3*s.* 4*d* A fat calf, 3*s* 4*d.* A fat lamb, 1*s* Wheat is not regiſtered, but the price of the year before is 8*s* 10*d.*

The ox is 24 buſhels.
The wether and calf, 3 buſhels.
The lamb, 1 buſhel.

Theſe at 6*s* 6*d.* are,

The ox, - -	£ 7	16	0
The wether and calf,	0	19	6
The lamb, - -	0	6	6

Which prices for ſuch cattle as the huſbandry of 240 years ago would ſupport, I conſider as high as any rates at preſent at *Smithfield.*

* * * *

There is an inexpreſſible difficulty in diſcovering the proportion between the prices of antient times and thoſe of the preſent. Till the 43d of *Elizabeth*, the coin varied perpetually, ſo that the number of grains of fine ſilver in the ſhilling vibrated between 20 and 264, the proportions between thoſe numbers and 86 mark the proportions between the ſhilling of that age and of this. Thus, when the writers of *Hen* VIII and *Ed* VI's time complain of the prices of all commodities riſing to *huge*, *immoderate*, and *exceſſive* prices, and attribute it to incloſures, we have the cleareſt evidence of their errors, by turning to the value of money; there we find that thoſe princes ſo debaſed their coin as to reduce the fine ſilver in the ſhillings down to 40 and even to 20 grains The immediate conſequence of which was, a prodigious con-

confusion in prices, which created an alarm that made most things rise greatly

For the better understanding antient prices, I shall here insert a table of the variations in our shillings.

One shilling contained of fine silver,

28	*Ed.* I	— 1300 —	264 grains.
18	*Ed* III.	— 1345 —	236
27	*Ed* III	— 1354 —	213
9	*Hen.* V.	— 1422 —	176
1	*Hen.* VI.	— 1422 —	142
4	*Hen* VI	— 1426 —	176
49	*Hen* VI.	— 1471 —	142
1	*Hen* VIII.	— 1509 —	118
34	*Hen.* VIII	— 1543 —	100
36	*Hen.* VIII	— 1545 —	60
37	*Hen* VIII	— 1546 —	40
3	*Ed* VI	— 1549 —	40
5	*Ed* VI	— 1551 —	20
6	*Ed* VI.	— 1552 —	88
2	*Eliz.*	— 1560 —	89
43	*Eliz.*	— 1601 —	86

And so has remained ever since *.

But having found the proportion between the shillings, there then remains a farther difficulty. which is, the difference in the value of money This is impossible to be discovered with accuracy, but conjectures upon it are numerous. Lord *Lyttelton* observes, that some reckon the proportion between the value of money, *for some centuries after the conquest*, at 20, some at 15 or 16, and some at 10 times the present rate, but his lordship calculates it at only 5 times †. His reason, however, appears to be very fallacious, for he founds it on making the prices of those days correspond with the present, which they very probably did not Mr. *Hume*, upon better grounds, calculates it at 10 times ‡, a proportion I should be

 inclined

* *Lowndes's Extract from the Mint*, p 69.

† *Hist of Henry* II vol 1 p 403

‡ *Hist of England*, vol 1 p 228

inclined to follow; he further adds, that considering we have six times more industry, and three times more people, we may multiply the sums mentioned by historians *for some reigns after the conquest* by 100. That ten times is not at all extravagant, we may gather from the conclusion of Bishop *Fleetwood*'s elaborate enquiry, who made the proportion between the reign of *Hen* VI. and that of Queen *Anne*, *six times*. Now, whoever considers the immense rise of prices since the beginning of this century, will allow that ten times, taken for the present period, is moderate.

But the difficulty continues after the 43d of *Eliz.* when the present standard was fixed; for there certainly is an immense difference between the value of money, for instance, in the reign of *James* I. and the present time interest was then 8½ *per cent.* and land sold at 14 years purchase. But what the general proportion is, remains, nevertheless, a great difficulty, in which every man, who has reflected much on these subjects, must be left to form his own conclusions

The most remarkable rise of prices was in the reign of *Elizabeth*, when the produce of the *Spanish* mines had circulated throughout all parts of *Europe*, that had any industry I should apprehend the value of money to be now ten times greater than it was before that period, and that for a long time afterwards, perhaps till late in the reign of *Charles* II *five times* might be the proportion. And that since that period the fall has been gradual.

If this idea (or indeed any moderate one that may be started, which takes in all circumstances) be considered, it will be found that those modern writers who complain of the *high* prices of the necessaries of life in the present period, compared with those of remoter ages, have very much mistaken the case. A few instances will shew this.

3 We

We find in *Fleetwood* *, that in 1302, a fat mutton ſold at 1 *s* , as there were 264 grains in the ſhilling, this in preſent money is about 3 *s.* which multiplied by 10 gives 1 *l.* 10 *s.* not a low price at preſent.

At the ſame time a cock or hen ſold at 1 *d* ½, which at preſent would be 3 *s.* 6 *d* —much higher than our prices

Hogs (I ſuppoſe fat) came to 3 *s.* 2 *d* ¼, which makes at preſent 4 *l.* 15 *s* 7 *d* ½, the price of our largeſt hogs

In 1314 the ſhilling continuing the ſame, a fat gooſe is 2 *d.* ½, or 6 *s* 3 *d.* preſent money, a very high price —I have taken very moderate articles, ſome oxen and ſheep run up to ſuch prices that we rarely know any thing like them, for inſtance, in 1314 a ſtalled ox ſold at 1 *l.* 4 *s* equal to 36 *l.* at preſent, which for ſuch oxen as theirs would be moſt enormous, even a graſs fed one at 16 *s* which now would be 24 *l.* An ordinary cow 10 *s.* or 15 *l.*

In the ſame year, four pigeons ſold for a penny; this is 2 *s.* 6 *d* preſent money, or 7 *d.* ½ each, which is a high price.

In 1315, and 1316, wheat 1 *l* the quarter, which is 30 *l* at preſent, but it was a great dearth Some records make it double that price. But the changes were ſo great, that in the ſame year it was 4 *l.* and alſo 6 *s* 8 *d*

In 1336, wheat reckoned very plentiful, at 2 *s.* the quarter, yet that would now be 3 *l.* A fat ox, 6 *s* 8 *d* which makes 10 *l* In 1344, a cow, 5 *s.* or 7 *l* 10 *s* , a good price now.

In 1348 (the ſhilling 236 grains) commodities were reckoned to ſell very cheap. A good fat ox at 4 *s.* which now would be 5 *l.* 10 *s.* In 1349, a fat ox, 6 *s.* 8 *d* now 9 *l.* 3 *s* 4 *d* In 1407, a cow, 7 *s* which would now be 8 *l* 15 *s.* Labour in this period was

* *C[illegible] Prec[illegible]*, p 66.

enormously dear, which, from many circumstances, particularly the small number of people, and still less industry, might easily be conceived In this year a thresher had 2 *d* a day, equal to 4 *s*. 2 *d* at present. In 1425, a sawyer and a stone-cutter had 4 *d* a day, equal to 5 *s*. 5 *d* at present. Threshing a quarter of wheat, 3 *d* ½, equal now to 4 *s* 7 *d*. At the same time a day horse for a prior came to 1 *l* 6 *s*. 8 *d*. which now would be 21 *l* 10 *s*

In 1444, a calf, 2 *s* As the shilling then contained 176 grains, this is equal to 40 *s* at present, a good price for fat calves. A porker, 3 *s* equal now to 3 *l* which is a great price. A goose, 3 *d* now 5 *s* Pigeons, the dozen, 4 *d*.⅛, now 6 *s*. 10 *d*.½.

In 1445, hay, the load, 3 *s* 6 *d* ½, which is 3 *l*. 10 *s*. 10 *d*. a very high price in any part of the kingdom such a price of hay explains the high price of cattle, yet rents were low Oats, 2 *s* a quarter, equal to 40 *s* at present. Bullocks and heifers, 5 *s*. each, equal to 5 *l*. now.

In 1449, sheep, 2 *s*. 5 *d* ½ each, making now 2 *l* 9 *s* 2 *d*. Hogs, 1 *s* 11 *d* ½, now 1 *l*. 19 *s*. 2*d*. and not said to be fat In 1459, wheat, the quarter, 5 *s*. equal now to 5 *l*. Two years before it was 7 *s* 8 *d*. or 7 *l* 13 *s* 4 *d*.

The ideas of parliament in those days were consonant to these prices, so high on comparison with ours. In 1463, it was enacted, that no corn should be imported if wheat was not above 6 *s*. 8 *d*. rye, 4 *s*. barley, 3 *s* the quarter, which now would be for the wheat, 6 *l*. 13 *s* 4 *d*. the rye, 4 *l* the barley, 3 *l*. It is plain that these prices were not at all oppressive.

In 1475, a load of hay, 6 *s* 8 *d* equal now to 5 *l* 8 *s* 4 *d* And in 1498, it came to 8 *s*. 2 *d* which now is 6 *l*. 10 *s* Nay, *Stow* makes it half as much again, and says, the *usual* price was 5 *s*. equal now to 4 *l*

In 1510, a load of hay, 9 *s* equal now to 6 *l* 2 *s* 6 *d*.

In 1533, the statute price of beef was ½ *d* *per* lb. equal now to 6 *d*. Mutton, ¾ *d*. equal to 9 *d* at present, proportions decisive in the present argument.

In 1551, a load of straw, 5 *s.* which, as the shilling contained but 20 grains, is equal to 10 *l* at present, another sign how unimproved their tillage must be, and how miserably they must support their cattle in winter. In the same year wheat, 8 *s* a quarter, that is at present, 16 *l* In 1562, a load of hay, 13 *s* 4 *d* or 6 *l.* 13 *s.* 4 *d.* A load of straw 6 *s.* now 3 *l*

After this period (the beginning of the reign of *Elizabeth*) the method of computing must be changed: the shilling contained the same number of grains as at present, and instead of multiplying by 10, we must multiply only by 5.

In 1574, beef, at *Lammas*, 1 *s.* 10 *d* a stone, equal to 9 *s.* 2 *d.* at present, but it is called very dear it shews that their *scarcities* happened in meat as well as wheat

In 1595, a hen's egg sold at 1 *d.* equal now to 5 *d.* A pound of sweet (I suppose *fresh*) butter, 7 *d.* equal to 2 *s.* 11 *d.* at present, but it was then a high price.

I think all these proportions prove, in the most satisfactory manner, that the writers who complain of the prices of meat and cattle being at present out of proportion to what they were in former ages, have utterly mistaken the difference in the value of money, and from that mistake have been led into declamation upon our present misery, which has raised riots among some of our poor, and infused discontent into the minds of the rest.

To say, in answer to this, that their pay is not now equal to what it was then, is no answer. for, in the first place, if the importance of bread be considered, and we were to set down *all* the old prices and compare them with the present, I am mistaken if the present pay will not be found equal to that of old. In the ſecond place, we ſhould reflect on the want of people and induſtry, the civil wars and confuſions common, the number of labourers kept in ſubjection to the barons, and the want of communications for the ſupply of one place from another if all theſe circumſtances are conſidered, it will be found that labour muſt have been very dear, without any reference to the price of proviſions

I muſt alſo deſire the reader to keep in his mind what I advanced at page 135, &c concerning the difference between the oxen of thoſe days and the preſent. They had no turnips, and the price of hay and ſtraw was ſuch, that very little cattle could be wintered, and thoſe which were muſt have been almoſt ſtarved, ſo that they could ſcarcely have any thing like the oxen now ſold at *Smithfield* In confirmation of this, I may quote the practice recorded in 1321, of ſalting all the oxen and ſheep that were conſumed in the winter, a circumſtance deciſive of what their huſbandry and their cattle muſt have been

It may poſſibly be ſaid, that the prices of commodities did not riſe and fall in ſuch exact proportion to the quantity of ſilver in the coin—This may be true, and may not be ſo—but the prices in the preceeding pages will, without injury to my argument, admit deductions on this account—But I am not inclined to admit this reaſoning, for we find in our hiſtories, that the *clamour* and *confuſion* ariſing from alterations in the coin, were very great, and if ſo, I ſhould ſuppoſe that the general alarm would raiſe prices *beyond* the true proportion.

NUMBER XII.

People gathering into Towns do not depopulate.— Page 71.

DR. *Campbell*, in his *Political Survey of Great Britain*, just publiſhed, vol. ii p. 254, a work which ſhews how deeply the author has reflected on theſe ſubjects, has a remark which I ſhall tranſcribe, being much to my purpoſe.—"Many think the great increaſe of towns, and the reigning inclination of people to reſide in them, hath a viſible tendency to depopulate the country, and thereby leſſen its produce. But whence does this deſire of living in towns proceed? Becauſe induſtry enables people in towns to live better. Numbers living better muſt create an increaſed conſumption. But of what? Moſt clearly of the produce of the country. If therefore the conſumption be enlarged, the cultivation muſt be augmented in proportion, and thoſe employed therein be conſequently benefited thereby? The voice of reaſon ſeems loud, but the language of facts is ſtill louder All the lands in the neighbourhood of theſe towns, from which lands the inhabitants, occaſional viſitants, and paſſengers, are ſupplied with milk, butter, cheeſe, lamb, mutton, veal, and beef, are much raiſed in their value, and not a little improved by plenty of manure which towns conſtantly ſupply It may be ſaid, this regards only paſturage It would be ſaid with truth if theſe people ate no bread. But by the help of their turnpike roads, they may receive corn and flour from even diſtant markets"

In another paſſage the Doctor reaſons very ſenſibly in favour of incloſures—"As to the popular clamours formerly againſt incloſures, they might have ſome foundation as tillage was then neglected, we had few manufactures and little commerce, ſo that the common people

people had few resources. But this has little to do with the present state of things. By the depopulation complained of must be meant a local, not a national loss of people, which however would be difficult to prove, since the villages and towns in the vicinity of these inclosed commons are as well or better inhabited than ever. As to the nation, the consumption and price of provisions *shew our people in general do not decrease*. In truth, this spirit of inclosing proves it. For the intent of inclosing is to encrease the quantity of provisions, and nothing could excite, or at least nothing could sustain this, but an increased demand. In respect to decreasing tillage, it also is hardly to be proved. It is certain the produce of arable lands in general is greatly augmented, that the tillage of commons was inconsiderable, and a great part of it beans. In respect to the poor (to whom the greatest regard is due) they only change the kind of labour; and this not to their disadvantage, for wages are higher, and employment in inclosed countries more easily obtained." Vol. ii. p. 278.

NUMBER XIII.

Inclosures.—Page 127

AS there has not been an age in which complaints against inclosures were not common, so no period has passed in which those complaints have not been satisfactorily answered. Of this I have given several instances—Another has occurred since these sheets were printed, it is taken from a pamphlet, entitled, *England's Interest considered in the Increase of Trade*, by *Samuel Fortrey*, 1663.—" 1 Our care should be, to increase chiefly our stock of cattle. First, by a liberty for every man to enjoy his lands in severalty and inclosure, one of the greatest improvements this nation is capable of, for want whereof we find by daily experience, that the profit of a great part of the land and stock of this kingdom, as now employed, is wholly lost And this appears, in that the land of the common fields almost in all places of this nation, with all the advantages that belong unto them, will not let for above one-third part so much as the same land would do inclosed, and always several.

" 2. But it may be objected, that inclosures would cause great depopulations and scarcity of corn, as hath been conceived by former parliaments.

" 3. To this I answer, corn would be nothing the scarcer by inclosure, but rather more plentiful, tho' a great deal less land were tilled. for then every ingenious husband would only plough that land he found most fitting for it, and that no longer than he found it able to bring him profit. And as to depopulation by inclosure, granting it increaseth plenty, as cannot well be denied, how increase and plenty can depopulate, cannot well be conceived. nor surely do any imagine that the people which lived in those towns they call depopulated, were all destroyed, because they lived no longer there, when indeed they were only removed to other

other places, where they might better benefit themselves, and profit the publick Certainly they might as well think the nation undone, should they observe how *London* is depopulated in a long vacation, when men are only retired into the country, about their private and necessary employments, and the like might they think of the country in the term time, yet a man is not thereby added or diminished to the nation

"4 Further, as many, or more families, may be maintained and employed in the manufacture of the wool that may arise out of one hundred acres of pasture, than can be employed in a far greater quantity of arable, who perhaps do not always find it most convenient for them to live just on the place where the wool groweth, by which means cities and great towns are peopled, nothing to the prejudice of the kingdom.

"5 Wherefore then, if by inclosure the land itself is raised to a greater value, and a less quantity capable of a greater increase and if it really causeth no depopulation, but at most a removal of people thence where without benefit to the public, or profit to themselves, they laboured and toiled, to a more convenient habitation, where they might with less pains greatly advantage both And if the manufactures and other profitable employments of the nation are increased, by adding thereto such numbers of people, who formerly served only to waste, not to increase, the store of the nation, it cannot be denied, but the encouragement of inclosure, where every man's just right may be preserved, would infinitely conduce to the increase and plenty of this nation, and is a thing very worthy the countenance and care of a parliament."

Authors much more ancient were of the same opinion. *Fitzherbert*, in 1534, recommends inclosures greatly as working an high improvement, keeping four times the number of beasts *Tusser* in 1590 is equally in favour of them. *Blythe* was of the same opinion in 1650, and *Hartlib* in his Legacy 1651, like *Fortrey*, answers the great objection to them, that

that of depopulation from laying down to grafs, in the following paffage:

"Pafture employeth more hands than arable, and therefore pafture doth not *depopulate*, as it is commonly faid, for *Normandy* and *Picardy* in *France*, where there are paftures, in a good meafure are as populous as any part of *France*, and I am certain that *Holland*, *Zealand*, *Friezeland*, *Flanders*, and *Lombardy*, which relye altogether on paftures, are the moft populous places in *Europe*. But fome will object and fay, that a fhepherd and his dog formerly hath deftroyed divers villages. To this I anfwer, that we well know what a fhepherd and his dog can do, *viz* look to 2 or 300 fheep at the moft, and that 2 or 300 acres will maintain them, or the land is extremely barren, and that thefe 2 or 300 acres being barren will fcarcely maintain a plough (which is but one man and two boys) with the horfes, and that the mowing, reaping and threfhing of this corn, and other work about, will fcarcely maintain three more with work through the whole year But how many people may be employed by the wool of 2 or 300 fheep, in picking, carding, forting, fpinning, weaving, dying, knitting, fulling, I leave to others to calculate And farther, if the paftures be rich meadows, and go on dairying, I fuppofe all know that 100 acres of fuch land employeth more hands than 100 acres of the beft corn land in *England*, and produceth likewife better exportable commodities And further, if I fhould grant that formerly the fhepherd and his dog did *depopulate*, that I may not condemn the wifdom of former ages; yet I will deny that it doth fo now for formerly we were fo unwife as to fend over our wools to *Antwerp* and other places, where they were manufactured, by which means one pound oft brought ten unwrought to them, but we fet now our own poor to work, and fo fave the depopulation. Yet I fay, it is convenient to encourage the plough, becaufe that we cannot have a certainty of corn, and carriage is dear both by fea ſea and land, eſpecially into the inland countries, and our commodities of wool do cloy the merchants * "

These obſervations are ſtrictly true at this day, if the compariſon is made with what it ought to be, the tillage of open field lands under the univerſal courſe of 1. Fallow, 2. Wheat, 3 Spring Corn, in which vile huſbandry not one of the modern operoſe improvements is to be found. The fact is ſo clear, that it is not to be wondered at that ſome of theſe writers ſhould appear to treat the contrary opinion with contempt, juſtly remarking, that it proceeded from people who knew little of huſbandry, and who therefore muſt be very ignorant of the employment in either caſe.

---

* Legacy of Huſbandry, p. 44

F I N I S.

Published, by the ſame AUTHOR,

Printed for W. STRAHAN; W NICOLL, No. 51, St Paul's Church-Yard, T CADELL, in the Strand; B. COLLINS, at Saliſbury, and J BALFOUR, at Edinburgh; and ſold by all the Bookſellers in Town and Country.

New Editions of

I. A SIX MONTHS TOUR through the NORTH of ENGLAND.

A SIX WEEKS TOUR through the SOUTH of ENGLAND.

The FARMER's TOUR through the EAST of ENGLAND.

In 9 Vols. 8vo. Price 2*l.* 7*s.* 3*d.* in Boards; or 2*l.* 14*s.* neatly bound in Calf.

Theſe TOURS contain the Regiſter of the Author's Journies through moſt of the *Engliſh* Counties, which were undertaken with a view of gaining as complete a Knowledge as poſſible of the preſent State of the Agriculture of the Kingdom. In them is deſcribed common Huſbandry in all its Variations; its Excellencies, Defects, and propoſed Improvements —The Journal of many Experiments communicated to the Author.—Plates and Accounts of new-invented or improved Implements of Huſbandry —The Prices of Labour and Proviſions, with the State of the Poor, Population, Induſtry, Manufactures, &c —Deſcriptions of the Seats of the Nobility and Gentry, and alſo of other curious Objects.

II. The FARMER's LETTERS to the PEOPLE of ENGLAND. The Third Edition. 2 Vols. Price 10*s* 6*d* in Boards.—Containing Miſcellaneous Obſervations on the Improvement of Eſtates—and on the national Protection and Encouragement of Agriculture.

Lately published, by the same AUTHOR.

III The FARMER's GUIDE in HIRING and STOCKING FARMS With Plans of Farm Yards, and Sections of necessary Buildings. 2 Vols 8vo. Price 10*s*. 6*d*. in Boards.

IV ESSAYS *for which the Society for the Encouragement of Arts, Manufactures, and Commerce adjudged the Premiums of* GOLD MEDALS, *viz.*

1 An ESSAY on the Management of HOGS, including EXPERIMENTS on Rearing and Fattening them.

2 An ESSAY on the Culture of COLESEED, for *Feeding Sheep and Cattle, including Experiments* The Second Edition. Price 2*s*

The Essay on COLESEED, may be had alone, Pr. 1*s*.

V The EXPEDIENCY of a Free Exportation of CORN With some Observations on the *Bounty*, and its Effects The Second Edition. Price 1*s* 6*d*

VI PROPOSALS to the LEGISLATURE for NUMBERING the PEOPLE. Containing some Observations on the Population of *Great Britain*, and a Sketch of the Advantages that would probably accrue from an exact Knowledge of its present State. Price 1*s*

VII OBSERVATIONS on the present State of the WASTE LANDS in this Kingdom Price 2*s*.

These, with the two following, are a complete Catalogue of all the AUTHOR's Works.

VIII RURAL ŒCONOMY. The Second Edition. 8vo Price 6*s*

IX A COURSE of EXPERIMENTAL AGRICULTURE, being the REGISTER of near 2000 Original Experiments 2 Vols Quarto. Price 2 [illegible] 10*s*.

Lightning Source UK Ltd.
Milton Keynes UK
UKOW04f0555030417
298192UK00011B/435/P

9 781170 479131